# Reengineering the University

WILLIAM F. MASSY

# Reengineering the University

## How to Be Mission Centered, Market Smart, and Margin Conscious

Johns Hopkins University Press    Baltimore

Johns Hopkins Paperback edition, 2017
9  8  7  6  5  4  3  2  1

Johns Hopkins University Press
2715 North Charles Street
Baltimore, Maryland 21218-4363
www.press.jhu.edu

*The Library of Congress has cataloged the hardcover edition of this book as follows:*

Massy, William F.
    Reengineering the university : how to be mission centered, market smart, and margin conscious / William F. Massy.
        pages cm
    Includes bibliographical references and index.
    ISBN 978-1-4214-1899-5 (hardcover : alk. paper) —
ISBN 978-1-4214-1900-8 (electronic) — ISBN 1-4214-1899-1 (hardcover : alk. paper) — ISBN 1-4214-1900-9 (electronic)   1. Universities and colleges—United States—Business management.   2. Education, Higher—United States—Finance.   3. Education, Higher—United States—Costs.   4. Educational change—United States—Economic aspects.   I. Title.
    LB2341.93.U6M374 2016
    378.1'060973—dc23        2015018663

A catalog record for this book is available from the British Library.

ISBN-13: 978-1-4214-2274-9
ISBN-10: 1-4214-2274-3

*Special discounts are available for bulk purchases of this book. For more information, please contact Special Sales at 410-516-6936 or specialsales@press.jhu.edu.*

Johns Hopkins University Press uses environmentally friendly book materials, including recycled text paper that is composed of at least 30 percent post-consumer waste, whenever possible.

*To my wife, Suzanne*

# Contents

This book is rooted in my conviction that America's traditional universities can be a lot better than they are and that they will have to change if they are to maintain their centrality. We may be the envy of the world, but a critical look from the inside reveals some significant warts and flaws. I have been speaking and writing about these problems for years, but the times just weren't right to effect systemic change. Now, however, the rise of disruptive technology and new postsecondary education models are threatening traditional universities to the point where such change is coming onto the agenda. This book aims to further that agenda.

I have tried to combine my analytical knowledge as a microeconomist and management scientist with my many years of experience as a professor, university officer, and consultant to produce a work that is both analytical in approach and intuitive in delivery. My goal is to provide practical guidance for people who want to effect change in their institutions, and, also, I hope to convince people who are on the fence that change is both necessary and practical.

The analytics may seem a little daunting in places, but I'd like to think that I've explained things in a way that's accessible to anyone willing to put forth a little effort. (The technical details are mostly relegated to the appendixes.) My hopes for the quantitatively oriented sections of the book were summed up in the recent *New York Times* article "When 'Money Ball' Meets Medicine": "Just as baseball and other sports have been transformed by our understanding of new numbers, public and global health can be, too."[1] Like medicine and baseball, higher education is awash in numbers—but the information they contain is insufficiently harnessed for purposes of decision-making. I disagree with those

members of the academy who believe that the rise of numbers is caus-
ing the "slow death of the University."[2] My thesis is that consideration
of numbers is not the same as "bean counting," though it may come to
that if academics don't play an active role in balancing academic values
with margins and market forces. How to effect that involvement is a
main theme of this book.

The "soft" portion of my work describes the values and behavior that
characterize traditional universities. I've tried to do this in ways that
boost understanding about what's happening, what needs to happen,
and why the changes are so important. A reviewer of the manuscript
described me as "[h]alf hopeless romantic about the value and high
purposes of higher education and half pragmatic engineer focused on
costs, efficiency, and metrics"—a combination that, he was nice enough
to add, is "just right" for present purposes. I think his comment was appropriate, and hope I have captured the best of both in this book.

One of my theses is that traditional universities not only are in great
need of reform, but their unique structure, circumstances, and culture
make such reform a worthy intellectual challenge. Universities are among
the world's most complex organizations. They produce multiple and
nuanced outputs, use highly specialized and often autonomous inputs,
and pursue nonprofit goals that are not easily quantified or even described coherently in subjective terms. They use complex and often
esoteric production methods, operate in competitive and dynamic
markets, and may be of large size. Such issues have been addressed in
many books, articles, speeches, and commission reports, but yet our
understanding remains incomplete. This limits rationality in decision-
making, deprives administrators of agency in key areas, and may allow special interests to exert a heavy influence on governance. It is the
confluence of these factors that makes the challenges of reengineering
so fascinating as well as so important.

Some years ago, I became convinced that the main problems of traditional universities do not stem from lack of intention. Most universities want to do better, but a large portion of these efforts have been
overwhelmed by other priorities. Complacency and self-interest play a
role, of course, but the root problem is a deeply held commitment to
traditional concepts and values. These were once eminently fit for purpose, but new technologies, insights, threats, and opportunities now

require significant revisions. While the needed revisions are significant, the reformers must be mindful that the essence of the traditional university must remain. That means understanding the fine structure of university values and activities so that one "does no harm" while effecting the needed cures.

Shortfalls in data availability, software systems, and computing power have made it hard to generate the data needed for reform. For example, my research and consulting produced a number of cost and productivity models that could be implemented on a small scale but which were impractical for the large-scale rollouts needed to produce campus-wide change. Similar limitations hobbled what could have been done with respect to teaching and learning, resource allocation, and other important domains of activity. These barriers now have been largely removed. Modern data systems, flexible as well as powerful software applications, and cloud computing have brought new ideas and technology within reach of most institutions. The conceptual underpinnings needed to deploy the technology, and indeed to reform universities generally, also have become vastly better in recent years. One objective of this book is to describe these concepts and demonstrate why they matter. This book could not have been written a decade ago, but I'm convinced that now the time for breakthroughs is at hand.

Real reform cannot be accomplished without leadership from the top. Presidents and provosts have other things on their minds and until recently most did not make reform a significant priority. This, too, is changing as more and more people—up to and including the president of the United States—have called for action. Universities need to pay attention, and increasingly they are. But what can be done (in management jargon) "starting Monday morning?"

I have tried to answer this question in an intellectually rigorous yet practical way: not preempting the academic judgments that must take place inside institutions but rather diagnosing problems and suggesting means for solving them within the scope of fundamental academic values and traditions. Each university must chart its own course, but I hope I have provided a roadmap and journey guide that include enough detail to move forward.

The material is organized into five chapters: (i) "Understanding the Traditional University," (ii) "The Reengineering Challenge," (iii) "The

New Scholarship of Teaching," (iv) "The Cost of Teaching," and
(v) "Financial Planning and Budgeting." The first two chapters provide the background needed to develop a reengineering program. The
last three cover the three major domains in which initiatives need to be
mounted, and a conclusion pulls the material together at the end. I
don't pretend to have resolved all the issues in these areas, and I'm sure
that particular arguments or recommendations will become lightning
rods for debate (and that's a good thing). However, I hope most readers
will agree that my intent is to preserve the traditional university sector's
essential characteristics while pointing the way toward changes needed
to ensure its sustainability.

The antecedents for these ideas span some thirty-five years, beginning with the publication of my award-winning work with David Hopkins, *Planning Models for Colleges and Universities* (Stanford University
Press, 1981). *Planning Models* described our efforts to improve Stanford's
productivity and resource allocation through the use of quantitative,
data-driven constructs, and in the process make the university's decision-
making more rational. This was an era of optimism as large numbers of
professionally trained managers and management scientists entered higher
education administration. All things seemed possible, but most of us
who worked in the field underestimated the difficulties caused by cultural factors, organizational and technical complexity, and lack of clarity
about university values and objectives. Notwithstanding these problems,
the work that began with *Planning Models* remained a touchstone as my
career in Stanford's academic and financial administration evolved and
my research and higher education consulting matured.

The Pew Higher Education Roundtables, organized by Robert Zemsky in 1986 to foster an informed national dialog on the changes facing
higher education, represented another milestone. I was the keynote
speaker for the first roundtable and continued as a participant for the
duration of the program. The roundtables opened my eyes to a broader
range of policy and governance issues than I had seen at Stanford.
Along with my experience at Stanford and my dozen years of service on
the Executive Committee of the Yale University Council, these discussions illuminated the need for new concepts and approaches and stim-
ulated my thinking about how to proceed. My return to full-time research and teaching in 1990 (which included research on academic

productivity with two federally funded National Centers), participating in the Forum for the Future of Higher Education's annual Aspen Symposium, and being a member of the Hong Kong University Grants Committee (the oversight body for the territory's eight universities) further broadened my experience base and spurred my impetus to write. More recently, my work with colleagues and students at the University of Melbourne's L. H. Martin Institute for Higher Education Leadership and Management helped to solidify my thinking. I believe that this book would not have come to fruition without the synthesizing opportunities afforded by my teaching and research in Australia.

I have tried to write in the spirit of Michael Hammer and James Champy's *Reengineering the Corporation: A Manifesto for Business Revolution* (HarperBusiness, 2003)—in a way that will appeal to people with a serious interest in the traditional higher education sector and who want to understand the problems and proposed solutions. I hope it will appeal to presidents, provosts, faculty, financial people, members of governing and coordinating boards, state and federal policymakers, and students in higher education programs, as well as, perhaps, to software developers and consultants who offer products and services related to the models presented in chapters 4 and 5. Some readers may wish to read quickly from end to end to get an overview of the issues and what can and should be done about them. The more technical portions may be skipped or skimmed without loss of continuity (I have indicated some of these places), but even a nodding acquaintance with them may prove valuable for charting the way forward. Readers who wish to implement the methods and models will find enough detail in the text and appendixes to point the way until standard methodologies can take over.

I would like to thank the many people who read portions of the manuscript and provided invaluable feedback. These include Robert Zemsky, Mike McPherson, Maureen Devlin, Candace Thille, Maria Anguiano, Lea Patterson, Will Reed, Mike Howard, John Curry, and Kelli Armstrong. Leo Goedegebuure, Lynn Meeks, and their colleagues at the L. H. Martin Institute provided important insights and opportunities. Tom Erlich, who reviewed my proposed outline, provided critical comments that shifted my direction toward the one represented here.

Lea Patterson of the Pilbara Group and Anthony Pember of Grant-Thornton LLP helped me perfect the activity and cost model described in chapter 4, and Ajith Prasad of the National University of Singapore helped me formulate the budget model described in chapter 5. Stanford's Candace Thille and Carl Wieman helped me with chapter 3's discussion of learning science and its applications. Andrea Wilger and my other colleagues and students at the National Center for Productivity Improvement in Higher Education were instrumental at key stages of my research. My colleagues on the Hong Kong University Grants Committee's Teaching and Learning Quality Process Review panels were instrumental in developing my ideas about process improvement, and Steve Graham and Paula Short contributed greatly to their introduction into the United States.

I also would like to acknowledge a few of the many friends and mentors who helped shape my thinking over the years: Bahram Bekhradnia, Dick Cyert, Peter Ewell, Nigel French, Bart Giamatti, Patti Gumport, Dean Hubbard, Dick Lyman, Bill Miller, Joel Meyerson, Ron Oxburgh, Frank Turner, Carol Twigg, Tim Warner, Marshall Witten, and Robert Zemsky. Finally, I want to thank Gregory Britton at Johns Hopkins University Press for seeing the potential in my manuscript and positioning it for appeal to a broad audience.

Suzanne May Massy, my wife and former college reference librarian, read every word of every version of the manuscript, offered extensive substantive and editorial suggestions, and engaged me in essential as well as delightful conversations about the content. This book could not have been written without her, and I am extremely grateful.

# Reengineering the University

# Chapter 1

# Understanding the Traditional University

President Barack Obama has promised to "shake up" higher education to improve performance and contain costs[1]—a goal that is shared by many governors and other political figures. Most independent commentators on higher education believe such a shakeup to be long overdue. There is no consensus on what should be done, but there can be no doubt that the performance of America's higher education system has been placed on the national agenda more centrally than ever before.

This book is about reforming traditional colleges and universities from the inside out in ways that preserve their academic values and essential strengths. It proposes changes that promise, in the president's words, to "offer breakthroughs on cost, quality, or both."[2] It aims at practicality in the sense of what can be done "starting Monday morning" to get the reforms underway. Most news reports have stressed the president's proposals for actions that could be imposed on universities: for example, the creation of a new performance rating system and linking it to federal student aid. However, my focus will be centered on what universities, and especially the traditional institutions that form the core of America's higher education system, can do for themselves.[3]

This book is based on research, experience, and insight gained during my years as a professor, vice provost and acting provost, and chief financial officer at Stanford University, and then as a consultant to higher education institutions and systems. As the title implies, this book focuses on methods and tools rather than a favorite set of "ultimate solutions." The initiatives are, for the most part, characterized by their relatively low costs and levels of risk. My hope is that readers will conclude that there is no reason not to begin implementing needed reforms on their campuses now—knowing that the details can and will be adjusted as they go along.

## Problems and Opportunities

Calls for reforming higher education have been forthcoming for decades. Indeed, I have been a regular contributor to these discussions.[4] The reasons for reform are manifold, and there's no need to go over that ground again here.[5] However, the following issues are sufficiently central to the proposals contained in this book to warrant mention:

- *Massive failures in the higher education marketplace.* The main failing is that would-be undergraduates and their families lack good information about how to choose among institutions on the basis of quality in relation to price.[6] This is partly due to the dearth of good measurement tools, but institutions also may keep negative information that *is* available secret in order to protect their brands.[7] In addition to its effects in the marketplace, such pursuit of prestige distorts internal incentives and inhibits quality improvement efforts. Similar problems arise with university rating systems that focus on inputs rather than educational outcomes.

  These failures prevent the "invisible hand" of competition from policing price, quality, and internal efficiency. They also have prevented "consumers" from developing the motivation and expertise needed to make intelligent choices—which tends to perpetuate the status quo. Efforts over several decades to mitigate or compensate for these problems through state and federal regulation have not worked well, and increasing reliance on markets without solving the information problem only makes things worse.

- *Loss of political confidence in traditional higher education.* Decades of criticism and calls for reform, amplified by a generally rising skepticism about "public goods," have come together to produce a skeptical, if not toxic, environment. One consequence is the erosion of public support for institutions, including higher education, which is driven by a combination of antitax beliefs and doubts about the value-for-money return on public investments.

  Regulation has proliferated in proportion to the doubts, and this has been amplified by growing perceptions about the universities' lack of responsiveness. Most proposed interventions are resisted fiercely, and those that are "successfully" imposed often are shunted aside with little more than lip service. One may be pardoned, however, for wondering whether the universities' defenses may be reaching the end of their useful lives.

- *Clear and present threats to traditional universities by disruptive innovators.* For-profit providers and new entities that bundle educational services in novel ways are threatening the traditional sector's hegemony. This is especially true in the online education space, as evidenced, for example, by the spectacular rise of MOOCs (massive open online courses).

  Higher education has always been a fertile ground for innovation, but the locus of these activities has largely been limited to individual entrepreneurs within institutions or largely separate online programs. Now, however, the impact of truly disruptive innovations is rising exponentially—to the point where it's no longer possible to ignore their systemic impact.

- *Lack of sufficient reform efforts by senior administrators, board members, and faculty.* On the whole, presidents, provosts, deans, and faculty have not embraced reform as a matter of urgent priority for their institutions. Nor have board members put reform on the agenda and insisted on systematic follow-through. Defense of "tradition" coupled with the many urgent issues associated with "business as usual" suck the oxygen from most campus discussions of reform and how it can be accomplished.

  The exception is in the area of technology. This does get a great deal of attention, and much time, effort, and money is being expended on it. Nevertheless, there is scant evidence so far that technology is transforming the fundamental character of traditional universities—as many of us believe is necessary if the reform agenda is to be successful.

The slow pace of reform has done more than leave traditional universities vulnerable to disruptive innovators and skeptical politicians. It has allowed continuance of the slow but seemingly inexorable shift toward maximizing the short-run goals of institutions and their constituencies, too often at the expense of students and long-term societal goals. Calls for change have become increasingly strident, but while individual instances of reform-triggering innovation can be discerned, the sector as a whole has proven to be remarkably impervious to pressures for changing the way it operates. In the not-so-long run, one fears, continuation of these trends may bring a tipping point that makes reform both more urgent and less easy to accomplish given greater constituent anger and a smaller resource base.

All this has brought us to what Bob Zemsky calls an "Ecclesiastes Moment—change may be all around us, but for the nation's colleges and universities there really is precious little that is new under the sun."[8] He goes on to point out that for the past thirty years, "the very thing each wave of reformers has declared needed to be changed has remained all but impervious to change." Even the language in which the various arguments and proposals have been couched—a language to which Bob and I have contributed in our joint and separate works—has remained essentially constant. For those of us who care deeply about reform, the situation reminds us of the subtitle to the Biblical *Ecclesiastes*: "The emptiness of all endeavor."[9]

Even with all the aforementioned problems, there is reason to think things may be different this time. The problems are bigger and understood more widely than at any time in the past, and the disruptive innovators are beginning to affect campuses in ways previously unimagined. And finally, of course, President Obama and some of the country's most influential governors and foundations have put reform squarely on the higher education agenda. The challenge is to leverage these forces to produce constructive rather than potentially destructive change.

One point of leverage can be found in Zemsky's observation that while "[d]etailed evidence of an existing problem has seldom proved sufficiently motivating" for faculty to embrace reform, professors are beginning to "sense that they can do better—for their students and for themselves." Further, "[w]hat is involved is not so much data or evidence as pride—of place and pride of scholarship."[10] Bob cites examples in which faculty radically reformed their curriculum in the context of explicit learning outcome objectives, helped shore up an institution's finances, and developed innovative new teaching and learning strategies based on technology and learning science.

This is consistent with Derek Bok's belief that "[m]ost faculty members do care sincerely about their responsibility as teachers to help their students learn. In fact, American professors seem to care more about this responsibility than their counterparts in other advanced nations in Europe and Asia."[11] Most reform examples involving faculty to be discussed in this book are underpinned by a belief that faculty want to do a good job.

To these insights about reform, I would offer two of my own:

1. It's never wise to expect faculty to adopt a reform agenda that appears alien to what they believe they know.
2. Faculty and academic leaders don't know as much as they think they know about how improvements, even ones that are mutually desired, can be achieved.

The first point is self-evident, and I can testify to it from many years of personal experience. The second, also rooted in my experience, is corroborated by Derek Bok's observation that "most professors are unaware of this large and growing literature [about reform]. . . . They periodically debate changes in the curriculum without much sign that research findings have played any role in forming their opinions. The methods of education they use do not undergo anything like the constant process of testing and revision common to many fields of research in which they engage."[12]

I believe that the aforementioned ideas, coupled with Zemsky's pride of place and of scholarship, will provide the leverage needed to get reform moving within colleges and universities. What's needed are initiatives that involve institutions and faculty step-by-step in meaningful change processes that generate understanding, buy-in, and increases in know-how as they go along—always encouraging midcourse correction on the basis of experience. The result can be a self-reinforcing sense of pride and scholarship that produces results and eases the adoption of subsequent proposals.

A corollary to the aforementioned points is that one should *not* try to settle on a full-blown solution at the outset. This generates resistance before understanding. Lack of experience and know-how begets fractiousness as the bright people within the academy struggle with the myriad possibilities without the evidence or experience to differentiate among them in an informed way. The fact that many proposed "solutions" eventually prove to have significant flaws raises legitimate concerns that important university values will be undermined—concerns that can morph into obstructionism. Marketplace and regulatory constraints join with the internal inhibitors to limit institutions' ability to test possibilities and learn from failures, yet such learning is essential for problem solving in the face of uncertainty. Introduction of one flawed "solution" after another has produced a stasis that has endured, now, for more than a generation. It is better to consider the problem as one of "active learning" on the part of institutions and faculty, and to develop interventions accordingly. That's what this book is about.

In April 2013 the American Enterprise Institute (AEI) published my "Initiatives for Containing the Cost of Higher Education."[13] In the preface to the series, AEI's Andrew Kelly described the essay as offering a "comprehensive reform agenda for policymakers interested in cost containment . . . [including] a national database of cost-containment practices, a 'race to the top' for college productivity improvement, and academic audit for all institutions."[14] Of particular importance was the essay's description of campus-level best practices for:[15]

- *Productivity improvement*: Getting more from the resources provided to universities and colleges by reducing the cost of operations, boosting the quality of learning, or (ideally) both. Further, such cost-reducing initiatives must be accompanied by robust quality assurance to avoid learning degradation in the interest of apparent cost-effectiveness.
- *Price moderation*: Holding down increases in net price to students—specifically, limiting the degree to which cost-saving productivity improvements are used to boost cross subsidies and amenities instead of limiting tuition and augmenting financial aid.

I have heard that the essay was well received and possibly read by staff members preparing President Obama's proposals.

One of my basic messages was that pundits, politicians, and other critics of the academy should not attribute malevolence to what really is bounded rationality and legitimate concern about risk. Beset by issues of affordability, politics, and disruptive innovation, most university leaders understand at some level that their institutions must change. But too often they feel powerless, or at least deeply concerned lest launching aggressive change initiatives produce serious blowback on their campuses—and for them personally. Obstructionism exists, of course, but to a considerable extent it arises from shortfalls in vision and know-how rather than irreconcilable differences in objectives or excessive risk aversion. This book's underlying proposition is that better vision and know-how will empower the many institutional leaders and professors who are open to or perhaps even wish for change, and that political leaders and change agents in foundations can facilitate this process. The problems facing higher education will be far easier to solve once such empowerment has been achieved.

Building such vision and know-how now appears to be an achievable goal. The state of the art is maturing rapidly, and enough is known to provide practical advice for institutional leaders and faculty. The ideas are not arcane and thus can be made accessible to all kinds of people inside and outside of the academy. Indeed, most will be seen as applications of common sense leading to "mutual wins" once the necessary evidence is marshaled and space for conversation provided.

## Assets Worthy of Preservation

This book is about "traditional universities"—that is, the vast majority of America's nonprofit four-year higher education institutions. These institutions are critically important, even in a world of for-profits, MOOCs, and other disruptive innovators. My focus on traditional higher education doesn't imply that other kinds of schools are unimportant or that they don't face their own problems. Some for-profit universities are very impressive, for example, and it should go without saying that America's community college system has done a great job over many years. Both are important for the nation's well-being, and it's imperative that they surmount their various shortfalls and address the criticisms being leveled at them. Nevertheless, the traditional sector represents the core element of today's higher education system: what Frank Rhodes, president emeritus of Cornell University, describes as "[t]he most significant creation of the second millennium . . . the quiet

but decisive catalyst in modern society, the factor essential to its effective functioning and well-being."[16] It's also the area where broad-based
reform is most urgent and difficult.

Clay Christensen and Hal Eyring argue in their recent book on higher
education that the capacity for "discovery, memory, and mentoring,"
defining features of the traditional university, should not be lost. They
cite online teaching to be the main disruptive force, but I believe that
"industrialized higher education" is more accurate. The industrialized
model is characterized quintessentially by the for-profit sector but not
limited to it. The model emphasizes top-down course design by small
teams of experts, optimized and controlled delivery (online or face to
face [F2F]) by what amount to adjunct faculty, and rigorous quality assurance based on largely quantitative criteria.[17] Christiansen and Eyring
argue that while the quality of such education can be very good (often
better than from the classic model applied in the traditional way), it
can't reach the potential of the classic model when applied with full
effectiveness. In their words, "[s]ome of the most important learning
outcomes [of higher education] can't be measured, and they are hard
to confer in the [industrialized] environment."[18] Traditional universities certainly can learn from the industrialized approach, but it should
not become the dominant paradigm.

The world badly needs to challenge young minds in ways that the
industrial model will not be able to match in the foreseeable future, and
it would be a mistake to limit such opportunities to students who can
afford expensive private institutions or can obtain extraordinary levels
of financial aid. This book's goal is to help make a high-quality traditional educational experience available to the broad middle of the student spectrum in an affordable and high-quality way.

Learning to scale a reengineered traditional education experience will achieve what Harvard historian Maya Jasanoff calls "local
globalization"—avoiding the downsides of making higher education
a commodity while continuing to reap the benefits of international
reach.[19] She likens the development and inevitable export of online university courses to Britain's export of industrial technology in the nine-
teenth and early twentieth centuries. It was immensely profitable but
eventually allowed the United States to climb the learning curve and
beat Britain at its own game. The industrialized higher education model

has the same attributes: capital-intensive development by small groups of experts delivered en mass through technology supplemented by lower-skilled (and lower-paid) knowledge workers. This would represent "progress" if the educational product could be as good as a properly scaled, more humanistic (i.e., nonindustrial) experience. However, because the experience is not and cannot be that good, unanswered disruptive competition from the industrialized sector would disadvantage America's learners as well as its universities.

Faculty research and scholarship provide a second reason why the traditional sector is so important. Research and scholarship in America are the envy of the world, and they have conferred innumerable economic and social benefits. America's research programs are doing well despite persistent concerns about funding—indeed, some critics complain they are doing too well because research sometimes siphons resources away from teaching. This book doesn't consider research in any depth, but I do address the joint production question—especially as it pertains to education quality, productivity, and cost containment.

Avoidance of stranded capital[20] provides a third reason for trying to reform traditional universities rather than replacing them with for-profit and other industrialized forms of higher learning. The years since World War II have seen vast public and philanthropic investments in the traditional sector's physical, human, and organizational resources. One can legitimately question whether this capital is being used effectively, but there is a strong argument for fixing the problems rather than declaring the investments to be "sunk costs" and essentially starting over. The argument gains special force in this era of constrained investment in public goods, which would prevent tax dollars from being used to replicate public universities' capital in other organizational settings. Such would require privatization on a large scale. Some might welcome such a move, but I am convinced it would be a disaster.

To get an idea of the consequences, let us consider the key distinguishing features of traditional universities. They lie in four broad areas: on-campus student bodies, faculty resources, research and scholarship, and the nonprofit organizational form. Each represents a unique kind of asset, and although there are downsides, the balance is strongly positive.

*On-Campus Learning*

Nothing characterizes traditional universities more than their large numbers of on-campus learners. By this I mean both residential and nonresidential (e.g., commuting) students, whether they are full time are not. Online learning by students enrolled on campus is included as well. Students who learn mainly online but who come to campus for periodic bursts of activity may be included or not, depending upon the circumstances and mix of activities. I'll refer to learning that does not meet these criteria as being "online," though we must keep in mind that an increasing amount of "on-campus" learning occurs online as well. An alternative term, "distance learning," could be used, but somehow it seems less modern and perhaps more confusing.

What distinguishes on-campus learning is its ability to bring people together on a regular basis for F2F conversations and other interactions. These can occur in online chat rooms and the like, but virtual conversations cannot be as rich as those that take place in person. Partly, this is a matter of bandwidth, the amount of information that can be transmitted in a given period of time, but in reality it's something more. People speak of "smelling the pheromones" as an advantage of coming together, which, arguably, taps something deeply human that developed in us through evolution. Less lyrically, F2F interaction allows people to get to know one another more quickly and deeply than through electronic means, and in most cases such knowledge facilitates the learning process. Those who participate in telephone conference calls know that conversations go better if one already knows the other individuals. Video calls are better yet, though still not as good as being in the same room. Today's electronic communications are vastly better than the snail mail "distance learning" alternatives of yesteryear, but they aren't equivalent to coming together on a regular basis.

The difference between electronic and F2F communication would not matter so much if the sole objective of higher education was to impart specific skills and abilities, especially those of a technical nature, to highly motivated and well-organized students. But neither premise is accurate. Much of what's important in undergraduate education is tacit rather than codified. For example, students ought to develop insights and people skills as well as tools and logical protocols. Some students are less motivated than others, or less able to organize their time as needed to be successful in the online environment. Again, my point is not to disparage online learning—which by any measure is vastly better than earlier alternatives such as correspondence and television courses. It is simply to point out that, cost considerations aside, online distance education isn't as effective as a well-executed on-campus alternative.

The logic behind this assertion begins with the unassailable fact that institutions are free to incorporate areas where online learning offers comparative advantage into their portfolio of on-campus offerings. Therefore, an on-campus program that includes an educationally optimal mix of classic and online elements can't do worse than a strictly online offering.[21] I discuss in later chapters how the optimal mix can be approached and why the results will be significantly better than the strictly online alternative. Resource limits may dictate trading off F2F benefits against cost, but this should be recognized for what it is—a substitution of dollar savings for quality to a greater or lesser extent.

The personal growth and transformation objectives of undergraduate education offer yet another reason for bringing students together in an on-campus setting, and while they are not always achieved, they are too important to be casually discarded. I have never heard anyone argue that these goals are better achieved online than on campus. The opportunity to bring students together to engage with their peers and selected adults in activities ranging from cultural to athletic to academic should not be undervalued.

Bringing students together also provides an opportunity to break down previously learned stereotypes and prejudices. One manifestation of today's electronic culture is its tendency to encourage people to expose themselves disproportionately to information that reinforces previous beliefs. This can also happen on campus, of course, and to some extent it occurs in one's choice of school and friends. However, most campuses try hard to broaden students' viewpoints, as much outside the classroom as in it. Students who sortie from the comfort of their home environments only for online learning experiences, especially in codified, tool-oriented subjects, will benefit less from the college experience than those who come together on a campus.

On-campus learning certainly has its downsides. For example, the student culture on many campuses leaves much to be desired. Binge drinking and other personally destructive activities have grown enormously in recent years, for example, and various studies have shown the amount of time students spend on course work to be steadily declining. Much of this is due to trends imported from the broader society, but mitigation by campuses is possible. Student services professionals are working hard on this. Feedback such as that provided by the National Survey of Student Engagement (NSSE) as well as the promotion of active learning, as discussed later, should help boost academic involvement.

*Faculty Resources*

The professoriate represents a huge pool of expertise and wisdom that would take generations to replace, if indeed it could be replaced at all, if many doctoral programs were to be downsized or eliminated. I have been as critical of faculty as most well-informed and independent commentators,[22] and where warranted I shall continue that criticism in this book, but it also is important to step back and view the big picture. To do so, let's imagine for a moment a world where the numbers and influence of today's faculty have been markedly diminished.

This world would be populated mainly by for-profit and other industrialized universities. All students except those in elite schools (which presumably would survive because of their endowments if nothing else) would receive their education from what one may call "journeyman faculty"—people who, though dedicated and perhaps reasonably well trained, would have less expertise and operate in a less rigorous and value-rich milieu than is available in most of today's traditional universities. (The journeyman faculty would be much like today's adjuncts, but they would be the mainstream teaching resource rather than auxiliaries.) Faculty recognizable in terms of today's criteria would be available for designing curricula and courses, but there would be many fewer of them and they would have much less influence on their students and their institution's value system, governance, and culture.[23] While critics might welcome such a world as being free of obstruction and unwanted intellectual, cultural, and political pot-stirring, I believe most people eventually would conclude that a great deal had been lost.

I'm led to this scenario by economic and organizational reasoning, not from any desire to defend faculty interests. To substitute lower-cost for higher-cost labor wherever possible is a central tenet of productivity improvement, and the market for journeyman teachers surely would undercut that for today's faculty. (Learning from student peers costs even less, but that only widens the gaps of wisdom and expertise.) Industrialized education's inability to measure all that's important, coupled with the absence of effective role models as discussed in the following sections, would tend to commoditize day-to-day educational delivery. We can see this trend already in the movement toward adjunct faculty usage. Though many adjuncts are well qualified and work hard, few would argue that they can do as good a job as well-motivated regular faculty supported by a robust departmental culture.

Another consequence of vastly diminished faculty numbers would be a breakdown in the nexus between teaching and research that has served America and other Western countries so well for more than a century. The Soviet Union and a few other countries performed research and teaching in separate institutions—the former in research institutes and the latter in universities, thus foregoing the synergies discussed next and in the following section. It's worth noting that the National Research Council's report on the measurement of productivity in higher education considers the nexus between teaching and research to be an essential part of American higher education.[24] This view is shared by Derek Bok, who argues that research and teaching "often complement one another to produce a whole greater than the sum of its parts." For example, "[t]eaching undergraduates helps to keep a research-oriented faculty from growing excessively specialized while giving the students a chance to learn from scholars working at the frontiers of their field. At a more prosaic level, because the undergraduate experience inspires unusual loyalty among its alumni, the existence of a [traditional] college makes possible much of the philanthropy needed to build the facilities, create the extensive libraries, and endow the professorships that allow universities to produce first-rate research."[25] In short, the nexus is of great help in sustaining the professoriate as a vital force.

The nation's top two hundred or so "research universities" train nearly all our PhD students, the next generation of faculty who not only will carry on with research and teaching but also will develop the conceptual structures and methods needed to guide both activities. The traditional sector, and indeed much of the industrial sector, could not sustain itself without this steady flow of top-quality new talent. Additionally, research universities and their faculty provide constantly evolving role models for most, if not all, of the remaining traditional institutions— models that help these institutions maintain themselves as serious centers of intellectual excellence in the face of the world's innumerable distractions.

On the whole, professors are an extraordinarily empowered and energetic group. The nature of faculty work makes it difficult to provide detailed direction or supervision, and therefore successful professors must be self-starting in problem identification and the development of solutions and workarounds. Much of the criticism of faculty stems from stereotypes based on a relatively few horror stories and bad actors. My experience, on the ground with countless faculty members, convinces me that for the most part, they are dedicated professionals who sometimes are caught in difficult circumstances. Business firms spend much time and effort figuring out how to instill the aforementioned qualities in their front-line workforces, whereas it "comes with the territory" in most academic departments.

As with on-campus learning, the faculty culture has its downsides. Professors can be insular, unaccountable, and resistant to change. They can be exasperating as individuals as well as in groups. Their tendency to obsess on institutional politics, personal goals, and the esoterica of academic disciplines is well known. Even desirable objectives such as research and scholarship may be carried to excess to further personal interest and career development. (Much of this must be attributed to the incentive structure within universities, but this is itself a product of faculty culture as it interacts with the marketplace.) Nevertheless, those who would solve the problem by shackling or even eliminating the professoriate as we know it should be careful what they wish for. As with the universities in which faculty operate, it is better to find ways to change the culture than to seriously weaken the whole enterprise.

### Research and Scholarship

Faculty research and scholarship often are mentioned in the same breath with faculty themselves. (For simplicity, I'll mostly refer to them as "research.") As noted earlier, research can be regarded as a necessary aspect of being a good university-level faculty member. Critics of higher education may deride these activities as a waste of resources, but, though there are doubtless many instances of waste, a rejection of the whole enterprise would produce great losses for universities and society in general.[26] I argue throughout the book that research and scholarship must be better managed than at present, but that's not at all the same as considering them as lacking in worth.

Research in traditional universities is viewed as being produced jointly with education. "Joint production" means the simultaneous creation of two or more goods from mostly the same inputs—in our context, teaching and research produced by the same faculty. In the language of economists, the joint products are "complements in production." The definition has many nuances, but the basic idea is that producing one good without the other will cause quality losses or cost increases. Joint production is different from production by a conglomerate, where multiple outputs are produced by disparate activities controlled by a single entity. Traditional universities should not be viewed as conglomerates because it's difficult or impossible to remove research and scholarship without fundamentally altering the production of teaching and vice versa.

I argue that this joint production is *the* major distinguishing feature of the traditional university. This is self-evident for research universities and schools aspiring to that status, but research is of great importance even for the many institutions that cannot properly be called "research intensive." One often-cited reason is that research activity is very important to professors' career goals, but there are also synergies with teaching.

It's difficult to cite hard evidence about the synergies between teaching and research, but I agree with the many commentators who believe that such synergies do exist in many circumstances.[27] An institution that engages in research is more intellectually vigorous than one that doesn't, if for no other reason than it has a better and more well-informed faculty. Looking to the research itself, even experienced senior researchers do better when they interact with fresh young minds. As Stanford's vice provost for research, I encountered many instances where famous scientists, usually quick to defend their own views, provided sincere encouragement when a student mounted plausible challenges. Indeed, a professor's instinctive response is taking pride in out-of-the box thinking by students and learning from it, which decalcifies established wisdom and contributes to the advancement of knowledge.

Financial synergies can exist as well. For example, the availability of inexpensive graduate student and postdoctoral labor cuts the cost of research as compared to, say, in a corporation or freestanding government laboratory. Research sponsors contribute to the university's fixed administrative and support costs, thus lowering the cost of education— provided, of course, that overheads are reimbursed at reasonable levels. While not exactly a synergy, the question of whether research subsidizes teaching or vice versa is a hotly contested aspect of joint production. The answer doubtless depends upon the circumstances. It's possible for research to subsidize teaching, but in today's environment it seems more likely that the reverse is true. Overheads rarely are fully funded, and many direct research costs remain underfunded as well. For example, some sponsors won't contribute to the academic-year salaries of researchers, even when they are expected to spend substantial amounts of time on their projects.

The benefits of research and scholarship are easier to understand when we recognize the breadth and relevance of the enterprise. Ernest Boyer's influential *Scholarship Reconsidered* identifies four distinct genres.[28] The scholarship of discovery, which includes traditional research, develops new theories and facts. The scholarship of engagement (originally known as the scholarship of application) applies research findings to real-world problems and brings the abstract analytical knowledge down to earth so a broader audience can appreciate it. The scholarship of integration provides reflective observations on both basic and applied research, observations that can be of great benefit in teaching. Finally, the scholarship of teaching, and teaching itself, draws heavily on the other three kinds of scholarship as well as on its own unique content domains. I elaborate on how the four genres contribute to teaching in chapter 3.

Universities vary in the degree of emphasis they place on each type of scholarship, but all are covered to some extent in nearly every traditional university. The four scholarships are mutually reinforcing because progress in one area can stimulate ideas in the others. It's difficult to imagine a world without, say, the scholarship of integration, let alone one where discovery and application are regarded as being of little importance, and we see in chapter 3 how the scholarship of teaching is on the verge of major breakthroughs. I am reminded of Charles Eliot's admonition about a life of teaching without scholarship: "Universities must change because they must be the best expression of a changing society. Don't expect professors to change them, though. Spending your life as a teacher makes one an 'unsafe witness in matters of education.'"[29] Eliot's concern was focused mainly on curricula, but I believe that it extends to teaching quality, cost, and the other subjects of this book. The business model for industrial higher education denies the importance of teachers as scholars, which is one reason why I believe traditional universities to be essential for the well-being of the country.

### Nonprofit Organizations

The fact that traditional universities almost invariably are nonprofit represents another asset that is worth preserving. Such universities march to the drummer of "intrinsic values," socially desirable objectives derived from their missions rather than "instrumental values" defined in order to further the private financial objectives of shareholders. It's not too much to say that *mission* manifests the identity of the traditional university, in contrast to a for-profit company's *market identity* or *brand*. (Universities have brands, too, but they are a means to an end rather than central to the end itself.) Traditional universities are similar to museums, symphony orchestras, and other nonprofits that have to "make it" in the marketplace, and also to the hybrid "benefit corporations" (B-corporations) that combine altruistic and shareholder objectives. Yale economist and law professor Harry Hansmann, who has written extensively on nonprofits, emphasizes that the main difference between for-profit and nonprofit enterprises is that the latter can't distribute profits to shareholders.[30] Nonprofits can and sometimes do accumulate surpluses, but the money eventually must be reinvested in the enterprise's work rather than distributed to owners in the form of dividends and capital gains. We tend to take this difference for granted, but it has some very significant implications.

The nonprofit organizational form is most desirable when the output of the enterprise is important to society—a "social good," so to speak. People need it, and few, if any, substitutes are readily available. In such situations, market forces may not motivate suppliers to produce enough of the desired outputs at sufficient quality levels: for example, because not enough people understand the need for them, the benefits are enjoyed in part by others (what economists call "externalities"), or the benefits are deferred to the point where purely financial calculations discount them to insignificance. A second and important example is where quality is difficult or impossible to evaluate, so buyers have to rely on suppliers to police value on their behalf rather than in the interest of owners who might line their pockets by shortchanging quality. Both examples illustrate situations where for-profit enterprises and market forces cannot be trusted to supply the needed social benefits at appropriate quality levels. The rise of nongovernmental organizations (NGOs) in recent years provides evidence to support these points, should any be needed.

A second condition, when it applies, provides yet another argument for maintaining a meaningful nonprofit sector: the desired output costs so much to produce that it would not be affordable if the enterprise had to recover its full costs. Maintaining access requires a public subsidy in this case, and nonprofits can't divert subsidy payments for the benefit of shareholders. (We'll see that resource diversion can occur in nonprofits, but the problem is not as direct as in for-profits.) Resource diversion is a clear and present danger if the subsidy comes in the form of institutional support, but it also can occur through price increases and aggressive marketing when governments provide vouchers or other direct payments to users. The perceived need for subsidies was one reason that traditional universities were organized as nonprofit entities in the first place.

Nonprofit organizations do suffer from a number of drawbacks. Among these is the fact that one's mission must be defined subjectively through an often-messy governance process, the dilution (but by no means the elimination) of internal incentives for efficiency and market responsiveness, and the difficulty of providing external oversight. But the alternative easily can be worse. This book is about how to fix the problems of nonprofit higher education without pushing a majority of students into for-profit institutions.

## Why Traditional Universities Do What They Do

Clarity about the differences between decision-making behavior in nonprofit enterprises and the more familiar for-profit ones is essential for understanding how traditional universities work. The basic characteristics of nonprofits, and why they are so important in higher education, were described previously. We now dig into the subject more deeply: first by describing the economic theory of nonprofit enterprises and then by discussing its implications for university costs, prices, productivity, and cross-subsidization of programs.

The tension between mission and market is central to nonprofit universities. Clark Kerr described the conflict as between the Agora (literally, "the marketplace") and the Acropolis, which represents mission-oriented academic values.

> In fact, universities began in Europe in early modern times precisely [to serve the market]. . . . The cherished academic view that higher education started out on the Acropolis and was desecrated by descent into the Agora led by ungodly commercial interests and scheming public officials and venal academic leaders is just not true. If anything, higher education started in the Agora, the market, at the bottom of the hill and ascended to the Acropolis at the top of the hill. . . . Mostly it has lived in tension, at one and the same time at the bottom of the hill, at the top of the hill, and on the many pathways in between.[31]

The late Gordon Winston, provost at Williams College, described the tension in more earthy terms as pitting "university as church" against "university as car dealer."[32] Universities exist to produce value rather than profit, but they also must wheel and deal in the marketplace. "Why Traditional Universities Do What They Do" (the economic theory of nonprofits) explains this seemingly contradictory behavior.

Economist Estelle James and I described the "why" of university behavior in separate publications beginning in the late 1970s.[33] Here is the semitechnical description I crafted for *Change* magazine a decade or so ago:[34]

> Rooted in the economic theory of the for-profit firm, the model describes nonprofit behavior as maximizing a subjectively determined value function by adjusting outputs and output prices subject to market, production, and financial constraints. The elements of the theory [and their relation to the topics of this book] are:
>
> 1. A *value function* that reflects the institution's mission. The "institutional value proposition" that's embodied in this function is discussed later in this chapter.

2. *Market demand functions* that reflect the preferences of (i) students and others who use the institution's outputs (e.g., students and supporters of research, based on "user value propositions") and (ii) those who provide its factors of production (suppliers of human and other resources). Chapter 3 discusses how the educational market can be made more efficient through better information on value creation.

3. *Production functions* that describe how the input factors are transformed into outputs of desired quantity and quality. Chapter 4 discusses the production function for teaching and learning.

4. A *financial function* that requires, on average over time, that the institution's "net margin," after deducting needed transfers to reserves and capital, equal zero (the budget limit). Chapter 5 discusses the financial function and a practical procedure for applying the budget limit.

In short, the traditional university seeks to produce the most value possible given its markets, its operating environment, and the need to balance its books. The idea of a single value function is, of course, a simplifying assumption. Real-world value functions, which reflect the views of many different actors, are cobbled together by messy processes of institutional governance.[35] The assumption leads to important insights, however, and some of the messiness is taken into account in the operational decision model presented in chapter 5.

### Rules to Aid Decision-Making

Nonprofit enterprise behavior differs significantly from its for-profit counterpart. Taught in countless beginning economics courses, the for-profit business model calls for maximizing the spread between revenue and cost, not an institutionally defined value function. In terms of the aforementioned definitions, this means that the financial function is the maximization target, not a constraint. The remaining constraints, relating to markets and production, are not different in principle from those faced by nonprofit entities.[36]

The two paradigms lead to different decision rules for resource allocation. The for-profit rule calls for a program or activity to be expanded until its

*incremental revenue = incremental cost,*[37]

where *incremental revenue* depends on the demand function and market prices and *incremental cost* depends on the production function and unit costs. Expanding an activity will increase profits until the equality point is reached; after that, further expansion will reduce profits.

The nonprofit model adds a *value* term to the decision rule. The program or activity should be expanded until its

*incremental value* + *incremental revenue* = *incremental cost*,

while maintaining

*total revenue* = *total cost*.

*Incremental value* represents extra fulfillment of the institutional value function associated with program expansion. (The user value proposition comes into the theory implicitly through the incremental revenue term—e.g., when students show up in greater numbers or are willing to pay higher prices.) For the mathematically inclined, the formulas are derived at the beginning of appendix G.

The three terms of the nonprofit decision rule can be described as *mission* + *money* = *cost*, or less formally as *love* + *money* = *cost*. This sums up the tension between "university as church and university as car dealer." Mission attainment can be thought of as "love," a subject notably present in churches, whereas "money" represents wheeling and dealing in the marketplace. The extra degree of freedom added by the "love" term adds to the complexity of university decision-making.[38] It is what distinguishes nonprofit from for-profit behavior.

The differences are profound. Mission competes with money in university decision-making. There may be arguments about how to interpret the mission, but its primacy in principle is above challenge. For-profits, on the other hand, want to maximize shareholder value, which depends on how the firm's activities are monetized in the marketplace. Nonmarket goals, the kind companies sometimes enshrine in "mission statements," rarely are overriding criteria for decision-making in for-profits.

As noted earlier, surpluses generated by nonprofit entities are reinvested in their missions, whereas those of for-profits exit the enterprise through payout to shareholders—who tend to be insatiable in their pursuit of investment return. This has important implications for the quality of outputs. The delivery of exemplary quality generally is an *intrinsic* goal in nonprofit universities and an *instrumental* goal in for-profit ones. The distinction is especially important when, as in higher education, markets find it hard to evaluate quality. Society has tended to favor nonprofits in this case because for-profits are motivated to cut corners in ways that boost profits while staying below the threshold of negative market reaction. Such entities perform well when quality can be evaluated with reasonable objectivity and consumers are informed and care about the variations, and not so well when many of the benefits are intangible or will accrue only in the future.

It's true that universities don't always deliver on their missions. Non-profit status is a necessary condition for mission primacy, but it's not sufficient. Constituency-based governance may twist the interpretation of mission toward participants' self-interest: for example, if a university caters to the special interests of faculty, staff, and alumni in ways that don't confer long-term societal benefit.[39] Improved governance can solve these problems, however, whereas shareholder self-interest is central to the for-profit's governance structure.

### "Cross Subsidies Are Us"

"Cross subsidy" sometimes is considered a dirty word when thinking about universities, but nothing could be further from the truth. To understand why, imagine a liberal arts college with just two programs, Business and Philosophy, each of which is being run with the greatest possible efficiency. Suppose, further, that Business's strong market demand produces positive margins but the demand for Philosophy is not sufficient to cover its costs, and that both situations are expected to persist over time. The results of the for-profit and nonprofit decision rule differ sharply in this case.

> The for-profit rule would close down Philosophy so the margin from Business can fall to the bottom line. The nonprofit rule would sustain Philosophy because its high intrinsic value offsets its financial losses, even though this means less money is available for Business. The academic payoff for sustaining Philosophy is greater than the payoff for expanding Business—by an amount sufficient to offset the former's negative margin.

This example should not be viewed as a rationalization but rather as the logical result of pursuing mission. The Business dean and faculty might argue that their school's market power entitles it to spend its surplus (e.g., on faculty research or salaries), but the provost could respond that a liberal arts institution is not complete without a Philosophy department and that Business benefits from being part of the broader enterprise. In effect, the argument that market power trumps institutional value is tantamount to saying customers should dictate priorities, which is not consistent with the goals of a traditional college or university.[40] Such issues don't arise in the for-profit world, where money-losing programs are downsized or eliminated because subsidizing them reduces the sums available for shareholders.[41]

The fact that *margin* can be more than an accounting construct is an important implication of the theory. To see why, we need only rearrange the terms of the nonprofit decision rule presented in the previous section to get:

$$mission\ contribution = incremental\ cost - incremental\ revenue$$
$$= -margin.$$

What this means is that, when thinking about the implications of expanding or contracting a department or program, *margin* (to be precise, "incremental margin") and *mission contribution* are mirror images of each other. When a well-managed traditional university decides to sustain a money-losing program (e.g., Philosophy), we know that the program must have high intrinsic value. A program that makes a lot of money (i.e., has a large positive margin) definitely has a lot of instrumental value, but its intrinsic value may be high, low, or perhaps even negative. Hence margin should be viewed as an important variable by academic leaders as well as by accountants.

I've described why maximizing mission as opposed to shareholder value is the primary objective in traditional universities, but doing so takes more than motivation: it requires the availability of discretionary funds with which to subsidize money-losing activities. There are two sources of discretionary funds: (i) positive margins earned by other activities as described previously ("cross subsidies") and (ii) net income from sources not associated with particular academic programs. I call the latter "fixed revenue" because, like fixed cost, it does not vary with student numbers, research projects, or other outputs. The prime examples are unrestricted income from gifts and endowments, and (for public universities) institutional support from the government. It's possible in principle for a university to subsidize all of its programs from fixed revenue, but this rarely happens in practice. What happens when overall revenue gets looser or tighter tells us a great deal about the behavior of traditional universities.

It turns out that the traditional university's ability to support money-losing programs—to exert its values over those of the marketplace—is directly proportional to its degree of budget flexibility. I demonstrate in appendix G that the nonprofit decision rule converges with the for-profit rule as money gets tighter and tighter. This means that financially strapped traditional universities behave just like for-profit ones! Traditional universities that are more affluent have more freedom to exercise their values, and those that face financial stringency must pay more attention to margin—and therefore to market pricing and cost control. Margin trumps mission when budgets are very tight and conversely, but most situations represent a blend of the two. An ability to appropriately balance mission with margin is what distinguishes well-led traditional universities, especially ones that face a degree of financial stringency, from their less effective counterparts.

The political strategy of "starving" universities financially, which appears to have been practiced in some states, can indeed force schools to become less costly. For most institutions, however, repeated budget reductions already have squeezed out the "fat" that accumulated during the years of plenty. In this case, stringent revenue diets simply reduce schools' ability to assert their values and drive them toward for-profit behavior. Those who would pursue "starving the beast" as a cost-containment strategy should think carefully about their universities' mission-related values (e.g., as laid out at the end of this chapter) and then ask whether the public good would truly be served by subordinating them to the shorter-term and narrower private goals of an ill-informed marketplace.

## Implications for Tuition and Cost Containment

While cross subsidies represent an unequivocally positive characteristic of traditional universities, the same can't be said for their performance on price, productivity, and cost containment. The performance is not necessarily worse than similar actions by for-profits, but it is not necessarily better either. I'll start with price, mainly represented by tuition and fees, and then go to productivity and its effect on the cost of teaching.

### Incentives for Price Escalation

One might think that being a nonprofit would remove the incentive for price escalation—that charging all the market will bear is associated only with profit maximization. This is a false assumption, however. The reason lies in the nonprofit's desire to deliver on its institutional value proposition to the greatest extent possible. Price increases "fall to the bottom line" as more discretionary revenue for subsidizing high-value activities, other things being equal. The higher the price, the greater the university's ability to deliver on its mission, which leaves it with a strong incentive to charge as much as it can.[42]

The higher education literature contains a famous quotation known as Bowen's law, which sums this up nicely: "Universities will raise all the money they can, and spend all the money they raise."[43] (Boosting tuition is only one way to raise money, but it certainly is an important one.) Also called the "revenue theory of budgeting," Bowen's law has become a touchstone for scholars who analyze the seemingly inexorable increases in tuition rates. They know that despite higher education's assertions about the need to boost price because of rising costs, institutions may well do so simply because they can. Cost-push can be a sufficient condition for price escalation, but it definitely is not a necessary one. As is noted in subsequent chapters, the problem is compounded by the market's lack of ability to differentiate quality and thus to effectively discipline price.

What, if anything, can be done about Bowen's law? The answer lies in the mission-related goal of maintaining affordability and in the university's desire to fill its classes with the kinds of students it wants. Today's traditional universities address these issues mainly through the medium of financial aid, but because many prospective students don't know the details of what the aid offers, the sticker price should not be neglected. Concerns about political blowback provide another reason for being concerned about sticker price.

Some institutions have taken, and publicized, self-denying ordinances with respect to large tuition increases, but the pressures to raise and spend more money usually overwhelm these good intentions. I believe that the only way to resist these forces is through changes in the budget process of the kind discussed in chapter 5 (i.e., the separation of pricing decisions from those pertaining to budget allocation). Bowen's law can be mitigated only when tuition rates are no longer used to "plug the budget gap" and advocates of price moderation get a powerful voice at the policy table.

### Why Productivity Improvement Is Problematic

Traditional universities benefit from productivity and efficiency gains (without quality diminution) in the same way that for-profit entities do. They know a penny saved through such gains is a penny added to discretionary revenue—and thus to the pool of funds available for subsidies. And since it is subsidies that enable universities to assert their missions, the incentives for productivity and efficiency improvement are indeed significant.

Unfortunately, the incentives are not as strong as in for-profits. First, it's easier to identify "unnecessary" expenditures when the benefits are calculable profits than when, as in nonprofits, they involve institutional values. As mentioned previously, institutional values are multidimensional and subjective—with many of the dimensions being hotly contested as various stakeholders seek to influence priorities. Conflicts about the degree to which a given expenditure supports the institution's mission and the opportunity loss associated with what might be done if it's not eliminated make it vastly harder to agree on cost reductions.

The lack of good quality metrics poses a second problem. The market is unable to police quality, and, as discussed chapter 2, the university also finds it hard to do so. Hence the danger that cost reductions will erode quality is ever-present. People who are close to the action (faculty) are in the best position to decide which costs can be cut safely, but they usually lack the incentives and knowledge needed to do so.

A third problem is the absence of external financial markets in which outside parties evaluate and discipline an organization's efficiency. A public company that lags behind in productivity is soon penalized in the stock market (and thus in the compensation of its top executives), whereas no such consequence occurs in the nonprofit sector. The traditional university's discipline must be mainly internal, at least until the state of the art in external oversight matures to the point where third parties can reliably detect productivity shortfalls. Internally generated concerns about productivity improvement and cost containment have produced a lot of talk but generally not much action. Hopefully, that will change as the concepts and tools discussed in this book gain currency.

### Barriers to Growth by Substitution

"Growth by substitution" means "stopping certain activities that are no longer of high priority" in order to make room for ones that have become more important. "Growth" in this context means improvements in quality, coverage, relevance, and the like, not increases in institutional size. Many schools have recently funded teaching and research programs on issues relating to the environment, for example, but doing so without increasing cost per student requires that certain less important programs be eliminated or downsized. The substitution of new teaching technologies for the traditional labor-intensive ones represent another example. Both kinds of substitution are necessary for a university to avoid proliferating activities to the long-run detriment of cost containment.[44]

Growth by substitution runs afoul of several aspects of the traditional university's culture. Imagine the following conversation between a dean and a department chair, for example: "I've got good news and bad news for you about one of your programs. The good news is that it continues to get good reviews from peers and students; the bad news is that I'm closing it down because it's losing money and I think other programs are more deserving of subsidy." Such decisions are unexceptional in for-profit entities, where the bottom line is easily measured and mission considerations are not a big factor. Not so in universities, where values are important, multidimensional, and subjective—and "deserving" may be asserted as lying in the eye of the beholder. University governance systems provide means for adjudicating serious value differences, but they can be slow, cumbersome, and subject to logrolling. Therefore, for budget purposes, the authority for making most of the value judgments is vested in deans, provosts, and other academic officers, who may develop systematic criteria for downsizing and apply them with an acute sense of due process. But even when this authority is accepted in principle, another factor makes growth by substitution exceedingly difficult.

In addition to being intrinsically valued, successful programs involve what educational economist Henry Levin calls "property rights."[45] Faculty feel vested in their programs and fiercely resist efforts to downsize them. Such behavior reflects more than ego. Because academics are so highly specialized, losing one's program can blight a career. Such cuts get appealed in the corporate world, but the appeals usually challenge facts or analyses. In universities, they also focus on equity—on violations of "property rights" that faculty have built up over a period of successful service. Adverse financial times make it easier to overcome vested property rights. Even then, however, growth by substitution requires carefully crafted processes and protocols as well as reliable data that are generally accepted across the institution.

It should come as no surprise that what's needed are pervasive and detailed data on the university's courses, programs, and operating units, as well as the revenues, costs, and margins associated with the activities. Chapters 4 and 5 describe these data in detail and provide some examples about how they can be used to gauge program efficacy. The sooner such data become routinely available, the sooner growth by substitution can become a regular process for improving productivity in traditional universities.

Provision of such data will enable the development of effective protocols for managing substitutions. Suppose, for example, that a provost, dean, or department chair has developed a "watch list" of activities where the data indicate actual or prospective weakness or an opportunity for improvement. No items may present a strong enough case to precipitate spontaneous action, but the list will prove valuable in two kinds of circumstances:

- An across-the-board target for budget reductions is put in place—either in response to a financial problem or as a general policy for stimulating productivity improvement.
- A high-priority item is being considered for funding, but the budget limit does not permit action unless something currently in the budget base is removed.

It's possible to identify potential budget reductions on an ad-hoc basis, but, given the need for comparative data analysis and consultation in advance with interested faculty, it's better to have a watch list in hand when the time for cutting arrives. Having such a list also helps instill a mindset that includes the possible need for growth by substitution.

Such a mindset will go a long way toward alleviating what Bowen and Tobin call "serious generic problems": (i) that "cost considerations drive decisions at hard-pressed institutions only when there is no other way to go—when 'muddling through' has hit the wall"; and (ii) that institutions may be pressed by legislators, trustees, and others to "move aggressively (with or without adequate faculty consultation) to introduce cost-saving technologies." Indeed, all the suggestions in this book respond to their plea for occupying Isaiah Berlin's "ungrateful middle ground, and dealing directly, up front, and unapologetically with trade-offs when that can be done thoughtfully and ahead of some make-or-break crisis."[46]

## Business Models and Value Propositions

Entities that operate in the marketplace must have business models that deliver value to their customers. In the for-profit sector, this is paramount. Management gurus Robert Kaplan and David Norton go so far as to say that "[s]atisfying customers is *the* source of sustainable value creation."[47] Universities also operate in the marketplace and thus must deliver value to customers, but they also pursue the intrinsic values embodied in their missions. This is what I mean by being "mission centered and market smart." Hence the business models of the two kinds of entities must be significantly different.

Figure 1.1 summarizes how the traditional university's business model for teaching differs from the for-profit university's model (or the model for any other business). The for-profit model is simpler, so we'll begin there. Everything starts with what's called the "customer value proposition," at the one-o'clock position in the left-hand panel, which describes how the firm will appeal to its customers. Next comes the market's response to the appeals, and this is followed by the production activities needed to deliver the goods and services. Then come cost and revenue, which the financial system processes into reported profits as

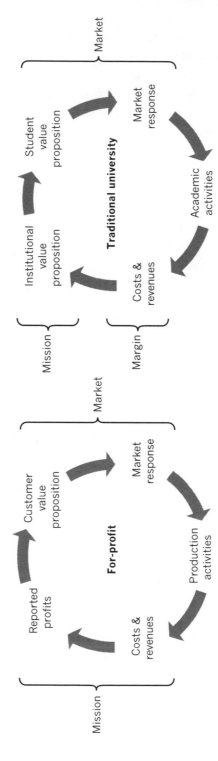

**Figure 1.1.** Business models in firms and traditional universities

required by the entity's mission—maximizing shareholder value. After this, the process starts anew, perhaps with changes in the value proposition and/or production activities.

The figure's right-hand panel depicts the business model in a traditional university. It differs from the for-profit diagram mainly in the area of mission, which appears at the ten-o'clock position. Rather than being a profit calculation based on cost and revenue, the university's mission is subjective and multidimensional. It's rooted in what I've come to call the "institutional value proposition," which describes the school's intrinsic values rather than the values that drive market demand. Costs and revenues have their own category, "margin," rather than being included under mission as with the business firm. That's because profit doesn't enter the university's mission but rather is a means to the ends described in the institutional value proposition. The other change substitutes "student value proposition" for the business firm's "customer value proposition," but both have the same purpose—to create market demand. (Some universities also consider value propositions for research sponsors, but they aren't relevant for the present discussion.) The three callouts around the edge of the university diagram correspond to the subtitle of this book: *Mission Centered, Market Smart, and Margin Conscious.*

Figure 1.2 elaborates on the business model as applied to undergraduates. It lists the elements of the student and institutional value propositions as I see them. There is a vast collection of literature about what universities do or should do to serve their students and further their missions. I shall make no attempt to review this literature but instead simply articulate what I believe to be representative undergraduate value propositions in traditional universities. Schools may explicitly articulate parts of the propositions or even write them down; other parts are implicit but nevertheless potent. Finally, the "organization of academic work" box at the bottom of the figure lists the three ways faculty activities differ from production in other kinds of entities. The value propositions, the idiosyncratic characteristics of academic work, and the ways these interact with market forces to produce flaws in the business model are elaborated in the next chapter. We shall see that the difficulty of obtaining feedback on the quality of education plays a critical role in these interactions.

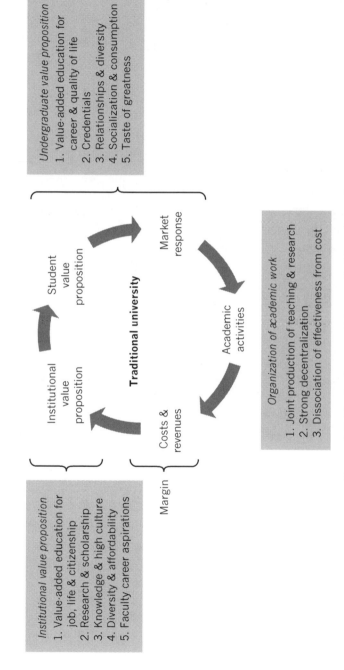

**Figure 1.2.** The business model as applied to undergraduates

The need for traditional universities to pursue *two* value propositions contributes strongly to the complexity so often cited in this book. Universities come close to being unique in this respect. They march to the drummer of mission, *and* they operate in highly competitive and important markets. For-profit firms operate in competitive markets, but their objectives are essentially one-dimensional and calculable from present and estimated future costs and revenues. Nonprofit foundations and NGOs may have complex missions, but they don't usually rely heavily on markets where service differentiation and price are hotly contested. Only universities and health care entities must simultaneously address the imperatives of both mission and market. Although it's possible that the two sets of objectives will coincide, such an outcome is highly unusual. This will become apparent as we illustrate the two value propositions.

### Undergraduate Value Proposition (Market)

The value proposition for undergraduate students is both critical to the university and problematic in application. It's critical because there are so many undergraduates, whose share of tuition and (where applicable) state capitation grants is so large, and because they are so important for external stakeholders like alumni and governments. It's problematic because an undergraduate's goals are complex, and because student motivation and learning can be difficult to attain. The value propositions for master's and PhD students are more straightforward. Master's students generally seek, and get, well-defined professional and/or disciplinary training, and PhD students are apprenticing with faculty experts to become researchers. That is why, here, I concentrate on the user-value proposition for undergraduates.

1. *Value-added education for job and quality of life.* Getting a job is the number-one goal for many students, and gaining access to relevant skill pools is a major goal for employers. Universities respond to this objective because it's in their interest to serve the marketplace and because they believe that it's the "right" thing to do. To quote Lumina Foundation president Jamie Merisotis, "We need to abandon our historic view in higher education that we don't train people for jobs. Of course we do. That doesn't mean it is the *only* thing we do, but to

deny [that] job skills development is one of the key purposes of higher education is increasingly untenable."[48] Many students and parents also value nonmonetizing outcomes such as the ability to make good personal decisions, enjoy meaningful activities, and relate well to others.[49] The work and quality-of-life goals often are considered separately, but in fact they are highly synergistic—if for no other reason than students' need to interact with other people and adapt as jobs and circumstances change over their lifetimes. Universities vary greatly in how their curricula reflect and their courses deliver on these goals,[50] but few academics would say that the delivery of these benefits is not a high priority.

2. *Confer credentials.* Credentials assure employers and other external stakeholders that students have met the criteria set forth in the school's catalog. Credentials take the form of degrees and certificates, credits for academic work, GPAs, and the like. The credentialing associated with selectivity can be important as well: students who have gained entry to selective institutions benefit from the certification implied by admission itself, even if they don't take full advantage of the opportunities their institutions have to offer. Some critics say that the spread of licensure programs will make institutional credentialing irrelevant, but it's important to remember that licensure only can certify threshold competencies in skill-related areas.

3. *Relationships and diversity.* Involvement with a diverse group of students who have passed the institution's selection hurdles but who may have different ethnicities, perspectives, and interests also provides important life-changing experiences. Benefits include peer-to-peer learning, an appreciation of multiple ethnicities and perspectives, lifelong networking contacts, and perhaps even a mate.

4. *Socialization and consumption.* These have long been associated with the college experience, especially for students in university housing and those who live near the campus. They can include social activities, life-enhancing amenities, and an attractive campus setting. Institutions work hard to mitigate the downsides of some of these activities (e.g., binge drinking), but on the whole they are seen as important parts of the undergraduate value proposition—and ones that many families are willing to pay for. Commuter students get fewer of these benefits, but they do get some.

5. *Taste of greatness*. Being in an institution that discovers and applies new knowledge, facilitates exposure to high culture and serious athletics, and in other ways is "part of something big" can open life-changing windows that may not be available later in life. Students engage through course work, extracurricular activities, athletics, and involvement in campus events.

These five propositions apply to most, if not all, traditional universities. In fact, when taken together they define what one can reasonably expect from being an undergraduate at a traditional university. The emphasis varies from school to school, of course. For example, selective schools offer the most potent credentials. Research universities stress the taste of greatness more so than public comprehensives. Private institutions generally focus on consumption values to a greater extent than public ones. Nevertheless, few traditional universities will deny that each of the five propositions is relevant for attracting and satisfying students.

Universities believe in their undergraduate value propositions for the same reasons business firms believe in their customer value propositions: because they need to serve the marketplace. Well-run enterprises know that good quality helps sustain future demand and gives the workforce pride in a job well done. Critics who claim that traditional universities don't care about their students are overstating their case. The academic business model harbors significant flaws, but "not caring about students" usually isn't one of them.

## Institutional Value Proposition (Mission)

There is considerable overlap between the user and institutional value propositions, but the two are definitely not identical. In fact, the differences between the two are what distinguish the nonprofit sector. The main elements of the institutional value proposition are listed as follows:

1. *Value-added education for job, quality of life, and good citizenship.* Except for creating an educated citizenry, this is the same as "value-added education" in the undergraduate value proposition. The importance of "educating citizens" was summed up by Thomas Jefferson in his defense of higher education in a democracy: "Only an

informed citizenry would be able to see through the ruses used by governmental authorities, and exposure to the competition of ideas would allow citizens to judge who could best represent their interests. . . . Orders of men [sic], watching and balancing each other, are the only security; power must be opposed to power, and interest to interest."[51] Yet such informed skepticism should be tempered by the willingness and ability to participate constructively in finding solutions to the difficult problems facing governments and the even more difficult ones of adopting and legitimizing new social norms. To quote Wesleyan president Michael Roth: "Guided by a liberal education, [students] will increase their ability to find together ways of living that have meaning and direction"[52]—where "liberal education" goes beyond the liberal arts to include, for any subject, teaching in a broad conceptual and empathetic way. I might have included the informed citizenry goal in the undergraduate value proposition, but I doubt that many students consider it to be a defining personal objective. Universities do, however, because an educated citizenry is a critically important public good.

2. *Research and scholarship.* Pushing back the frontiers of knowledge is of critical importance for the nation and the world. It is viewed by many academics as the highest calling of a university, but, true or not, there is no denying its high priority both for institutions and faculty. Success, which can be measured through publications, citations, and prestige surveys, seems to be of ever-greater importance in the minds of academic leaders and faculty. I've already discussed the importance of research and scholarship at some length.

3. *Preservation and exchange of knowledge and culture.* Universities have long seen themselves as repositories of knowledge and high culture, even in areas where public interest and market demand are lacking. They make investments and stage events in the face of marketplace indifference because they believe that these have intrinsic value. In a recent extension of the concept, universities are becoming "entrepreneurial" by engaging as active knowledge exchange partners in areas where market demand has yet to materialize. This is done through cooperative projects, consultancies, joint ventures, and the like. Entrepreneurship offers a number of advantages: the university becomes a proactive force for the adoption of its ideas, commu-

nication is two way rather than mostly one way as in traditional dissemination, and it eventually may be possible to monetize these activities through profits and royalties.

4. *Diversity and affordability.* Universities want to provide opportunities for disadvantaged students and maintain affordability for all students—to benefit their own programs and on behalf of the society at large. These represent additional public benefits that, while overlapping with the private benefits of participating in diverse and high-quality educational experiences, offer powerful levers for short- and long-run societal improvement. Evidence for why this goal needs to be reaffirmed, should any be needed, can be found in the startling statistic that children of parents in the bottom socioeconomic (SES) quartile who score the highest on eighth grade test scores are now slightly less likely to graduate from college than the lowest-testing children of parents in the top SES quartile (i.e., 29 percent vs. 30 percent).[53] Harvard sociologist Robert Putnam makes the powerful point that, in addition to the ethical problem posed by this statistic, it reflects a poor prognosis for the productivity of our economy, the stability of the country, and the quality of life for all of us.

5. *Faculty career aspirations.* Advancing the career aspirations of those who work at the institution, especially the faculty, may seem self-serving, but there is more to it than that. Traditional universities strive to advance the long-term intellectual vitality of society. This includes facilitating and rewarding the work of professors, whose value, many believe, stems from who they *are* rather than simply from the labor they provide. Professors represent "seed corn" for society's future intellectual development. Overexploit the seed corn in the present and one stunts future harvests. That said, it certainly is possible for individuals' career aspirations to dominate the institutional value proposition to an inappropriate degree.

How the propositions manifest themselves in particular universities depends on the interpretation of mission by academic leaders, faculty governance groups, and governing boards.[54] These interpretations can shift in response to changed circumstances: for example, when a liberal arts college that is hard-pressed financially decides that a potentially profitable Business program no longer conflicts with its traditional mission. It's also possible that people responsible for governance will form a self-reinforcing circle that, over time, warps the institutions' values in ways most stakeholders see as unfortunate. In general, however, I believe that universities want to deliver on their institutional value propositions.

# Chapter 2

# The Reengineering Challenge

To succeed at reengineering, one first must probe the details of the problems that need to be solved. In our case, that means examining what I've come to call the "academic business model," which describes how the values defined in the previous chapter are, in fact, created. This requires a close look at teaching and learning—the "business of the business" in universities. Some might consider the juxtaposition of "academic" and "business" to be an oxymoron, but this isn't so. Business models are essential for strategy development and implementation, and thus are as applicable to academic as to other kinds of organizations. Academic business models have been largely implicit (and therefore unexamined), but today's challenges require explicit consideration. This chapter examines the problems that need fixing and describes how to go about getting the job done. The details of the "fixes" are presented in chapters 3 through 5.

I deal only with the academic side of the university. Elements such as administration, support services, and asset management, while important, are beyond the scope of this book. My concern is with what makes the university's academic operations unique as compared to most other organizations, the emergent flaws in traditional ways of thinking, and what can be done about them.

## Flaws in the Academic Business Model

The following narrative, hypothetical but deeply rooted in experience, raises some fundamental questions about the academic business model.

The provost of a large university was pondering a sharp question that had been raised by a trustee at the last board meeting: "Just what is our university's academic business model? I understand the nonacademic parts of the business model (revenues, expenses, support services, and so on), but the academic side eludes me.

"We say that our goal is excellence in teaching and research, and that the two are equally important. But what does that really mean? How do we manage the joint production so neither one crowds out the other? Research gets evaluated in many ways, but do we have a firm grip on what it takes to produce educational excellence? What are we doing to eliminate excess expense and improve our cost effectiveness? Why, for example, do we continue to support money-losing programs? How do we think about academic productivity, and how do we gauge its improvement?

"I know you can't improve something if you can't measure it, so I'd like to understand how we assess student learning. Business quality gurus say that the objective is to delight the customer, but I agree with the faculty that it isn't right to rely mainly on students for quality assessment. Surely, however, marketplace priorities should influence what we do. Am I missing something, or is there confusion and perhaps inconsistency at the heart of our billion-dollar enterprise?"

The questioner, from the business community but highly sensitive to the differences between universities and corporations, was dead serious. She had studied the voluminous planning documents and board data books and could recite the standard arguments for why her concerns were unfounded, if not misguided. But the wealth of details and anecdotes had left her unsatisfied. She knew that some elements of her profit-oriented business experience didn't apply (e.g., the university should not march to the drummers of money and the marketplace), but just what should replace the money and market model?

The provost respected the trustee and wanted to provide a well-thought-out response. But what should that response be?

This narrative highlights some fundamental disagreements and misunderstandings that bedevil traditional universities—problems that are serious enough to call forth a "reinventing" of the academic business model.[1] Understanding these problems, and the business model itself, poses the problem faced by blind men and the elephant. Each person understands a piece, but no one has a firm grasp of the whole.

Universities are very complex places, and this complexity makes them hard to manage. It is even harder to convey the reasons for management decisions to stakeholders outside the institution.

But the problem runs deeper. My thesis in this book is that the academic business model as currently exercised by traditional universities harbors some fundamental flaws and indeed is no longer sustainable. The flaws have been masked by the sector's complexity and, until recently at least, its dominance in the marketplace. Now, however, the rise of technology-enabled disrupters is making the flaws too significant to ignore. I focus on the academic functions in traditional universities: the things that make such universities special places and distinguish them from other kinds of entities. The objective is to mitigate the flaws in order to restore sustainability in ways that do not jeopardize the enterprises' fundamental values or comparative advantage.

Decades of experience, research, and consulting have convinced me that the most serious flaws fall into the following broad categories: (i) overdecentralization of teaching activity, (ii) unmonitored joint production, (iii) dissociation of educational quality from cost, (iv) lack of good learning metrics, and (v) overreliance on market forces. These flaws have become deeply embedded core elements of the academic business model. They have evolved for good reasons, however, and reengineering initiatives that don't take these reasons into account will risk damaging the university's distinguishing qualities.

## Overdecentralization of Teaching Activity

While clearly employees of their universities, professors often are viewed, and view themselves, as autonomous agents whose job it is to pursue self-defined teaching and research goals rather than to function mainly as team members in a larger enterprise. This goes back to medieval universities like Bologna, Paris, and Oxford, where professors were, in fact, independent contractors paid by students at the conclusion of lectures. Another cause stems from the granular structure of knowledge itself. Traditionally, the "scholar" (teacher or researcher) was an expert in a particular content domain. General disciplinary expertise may have been shared among departmental colleagues, but a professor's true comparative advantage lay at the branch tips of the tree of knowledge.

"Content is king" in traditional university education, and individual faculty expertise is the key to content. Students have been viewed as "sitting at the feet of scholars," figuratively if not literally, so it's not unnatural for professors to view themselves as content sages. This is why the academic culture generally holds that faculty should be solely responsible for the curriculum, and that courses should be the responsibility of individual faculty members.[2] Professors develop courses and then teach them according to their own ideas about both content and teaching method. Basic courses may involve the effort of several faculty members, but even here it's usually understood that individual professors should maintain autonomous responsibility for the sections they teach. Professors also can develop advanced courses, for which they negotiate entry into the school's catalogue and credit in terms of their teaching loads. Curricular design usually takes the form of listing catalogue entries, with occasional requests for new course development to fill particular content gaps. Faculty committees have long taken responsibility for curricula and for ensuring that what gets taught is appropriate to the discipline and at university level (e.g., that "science" is really science), but faculty autonomy requires that most other decisions be left to individual professors.

Faculty autonomy is closely linked to academic freedom and intellectual diversity.[3] Overt threats to academic freedom are, of course, all too familiar: for example, speaking truth to, and about, power can be dangerous. Peer-based threats also can be significant. The downside of dedicating oneself to a team of peers is that to innovate, one must convince others that his or her proposal is worth adopting. These threats manifest themselves in many small ways, for which the effects can accumulate over time, even when there is no coercive intent. Intellectual diversity has flourished because professors have been free to adopt new concepts and methods in noncoercive and relatively forgiving environments rather than having to take everything to a committee. Furthermore, this diversity has been played out on a massive scale rather than being limited to a few well-placed individuals.

The benefits of such decentralization are substantial, but a heavy price is extracted when it comes to the systemic improvement of teaching and learning. Developing courses that juxtapose discipline-based knowledge paradigms with student, employer, and societal needs requires a good deal of time, and devising scientifically valid and cost-effective teaching methodologies to deliver learning requires even more. Doing these things well requires more sustained effort than can usually be supplied by individual professors working autonomously. They require a collaborative effort, often supplemented by professionals in fields such as survey design, learning science, service science, and information technology. Unfortunately, the academic culture of strong decentralization discourages this kind of collaboration and support.

Research has a lesson to teach us here. It was not so long ago that individual professors, supported by a few graduate assistants, postdocs, and perhaps technicians, conducted nearly all traditional-university research. As the work became more complicated, however, the individuals began collaborating in small groups and then larger ones. Centers and large laboratory groups were formed to provide needed infrastructure, and nonfaculty professionals were hired to mainline positions under the principal investigators. Many fields of science now require large teams to accomplish anything worthwhile, and it's not uncommon to see a dozen or more coauthors on publications. All this was forced by the increasing complexity of the work, and it was enabled by the financial support available from universities and research sponsors. For-profit educational providers and, recently, developers of large online programs such as MOOCs have adopted a similar model. However, teaching in traditional universities generally remains mired in the "artisan" modality because that's the only viable approach in a strongly decentralized system.

*Unmonitored Joint Production*

The unmonitored joint production of teaching and research is another serious flaw in the academic business model. By "unmonitored" I mean that decisions about how much of each to produce lie mainly in the hands of individual professors, with relatively little oversight from department chairs—let alone deans and provosts. (This is consistent with the decentralization described in the previous section.) Universities have policies for the fraction of time professors should spend on teaching, research, and service, but they lack effective means for enforcement. It is understood, correctly in my opinion, that the nature of faculty work precludes "punching time clocks" or even monitoring the number of hours spent on specific tasks as is done by lawyers and consultants. Measures of teaching load allow for a modicum of monitoring, but, as we shall see in chapter 4, the actual time spent is subject to a great deal of variation. The lack of monitoring would not be problematic if faculty incentives for the two outputs were evenly balanced and both the quality and quantity of teaching and research could be assessed accurately. Unfortunately, neither condition is even remotely true.

The conclusion that "research, not teaching, gets the lion's share of rewards conferred by institutions and colleagues" is a common theme in the academic literature.[4] For example, more than 90 percent of professors interviewed by staff of the National Center for Postsecondary Improvement in the 1990s cited tenure and promotion as their top priorities along with their belief that research counts far more than teaching in performance reviews. While concerns about teaching quality have increased in recent years, the pressures to do research have increased as well. The result is a tendency for research and scholarship to "crowd out" time spent on teaching and its improvement. Bob Zemsky's and my concept of the "academic ratchet" describes the steady erosion of attention to teaching as research pressures grow.[5] Corner-cutting becomes more and more the norm as professors come to "satisfice" on their educational tasks. They may do what's necessary to achieve a high-outcome standard, but then, with relief, they turn their attention to research. Unfortunately, satisficing is the antithesis of continuous quality improvement (discussed in chapter 3) because it substitutes "good enough is" for "good enough isn't."

The consequences of the academic ratchet are depicted in figure 2.1, originally formulated by the distinguished economist Mark Nerlov.[6] This stylized diagram displays a department's educational quality on the vertical axis and research intensity on the horizontal one: with, importantly, the number of faculty and students being held constant. The positive slope on the left-hand side of the diagram indicates "complementarity in production" as defined in chapter 1, because more research begets better education quality. But research and education quality eventually become "substitutes" as the more intensive research program presses on faculty time and crowds out attention to educational tasks. At this point, the positive synergies become overshadowed by the losses in time spent on teaching and mentoring students.

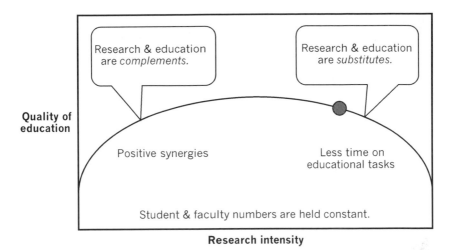

**Figure 2.1.** Teaching and research: Complements or substitutes? *Source*: Massy, *Honoring the Trust*, 97.

The gray dot on the diagram depicts a situation where research and teaching are compliments on average but substitutes at the margin. Quality is better with this amount of research than it would be with none, but further increments to research reduce educational quality. The lack of monitoring noted previously makes it hard to determine any given department's position on the curve. However, there's no reason to believe universities always, or even usually, operate in the upward-sloping range where more research improves education quality.

The crowding-out problem undermines the proposition that excellence in research implies excellence in teaching—a proposition that is reflected in countless ranking and evaluation schemes. "Prestige," based largely on publications, citations, and other measures of research prowess, has come to signify quality in the traditional university sector. This is unfortunate because it has tended to mask what's really happening. The use of research as a surrogate for educational quality has become so deeply embedded within institutions and among their stakeholders that it is no overstatement to say that it's a very important, albeit deeply flawed, element of the academic business model.

The last problem associated with unmonitored joint production is that much research nowadays is too specialized for direct relevance to undergraduate education. Few undergraduates can even approach the state of the art. Students may be encouraged to take part in faculty research projects, but only the better and most highly motivated ones take full advantage of these opportunities. (Even they must be careful not to get stuck with menial jobs—the iconic example of which, in psychology, is cleaning the rat cages.) Hence most students read or hear about research second-hand, which they could do nearly as well in an institution not so highly dedicated to advancing the frontiers of knowledge. Yet the lack of good educational quality measures (to be discussed shortly) prevents institutions from looking through the anecdotal evidence to challenge the traditional assertions about synergy.

### Dissociation of Quality from Cost

The dissociation of quality and cost, particularly in teaching, is another key differentiator of traditional academic work. In most industries, people who are integrally familiar with the details of production make the inevitable trade-offs between cost and quality. This isn't true for traditional universities. Professors bring expertise about the quality of teaching and learning, but cost is outside their domain. Worse, they tend to believe that, with quality held constant, the cost of teaching is fixed. This implies that boosting quality requires more resources, and conversely, which contradicts the very idea of productivity improvement. Professors do the best job possible with the resources they have been given and lobby for more at every opportunity, but they don't see the reengineering of teaching to improve cost-effectiveness as part of their job description.[7]

Professors aren't trained in cost analysis, and their experience as autonomous agents seldom brings them into contact with people who are. The academic culture maintains an arms-length relationship with the finance side of universities, and most professors speak rather disparagingly of the "bean counters" in their institutions' financial offices. (I was something of an exception as Stanford's CFO, because I was also a tenured full professor who had served as a vice provost and acting provost, but I had to tread lightly in the area of teaching cost.) Professors worry that a narrow view of "efficiency" will cause intangible but extremely important educational quality considerations to be swamped by hard data on costs, revenues, and margins. The fact that few professors know or care enough about accounting to refute inappropriate challenges on their merits exacerbates this worry, and so does the widespread confusion at all university levels about how to balance mission and margin—a subject I take up in chapter 5.

Unfortunately, the dissociation of effectiveness and cost leads to serious problems. Trade-offs between cost and educational effectiveness are made far from the action, necessarily using abstract criteria and fairly aggregative data. Making those trade-offs without detailed knowledge of how teaching and learning are accomplished in particular circumstances requires one to ignore many critical factors—ones that can have a powerful effect on quality. The task might be performed well enough when resources are plentiful (which means there can be a lot of what's called "organizational slack"[8]), but it becomes problematic when money is tight.

Schools try to find magic bullets for cost containment: for example, online courses (and now, especially, MOOCs) that can be initiated by high-level administrators and implemented by small teams outside the regular academic line. Real reform, however, requires trade-offs in the trenches with respect to the fine-structure of activities in many courses, modules, and even individual learning experiences. To be effective, this work will have to involve significant numbers of professors who can address *both* quality and cost.

Work on sponsored research projects shows what happens when professors care about making fine-structure cost-effectiveness trade-offs in an environment where both effectiveness and cost are well understood and measured. Principal investigators (PIs) make such judgments on a daily basis as they optimize their grant and contract expenditures. They consider cost-effectiveness alternatives, try out promising new ideas, and document the results—because failure to do these things will disadvantage them in the competitive market for funding and, eventually, publications. PIs don't hesitate to work with financial people when they need to, but, subject to funding constraints, ultimate decision-making power rests with the PI. Universities could apply a similar model to their teaching programs.

*Lack of Good Learning Metrics*

Despite the key role of student learning in the academic business model, guidance about how to assess its quality is conspicuous by its absence from most university planning. Other industries include quality assessment and assurance as integral to their business models, but the academy has yet to do that. This shortfall has profound negative consequences for both institutions and the higher education marketplace.

The National Research Council's report on measuring university productivity recently concluded that while great progress is being made, definitive quality metrics are "unlikely to be practical anytime soon."[9] More than two decades of effort have failed to produce the kinds of results hoped for by, for example, progenitors of the widely adopted "student assessment movement."[10] But while no magic bullets have been found and none are in the offing, several developments are worthy of mention. For example, campus-level learning outcomes can be assessed by the Measure of Academic Proficiency and Progress (MAPP), produced by the Educational Testing Service; the Collegiate Assessment of Academic Proficiency (CAAP), produced by the ACT Corporation; and the Collegiate Learning Assessment (CLA), produced by RAND and the Council for Aid to Education. CLA comes closest to measuring institutional value added between the freshman and senior years, although to some extent all can be used to make such inferences.

Surveys of student engagement measure the necessary conditions for learning as opposed to the learning outcomes themselves. Examples are the National Survey of Student Engagement (NSSE), the Community College Survey of Student Engagement (CCSSE), the Student Experience in the Research University (SERU), and the Cooperative Institutional Research Program (CIRP), which provide insight about the experiences of students enrolled in a given institution. But while useful, the link between engagement and learning must be considered carefully. Inferences about learning can be confounded by differences in discipline, student background, and social factors. Finally, all student surveys suffer from a kind of "moral hazard" in that the students who take the surveys and tests have much less at stake than does the institution that administers them.

The kinds of measures described previously operate at the institutional level or at the level of major segments within the institution. But while valuable for assessing aggregate strengths and weaknesses, they provide little guidance for professors who wish to improve their courses. Put another way, the measures don't focus on the fine-structure distinctions needed to decide whether one approach to learning is better or worse than another. It seems doubtful, moreover, that further development of these measures will generate the kind of "resolving power" needed for continuous education quality improvement. Much more promising is the refinement of methods by which professors measure learning in their own courses for their own purposes—a topic I take up in chapter 3.

A similar difficulty arises in efforts to study variations in learning across the student population. For example, it can be important to know whether learning is concentrated among students with high academic aptitude or whether it occurs equally, or at least proportionally, among those who are less well endowed. The relation of learning to student characteristics not highly correlated with aptitude also can be important: for example, to ascertain the effect of differences in learning objectives and style. There is no reason in principle why these things can't be analyzed, but study designs usually are not up to the task. Such studies require pre- and post-learning measurements for the same group of students, for example, which aren't available from standard datasets.

The aggregate measures' usefulness as quality indicators for the marketplace also is limited. There is no consensus about the efficacy of the various measures: all have their good points, but all have flaws as well. Differences in the circumstances of individual institutions (e.g., in the profiles of entering students, majors, and degrees) make comparisons among them difficult. The problem is compounded by the fact that samples often are too small for one to have confidence in small differences. Lack of transparency is another impediment to the measures' use as sources of market information. Institutions tend to resist the publication of results, so there is as yet no critical mass of discussion about efficacy and importance. There may be good reasons for such embargos, but one also suspects that many schools simply fear the prospect of looking bad. It's easier to hold the data close, and maybe discreetly discredit less-than-stellar results, than to disseminate and take on the consequences. Unfortunately, this strategy deprives the market of important information and inhibits improvement of the various metrics over time.

Surrogates for quality such as time to degree, graduation rates, and employment uptake and salaries have become popular as workarounds for the aforementioned problems. A number of foundations are active in this space, and a recent report by the National Governors Association offers specific proposals that state governments can adopt to oversee their institutions.[11] There's much to be said for such surrogates, but it's also necessary to understand their limitations. First, they do not address the value-added problem. Selective institutions almost always do better on the popular surrogates than do nonselective ones, yet the latter may be doing an excellent job in light of their missions. Second, because the surrogates usually function at an aggregate level, they aren't useful for professors who want to improve their courses. Similar problems stem from the time lags associated with many of the surrogates. It takes a number of years for changes in curriculum and teaching method to have an effect on degree completion, for instance, and even longer for the effect to propagate into the labor market.

### Overreliance on Market Forces

Most product and service providers rely on markets as the ultimate arbiters of quality and price. A former mentor of mine, one-time president of a major auto company and dean of Stanford's business school, described this thusly: "At the end of the day, all is well if the dogs are eating the dog food." In other words, delighting consumers by having the right user value proposition and then delivering on it effectively are what ultimately matter. This is not so in traditional higher education.

There are two reasons for this. First, as discussed in chapter 1, traditional universities pursue mission- as well as market-related values, and the institutional value proposition sometimes trumps the user value proposition. Second, there is little incentive to provide prospective students and their parents with detailed information on educational value added as opposed to, say, imperfect but self-serving surrogates for value added. Hence the market cannot play its normal role as arbiter of quality and price.[12]

The student marketplace also lacks indirect information that might be used to infer quality. Does a school deploy state-of-the-art technology and learning science, for example? Will the school be right for particular students, given their backgrounds and learning styles? The unfortunate fact is that most schools can't answer such questions authoritatively, let alone communicate the answers to the marketplace. Most of their information is anecdotal: for example, that they use cutting-edge technology in a few courses, that some students have written fine papers or participated in research projects, that others have been helped to surmount shortfalls in academic preparation, and that many alumni have gone on to graduate school and good jobs. But what does this mean for, say, the broad middle group of students—those with adequate admissions credentials but who may not be "turned on" by traditional academic work?

A huge industry has developed to supply information to the marketplace. Much data are available about credentialing, exposure to research, selectivity, diversity, graduation rates, times to degree, and consumption values. Some information is available on employment uptake, and this appears to be getting better over time. What's lacking, however, are data about how well students actually learn and what universities are doing to improve learning performance. Until this shortfall is mitigated, it will be exceedingly difficult for the market to police educational quality.

Another reason why the market is ineffective at policing quality derives from students' lack of experience and perspective. The vast majority of prospective undergraduates don't know what questions to ask, let alone how to find and interpret the answers. They make an enrollment decision only once or a few times in their lifetimes, so they are unable to build up the kind of experience that informs purchasers of most other goods and services. (Prospective graduate students generally do better because they already have some relevant experience.) High school counselors and college choice consultants offer as much advice as they can, but they too are shackled by the lack of good data about learning quality.

Markets are expected to discipline price as well as quality. Bob Zemsky, Greg Wegener, and I put it this way in our compendium of the Pew

*Policy Perspectives* to which we contributed during the 1990s. "It was expected that the market would extract some kind of accountability from the nation's colleges and universities as it was already extracting from the nation's manufacturers. . . . Better-informed consumers would make better decisions, sending the message that colleges and universities with ever-escalating prices would not be tolerated and educational processes that ignored what the customer wanted and needed would no longer suffice."[13]

It hasn't happened. Data shortfalls have caused the market to place extra emphasis on expensive activities such as research and provision of consumption values such as gourmet food and climbing walls—the "winner takes all" arms race referred to earlier. Again, to quote our compendium: "Each institution seeks an edge it can neither win nor hold, but joins in the competition fearing that unless it joins the race it will be left behind." Selective institutions, in particular, will spend all they can in order to attract the high school seniors everybody wants. The universities that do well in this race enjoy market power that, given their selectivity, can be used to raise price.[14] These increases provide a pricing umbrella that allows other schools to boost price as well: for example, "Our $25,000 tuition doesn't seem so bad when Stanford charges twice as much."

In an ironic twist on the arms race, there is a growing tendency for tuition payers to associate price with quality. Price increases may actually boost prestige in and of themselves, quite aside from the enhancements the extra revenue allows the entity to build into its product or service. When confronted with two vials of perfume, for example, the uninformed consumer is likely to view the more expensive one as being better.[15] It should not be surprising that relatively uninformed consumers would make the same associations in evaluating colleges, or that colleges would, sooner or later, begin to exploit this phenomenon. This may be fine in the marketplace for private goods, but it is not fine for a largely public good where affordability is an issue.

Skeptics say that students and their families would not pay attention to value-added learning measures even if they were available, but this ignores the fact that the market has had no experience with such measures. Steve Jobs taught us that one shouldn't wait for users to demand new functionality that they have yet to experience or even visualize. The fact remains that quality is the core element of most university value propositions. In particular, the market-facing user value proposition is grounded in the belief—valid in my opinion—that, in the end, students and parents do care about educational value added. This suggests that "[i]f we build them (the measures), they (the users) will come," and that the rate of adoption will accelerate as intermediaries such as rating entities, publishers, and consultants rush in to publicize and apply the new information.

Higher education's regulators have long understood the market's inability to police quality and price. They attempt to compensate by imposing their own accountability processes. The assessment of student learning has been a major tool for accountability. (Cost measurement is another, as discussed in chapter 4.) Quality assurance expert Peter Ewell's landmark paper "Assessment, Accountability, and Improvement: Revisiting the Tension" argues that the current demands for accountability in this area will not go away. "Colleges and universities will not only have to demonstrate sincere efforts to improve student learning but will also have to prove that their students are achieving adequate levels in the first place. This will increasingly mean reporting actual learning outcomes in comparative or benchmark forms as well as being transparent about internal efforts at continuous improvement."[16]

He goes on to state, as I have on numerous occasions, that most traditional universities don't know how to continuously improve either learning itself or the methods for measuring it.

## Building a Reengineering Portfolio

Mitigating the flaws described in the previous section will require organized and sustained initiatives—what some experts call "whole-model" innovation. The initiatives need to be carefully designed and implemented so as first to attain adoption by faculty and then to avoid or mitigate the inevitable unintended consequences. Chapters 3 through 5 offer specific suggestions about what to try in the areas of teaching quality, cost containment, and planning and budgeting. The ideas don't map neatly into the scheme I used to classify the flaws, but in the aggregate I believe that they cover the main areas that need to be covered. (I will refer to impacts on specific flaws from time to time.) Before diving into the detail of the initiatives, however, it will be useful to consider the *strategy* of reengineering. This involves building a reengineering portfolio and understanding how its various elements are likely to evolve over time and across categories of activity. The emphasis throughout is on "starting small" in order to focus on the adoption process, but "thinking big" so as to generate momentum toward scalability.

Scalable reengineering initiatives generally require some kind of central impetus: for example, provision of seed money or tools, a change in incentives, or an adoption decision by the budget office or another administrative and support entity. Then they propagate outward to schools, departments, and other operating units, where eventually they become part of established routines. The barriers to propagation depend on the amount of change required and the number of people who need to be brought on board. Small changes by a few people are easier than large ones that must be adopted by many.

Figure 2.2 describes the kind of portfolio I have in mind. The vertical axis categorizes the "focus of involvement": whether the central administrators, schools, departments, or faculty members have the main action at a given stage of adoption. *Central* initiatives are undertaken directly by campus administrators; *school* and *department* initiatives require deep involvement of deans and department chairs (and their close colleagues); and *faculty* initiatives require significant involvement by rank and file professors. The horizontal axis categorizes "types of change" as evolutionary, discontinuous, and disruptive.[17] *Evolutionary* changes represent variations on current themes, *discontinuous* ones reflect new departures within existing paradigms, and *disruptive* ones upend the current modes of thinking. The difficulty of gaining adoption for an initiative depends both on the breadth of involvement sought and type of change required.

## Classes of Initiatives

The shapes in the body of the diagram depict the three classes of initiatives listed earlier: rectangles for initiatives that improve teaching and learning, ovals for cost-related initiatives, and hexagons for initiatives to improve financial planning and budgeting. The solid curves show the expected evolutionary paths, and the dotted curves show important synergies among the initiatives. Achieving adoption usually gets harder as one moves upward in the diagram, from the central ad-

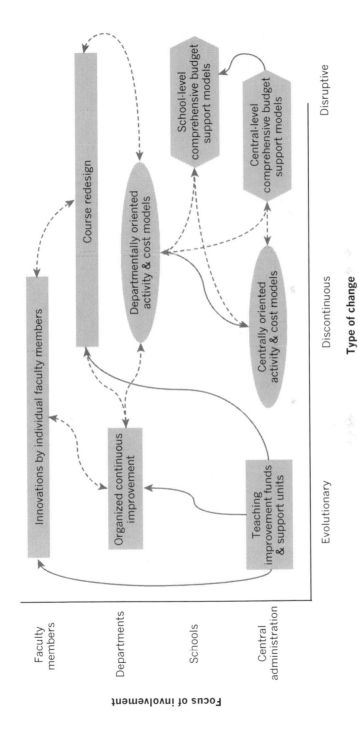

**Figure 2.2.** The reengineering portfolio

ministration to individual faculty members, and also rightward, from evolutionary to disruptive change. Efforts to propagate scalable initiatives generally begin with action by the central administration and then move upward and/or to the right. Later chapters make the case that none of the initiatives is terribly costly, though, of course, material investments of time and money will be required.

Quality initiatives usually start with the creation of teaching improvement funds and teaching support units. These stimulate and facilitate innovations by individual faculty members as well as team-oriented course redesign projects as described in chapter 3. They can arise spontaneously within the faculty, but progress will be greatly accelerated with central support. Organized continuous improvement, also described in chapter 3, provides more forward-leaning interventions—though it can start in a purely evolutionary way. Course redesign is an example of an initiative that starts as discontinuous, because it changes only a few courses, but becomes more disruptive if pursued at scale. (Other teaching-related activities also can be redesigned: e.g., as with the University of Michigan's grants to "let 19 schools and colleges at Ann Arbor use technology to tailor advising to individual students."[18]) Teaching activity and cost models, the subject of chapter 4, are implemented initially by and for the central administration and perhaps the schools, but the ultimate goal should be to make them useful at the departmental level—where, among other things, they can be a useful stimulus for course redesign. Likewise, the financial planning and budgeting models discussed in chapter 5 will be implemented first for the central administration and then, hopefully, propagated out to schools and perhaps departments. I show these as disruptive innovations because of their potential for changing the way institutions think about resource allocation, though many nondisruptive applications also are possible.

A few institutions are extending the scope of their teaching initiatives to jump immediately to disruptive change. In early 2014, for example, Georgetown University established a teaching innovation center called "Designing the Future(s) of the University." An avowed goal of this initiative is to break the conventional constraints.[19] The nature of its work is illustrated by a document titled "Five Pump-Priming Ideas for New Ways to Deliver a Georgetown Education and Experience: A Discussion

Draft to Identify Boundary-Pushing Experiments." Design approaches were sought for:

- flexible curricular and teaching structures,
- competency-based learning,
- expanding mentored research,
- new work/learn models, and
- four-year combination BA/MA.

Numerous responses were received, and the center has begun work on redesigning education around high-impact learning and a combined BA/MA program. The Center's strong emphasis on design is essential for developing constraint-busting initiatives. It works with faculty in the relevant areas to design the innovation, which then can be pilot tested and rolled out for regular use. This approach is fundamental to successful reengineering.

### Synergies among the Initiatives

The benefit of mounting initiatives in all three classes can be summed up in a single word: synergies. One's chance of success in propagating a class of initiatives across the institution and moving them toward discontinuous or even disruptive territory is greatly enhanced if one understands and exploits the synergies. This can be demonstrated by a few examples.

The major synergies among the initiative classes, depicted by the dotted links in figure 2.2, are as follows (the flow moves clockwise from the upper left):

- Between *innovations by individual faculty members* and *organized continuous improvement.* Experimental results by individuals feed naturally into the department's collective efforts, and the collective experience motivates and informs new experiments.
- Between *innovations by individual faculty members* and *course redesign.* Individuals' experimental results can inform team-oriented redesign, and new needs surfaced in redesign can inform new experiments.
- Between *organized continuous improvement* and *course redesign.* A redesigned course provides a new baseline for continuous improvement.

- Between *course redesign* and *departmentally oriented activity and cost models*. The analysis of activities and costs is an integral part of course redesign, so experience with one helps work on the other.
- Between *departmentally oriented activity and cost models* and *organized continuous improvement*. Whether and how the model's results are incorporated into departmental decision-making is a fit subject for continuous improvement.
- Between both departmentally and centrally oriented *activity and cost models* and *comprehensive budget support models* at the central and school levels. Data from the activity and cost models inform the budget models, and the budget models motivate greater use of activity and cost models.

Reengineering portfolios that omit one or more of the initiative classes will forgo important synergies. I stated earlier that university leaders can't do everything at once, but they should develop strategies for moving each type of initiative through its evolutionary process and harvesting all available synergies along the way. The initiatives will evolve at their own rates, but conscious planning about how to achieve the synergies will pay dividends at every stage. Details will depend upon local circumstances, but certain common elements that increase the likelihood of success can be identified. My advice is to "think big but act in manageable steps." Trying to do too much at once often is a formula for failure. However, not calling out the program's expected scope at the beginning, when the ideas are fresh and one has the organization's attention, may well forfeit the opportunity for achieving profound change.

## Implementation Considerations

Change on the academic side of traditional universities does not occur monolithically, and people who try to implement it in that way are in for big disappointments. It occurs bit by bit as professors and departments begin experimenting with the new initiatives and then, hopefully, build them into their normal routines. (I described this earlier as "starting small" but "thinking big.") Senior leaders need to initiate and drive change, but they must do so in a way that encourages and empowers faculty. The socioeconomic literature on the adoption of innovations provides some useful insights about how to do this. We will review those lessons next and then apply them to the implementation of reengineering portfolios.

### Adoption of Innovations

Potential users do not automatically adopt new science and technology applications, even when their advantages are readily apparent. The adoption process has its own dynamic, and there is a vast literature on the subject.[20] Figure 2.3 shows that adoption generally starts slowly and then accelerates as information and influence diffuse from one person to another through a process called "contagion." It slows as the population of nonadopters is depleted, but a new innovation cycle may begin at any time if new markets or applications are uncovered. Researchers typically define five stages of innovation in terms of the populations called out in the figure: innovators, early adopters, early majority, late majority, and diehards.

The innovators, who generally represent only a few percent of the relevant population, reduce the new ideas to practice and begin working out the bugs. They shoulder the substantial risks associated with whether the innovation will work out as planned and produce the expected consequences. (Innovators sometimes are described as "pioneers with arrows in their backs.") The next 10 percent or so of the population, the "early adopters," adopt after feasibility has been demonstrated. They legitimize the innovations and extend their scope of application, which still is risky but less so than initial adoption. The "early majority" also takes risks, but these have more to do with scaling up and moving into new niches than whether the idea will work at all. By the time the "late majority" comes on board, people have begun to ask why the innovation should *not* be adopted instead of why it should. Finally, a few diehards never adopt: they stick to the old ways, but eventually they retire or are pushed from the scene.

Early studies of the diffusion process included farmers' adoption of modern techniques, the railroads' adoption of diesel locomotives, physicians' adoption of new drugs, and the American public's adoption of color television.[21] But for each success there are countless failures— innovations that look promising at the start but stall out at the innovator or early adopter stage. Adoption processes have been speeding up

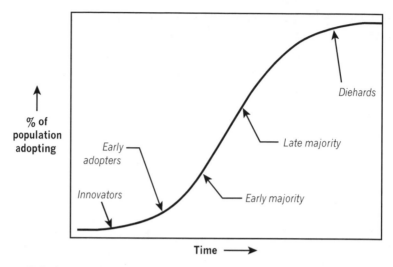

**Figure 2.3.** Stages of technology adoption *Source*: Massy, *Honoring the Trust*, 126.

over time, but it remains impossible to gauge the eventual success of an idea from the early data on adoption. The problem is compounded because for most important innovations there is not one but a series of adoption process—a cascading of S-curves, so to speak—as success in one area opens the way for further progress.

One reason for these difficulties is that early applications may be relatively crude. As Clay Christiansen points out in his works on disruption, the new technology's initial niche often is to "serve the underserved": for example, in situations where the old approach can't be used effectively.[22] A second reason is that, because innovation can be viewed as relaxing constraints that stand in the way of progress, the success of one initiative may depend on success with another. How the electric motor "flattened the factory" illustrates the successive elimination of constraints.

The factory of the mid-nineteenth century was a multistoried affair, expensive to build and inefficient in organizational structure and materials handling. This was dictated by the limitations of the steam engine, which, given the bearing technology of the time, had to be linked to machines mainly by vertical rather than horizontal driveshafts. The first electric motor simply replaced the central steam engine, leaving the other constraints in place, but in time it became possible to distribute the motors to individual workplaces. This provided much greater flexibility. Eventually, people learned to restructure the whole manufacturing enterprise, to "flatten the factory," and thus eliminate the inefficiencies of the multistory mills.[23]

The electric motor has much to teach us about the adoption of innovations in teaching and learning. Traditional universities are rife with constraints that reinforce the status quo: for example, incentives, faculty workload definitions, academic calendars and class schedules, the fact that most professors are very busy, and, of course, the academic culture itself. The multiple constraints need to be surmounted, which can't happen all at once. Nevertheless, it seems clear that the adoption at least some of the initiatives of figure 2.2 have reached the innovator or early adopter stage. While the numbers of adopters remain small, this could change rapidly as the modern ideas gain currency and successive constraints to adoption crumble. Institutions have an opportunity to get ahead of the wave without taking inordinate risks and doing so will confer significant and lasting first-mover advantages.

*Pilot Projects*

Pilot projects have proven to be a good way to jumpstart the adoption process in many circumstances.[24] They can be organized by people at any level, which allows for more proactive leadership than simply announcing the availability of funds and then waiting expectantly for takers. Pilot projects provide opportunities for innovators to work the bugs out of the new initiative or early adopters to bring it to scale. But while recognizing the importance of these benefits, the leaders of a reengineering program should never forget that the ultimate goal is to progress past innovation and early adoption to the stages of majority adoption—where the phenomenon of contagion can be expected to carry the initiative across the campus.

Suppose a university has decided to implement the teaching activity and cost model described in chapter 4. The model, which can be acquired by the central administration with relatively little effort, will aid financial managers immediately. Faculty involvement can be modest at this stage because cost analysis is regarded as an administrative rather than academic matter, and nearly all the requisite data already reside in the university's data systems. So far so good, but the full set of benefits will come only when faculty and administrators in schools and departments use the data in day-to-day decision-making. Simply directing departments to use the model will produce more resistance than adoption—which is where the pilot project comes in.

What's needed is a "coalition of the willing"—in this case, pilot departments that will spend enough time with the model to realize its potential. These departments may be obtained by offering financial or other incentives and then calling for volunteers, perhaps targeting people known to be sympathetic to activity and cost issues and the use of decision support models. The number might be in the range of three to five, depending on the level of resources available to support the project. Piloting in multiple departments allows one to gauge response variation and ensure against accidents: for example, due to anomalies in the data for the department or a chair who gets cold feet about participating. Ideally, the pilot departments will span a number of different disciplines. For example, the pilot described in chapter 4 involved chemistry, mathematics, and psychology.

I've found the following six-step program to work well for pilot/demonstration projects. Variations in detail are to be expected, but performing all the steps in the order given will boost the likelihood of success.

1. *Explain.* Briefings and seminars inform faculty and staff about the model and its benefits, and workshops provide hands-on familiarization using actual data. A major goal of the exercise is to generate enthusiasm (e.g., by sparking connections with previously known problems, as occurred in the pilot test described in chapter 4).
2. *Plan.* Faculty and staff reflect on the model's capabilities, describe how they plan to use it and who should be responsible for each activity, and write up the benefits they expect to get. The plan need not exceed a few pages (e.g., a series of bullet points), but setting pen to paper is critically important for shaping, and subsequently guiding, the work.
3. *Do.* Use of the model for actual decision-making. The plan should be taken seriously, but departments should feel free to deviate from it as experience is gained. Major activities and results should be documented as usage proceeds.

4. *Self-review.* Faculty and staff reflect on their experience with the model and describe the results in a brief report that will be disseminated within the university. The report should include recommendations for improving the model and data and, importantly, how the department plans to build on the experience during the subsequent year.

5. *Peer review.* A small panel of faculty from outside the department makes a one-day visit to discuss the pilot experience and self-evaluation, and then writes a brief report on their findings. The objective is to provide constructive criticism about what has been accomplished so that the department and others across the university will be able to benefit from the pilot experience.

6. *Adjust.* Make needed changes and re-up for the following year. All who participated in the project come together with university leaders to discuss what happened, what was learned, what should be done differently in subsequent trials, and—importantly—to recommit to a subsequent round of activity. Other objectives include celebrating the year's activities, disseminating information, and propagating momentum across the campus.

Readers may recognize steps two through six as a variation on the "plan-do-check-adjust" (PDCA) cycle used in business for the continuing improvement of processes and products. The "check" component has been expanded to "self-review" and "peer review" to meet the needs and sensibilities of academe.

All six steps will be aided considerably by the appointment of "implementation facilitators," who help faculty learn about the model, provide ongoing first-level technical support, and ensure that the project remains on track. Carl Wieman's "science education specialists" (discussed in chapter 3) played similar roles; they were postdocs in the department's discipline, but that level of training probably isn't essential when introducing activity and costing models. While not necessarily academics themselves, the facilitators should understand academic life and be able to gain the confidence of faculty.

Peer review (step 5) represents the greatest departure from PDCA. Such reviews are a well-accepted part of academic professional life, but they are rarely seen in business. The reviewers can come from anywhere in the university, though it will be helpful for some to come from a cognate discipline. Peer review offers two advantages in the present context. First, the faculty panelists become familiar with and often enthusiastic about the model and its benefits, which helps build acceptance across the campus and makes it easier to recruit volunteer departments for the next round of testing or rollout. Second, because departmental faculty know that a peer review will take place near the end of the academic year, they will be more likely to "stay the course" until the end of the trial. Professors hate to look bad in the eyes of their colleagues, even when there are few overt consequences, so they are more likely to bear down.

Consideration of the new design by additional departments becomes easier once it has been successfully implemented in the first pilot/demonstration round. Some peer reviewers carry the word back to their colleagues. Other professors learn from the campus media and word of mouth. Success with a second group of volunteer departments builds further momentum, and so on. One hopes that after a few rounds adoption can be pushed as a matter of policy, with recalcitrant departments coming to be viewed as out of step.

### The Improvement Cycle

Successfully launching an initiative in a department is only half the battle; one still must build momentum to the point of sustainability. It's useful to conceptualize the launch and subsequent steps in terms of an "improvement cycle": a virtuous circle of activities that hopefully will result in full adoption. (When I referred to "piloting" an initiative in, say, a department, I meant not only the initial launch but also the progression through the improvement cycle.) My work on organized continuous improvement with Steve Graham and Paula Myrick Short conceived the cycle as a circular track, like the one shown in figure 2.4, around which are arrayed the main "centrifugal forces" that can derail the change process.[25] The idea can be applied to departments, as discussed in the previous examples, or to any other work group that engages in annual cycles of decision making. To maintain generality, I'll refer to the participants as members of "work groups" from here on.

The "explain" arrow at the top of the diagram represents step one in the six-step process, and the five "stations" around the track represent

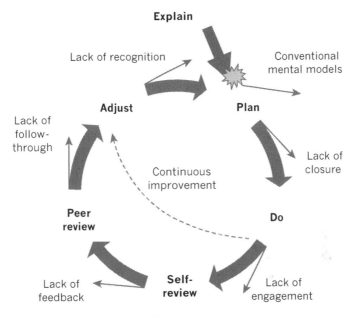

**Figure 2.4.** The improvement cycle

steps two through six. The potential derailers and the ways they can be mitigated are as follows:

1. *Conventional mental models* will cause work groups to reject the new ideas and thus block the adoption process before it gets started. The mitigation is to work with faculty who already are predisposed to give the innovation a serious try, and then to provide lots of information and hands-on facilitation.

2. *Lack of closure* reflects the academic tendency to argue endlessly over the fine points of proposed actions. Closure is produced by the need to deliver a timely project plan. Among other things, the plan should describe the actions to be taken and the criteria by which success will be gauged.

3. *Lack of engagement* causes the "doing" stage to falter partway through the trial period. I have already described the salutary effect the requirement for self-study and the prospect of peer review can have on engagement.

4. *Lack of feedback* prevents participants from achieving maximal benefit from the self-review. Peer review provides two kinds of benefits:

the substance of the reviewers' comments and the incentive to bear
down during the self-review process. As mentioned earlier, professors hate to look shallow in the eyes of their colleagues.

5. *Lack of follow-through* prevents the findings from the self-study and
   peer review from producing action and organizational learning. The
   mitigation is to organize a process by which deans or other administrators review the department's results and obtain new commitments
   about the way forward. Performance against these commitments
   should be tracked against agreed performance indicators wherever
   possible.

6. *Lack of recognition* for a job well done will dissipate commitment.
   The mitigation is obvious: administrators should celebrate successes,
   build the work into performance reviews, and, where the institution's
   standards for scholarship can be met, include it in evaluations for
   promotion and tenure. Professors are motivated by intrinsic rewards,
   but no opportunity for adding extrinsic ones should be overlooked.

The improvement cycle is designed to operate on an annual basis.
One can reasonably expect, after a few years of cumulative successes,
that a department will reach the point where formal self-study and peer
review aren't needed every year. This activates the shortcut labeled *continuous improvement* that connects *do* with *adjust*. The department
takes responsibility for performing these steps on its own without using
a formal process—this is, in effect, the "act" component of the PDCA cycle
mentioned previously.

### "Capability Maturity"

Assessing the degree to which an initiative has become embedded in
an entity's routines is extremely important, both for people at the grassroots level and for those higher up in the university hierarchy who need
to oversee and facilitate the adoption process. The peer-review teams
discussed earlier invariably make such assessments as by-products of
their efforts to provide formative feedback. When peer review of departmental quality assurance and improvement processes was first introduced
in Hong Kong and Tennessee, for example, my colleagues and I had little
difficulty discerning that little attention was being paid to good prac-

tices of the kind discussed in chapter 3. Later rounds showed great improvement. Such peer review should be built into nearly all reengineering initiatives. Few people who have internalized the concepts behind a particular initiative will find it hard to distinguish between the good, the bad, and the ugly when looking at the degree of implementation.

The "capability maturity" (CM) rating scale provides a powerful yet practical language for describing the degree to which an initiative has become embedded. Work groups can use the ratings to gauge their progress up the learning curve. University administrators can use them to identify areas where additional effort is needed and then facilitate improvements, and also to track the overall health of the campus's reengineering program. Use of the scale does not reflect a measurement fetish; rather, it provides a needed method for describing progress in a very important area.

The five-level CM scale was developed at Carnegie Mellon University to track the progress of advanced software development teams. Now it is used to aid process improvement worldwide in government offices, commerce, industry, and software development organizations. The version described in the following paragraph is the one my colleagues and I developed for the Hong Kong quality-process reviews, after which it was further refined for use in Tennessee.

Table 2.1 presents two versions of the capability-maturity scale:

- Column 1 shows the scale designator.
- Column 2 shows the scale designator as it is applied to a particular initiative: for example, a department's use of activity and cost models.
- Column 3 shows its application to the model's campus-wide rollout.

The scales are "criterion referenced" (i.e., they are anchored to descriptions of specific situations). The judgments are subjective, but, as mentioned previously, on-the-ground experience shows that faculty, in work groups and on peer-review teams, have little difficulty deciding where on the scale a particular activity lies. Fractional ratings are fine: it can be sufficient, for instance, to know that an entity is in the *emergent* to *organized effort* range rather than mired in *firefighting*. The first can be produced as by-products of the six-step process for a particular work group as described earlier, whereas the second one requires a

| Table 2.1. Capability-maturity scales for operating units and the campus as a whole | | |
|---|---|---|
| Scale value | Work group criteria | Campus-wide criteria |
| No effort | There is no initiative-based activity. Traditional approaches are used, and performance tends to remain stagnant. | There is no leadership from the central administration. Traditional methods dominate in nearly all the work groups. |
| Firefighting | Units respond to problems, but mostly with ad hoc methods. The reengineering initiative receives little attention beyond lip service. | Leadership from the central administration is weak. The reengineering initiative has been announced but receives little serious attention. |
| Emergent effort | One sees initiatives by individuals and some experimentation with the principles, but the incidence is far from critical mass. | There is some leadership, and some groups have reached the "emergent effort" level on certain aspects of the initiative. |
| Organized effort | Group-wide actions begin to be planned and tracked, methods are systematically rooted in the principles, and the unit has begun to develop performance metrics and norms. | The administration exerts active leadership, and some groups have reached the "organized effort" level on certain aspects of the initiative. |
| Mature effort | The initiative is embedded in the group's culture, continuous improvement is a way of life, and organizational learning is fully established. | The initiative is a key results area for the central administration and all the work groups. Some groups have reached the "mature effort" level, and the administrative is working with the others. |

peer-review procedure to track an institution's progress across multiple work groups, as will be discussed later.

One goal of any reengineering initiative should be to move the people who implement it from a low-ranked capability-maturity rating to a significantly higher one. My experience suggests that once a program gains momentum, progress can be made in a remarkably short time—perhaps in as little as a few years to reach the *organized effort* threshold and not much longer to reach *mature effort*. Professors are smart and self-directed, so they can solve complex problems when their heart is in the effort and they are supplied with appropriate information and resources. The language of the CM scale resonates with the case for organizational learning. Once it's accepted that a given initiative is important, it's hard to defend positions characterizable as "incapable" and "immature."

Capability-maturity ratings become relevant once an implementation has passed its start-up phase and begun to achieve tangible results. The focus should be on organizational units: academic departments, schools, degree program offices, and administrative units related to resource allocation. Multiple ratings can be made for work groups, such as departments, that are engaged with more than one reengineering initiative—for example, one for course redesign and another for the application of activity and cost models. As mentioned previously, the goal of reengineering should be to move work groups up the capability-maturity curve in all the relevant reengineering areas. The ratings allow progress to be tracked and communicated to interested parties both inside and outside the university. For example, I envision a time when presidents and governing boards get such reports on a routine basis.

## Responsibilities for Reengineering

To embark on a program of reengineering is one of the most strategic decisions a university can make. Leadership from the top, especially from the president and other senior campus leaders (including, importantly, the provost or vice president for academic affairs), represents an absolutely necessary condition for success. We have seen that reengineering must involve the faculty in a broad and deep way. The impetus can be anywhere in the organization, but getting the critical mass of reform that will be needed for competing in the twenty-first century requires serious and sustained leadership from the top.

### Leadership from the Top

The responsibility for reengineering a campus rests with its president or chancellor. His or her strong and visible support is essential for getting and sustaining the organization's attention, funding the chosen initiatives, and, above all, convincing people whose lives will be changed by reengineering that the task can be accomplished, the benefits for the institution are worthwhile, and the local impacts will be manageable or appropriately mitigated. Presidents and provosts are busy people, so, of course, it will be necessary to delegate much responsibility to others, but they must treat reengineering as an overarching priority and keep spurring the process until satisfactory results have been obtained and embedded in the university's culture.

The first task is to identify a "champion" to serve as the point person for the reengineering program. The champion provides senior hands-on leadership for reengineering. Much delegation will be required, but he or she needs to maintain a strong element of personal control: for example, to know when any part of the reengineering process is flagging and be proactive in getting it back on track. The champion also serves as the senior go-to person for alleviating the concerns of faculty and other on-campus influentials.

It also may be helpful for a university to engage or employ a "leadership coach" to help the champion and others (including the president and the provost) understand the innovation process and how people in the organization are reacting to it. Richard Martin, part of the Organization and Leadership Effectiveness Group at Ohio State, describes this person as "someone to confide in, and get advice from, about things you can't talk about with your superiors, reports, or peers."[26] I employed such a person when I served as Stanford's vice president for business and finance and found the experience to be very worthwhile.

Three elements of leadership are required:

- The champion and his or her senior colleagues must make a strong case for changing the status quo: why faculty and staff members should reallocate time and effort from their "day jobs" to perform reengineering tasks.
- They should lay out and fund a strategy for effecting the necessary changes: one that comes across as intrinsically practical and beneficial for the people involved.
- They should set up a system for encouraging experimentation, initiating pilot implementations and rolling out successful results across the institution, spurring their improvement, and then, importantly, following up to see that the improvements are sustained over time.

Failure on any of these dimensions will seriously undermine the reengineering program and thus limit the degree to which institutions can transform themselves.

Writing and promulgating a vision statement should be another early task. The statement describes the goals being sought, explains why achieving them will make the institution and its stakeholders better off, and provides assurances that the costs in time, energy, and lost opportunities will be reasonable. It should be specific enough to convey the desired messages but general enough to dampen the academic tendency toward nitpicking. Finally, it should provide an inspirational shorthand description (an "elevator speech") that people can refer to as implementation proceeds—one that will generate positive buzz and excitement across campus.

A good next step is to establish a "transformation council" to help generate ideas, advise on implementation issues, and facilitate the dissemination of results. Subcouncils may be established for individual initiatives. I introduced the council/subcouncil system at Stanford during the 1980s in my successful Quality, Service, and Productivity program for business and financial operations, and also used it in Missouri and Tennessee when working on academic quality work. Another step is to set clear lines of responsibility and accountability for getting each initiative accomplished. The people involved should know that the task is a significant assignment that offers opportunities for creative accomplishment—and will enter into performance evaluations.

The champion works with the transformation council to prepare the campus's reengineering strategy. At a minimum, this should include a first round of initiatives such as those described along the bottom row of figure 2.2. Often these will involve pilot projects. A more ambitious program will lay out a comprehensive portfolio of reengineering initiatives and a rolling plan for their implementation. The strategy should include performance metrics, robust processes for getting the data needed to track capability maturity, and a schedule for reporting on progress to the president and the board.

### Role of the Governing Board

Governing boards have the ultimate responsibility for making sure their institutions adapt to the realities of the twenty-first century. Hence their members should be prepared to intervene if the needed attention isn't forthcoming. This is an area where "no news is not good news." Boards cannot assume that the right initiatives are being taken without evidence that this is so.

It is the president's job to approach the board with a reengineering plan and then provide regular progress reports. But if this doesn't happen, even after a number of hints and nudges, the board should make clear that it insists such a plan be developed. It should make reengineering a key results area for the president and take it into account in annual performance reviews. Boards should make reengineering an important criterion when searching for a new president and include it in their own self-evaluations of performance.

In fairness, I should say that not everyone agrees that boards should be proactive in the promotion of reengineering. For example, some distinguished academics believe that teaching and learning (including its cost as well as quality) should be the exclusive province of faculty and academic administrators, and that boards should steer well clear of the whole area. I've heard it said that the board's role should be to wait for transformational initiatives to emerge from inside the institution and then support them financially. Unfortunately, there is overwhelming evidence that the waiting time for such spontaneity may well be unacceptably long. Board members have the ultimate responsibility for ensuring the long-run health of their institution, and solving the problems addressed by reengineering is simply too important for a hands-off strategy.

But despite the board's ultimate responsibility for reengineering, its members cannot and should not get too close to the action. Micromanagement by boards is a formula for ineffectiveness. I've served on and worked with numerous boards, and in the best ones the mantra has been "Good people working full-time (i.e., management) will do a better job than good people working part-time (i.e., board members)." Overly close contact also short circuits the administrative chain of responsibility and thereby undermines leadership, and, in any case, board members lack the expertise to micromanage academic reengineering. Boards must walk the line between trying to micromanage the reengineering program and failing to ensure that the job does, in fact, get done.

The initiatives described in this book allow board members to walk that line. The first requirement is that they understand what needs to be accomplished: in general terms but with sufficient detail to judge whether the right things are happening. I'd like to think that the main points in this book offer the needed understanding: that anyone who has internalized them will, when provided with appropriate data, be able to judge whether the institution is serious about reengineering and proceeding in an intelligent way. The material does not require training in an academic discipline and no more familiarity with university life and operations than should be expected of university board members.

So what kinds of data are "appropriate"? The threshold question that board members need to answer is whether the university has embarked on a purposeful and systematic reengineering program—of the kind described here or something of equivalent scope and substance. If it has not, it's very likely that reengineering is getting lip service at best and perhaps not even that. In my view, such a finding should trigger immediate board action.

An effective program will include metrics and feedback mechanisms like those discussed earlier. These will call out the kinds of reengineering, if any, that are being undertaken. It's possible for boards to tap into that flow of information: for example, by requesting regular reports from senior management that include reengineering goals, methods, and accomplishments to date. Targeted in-depth reports can be requested when questions arise or when the board simply wants to become better informed about a particular initiative. Probing questions, based in part on the conceptual frameworks described earlier in this chapter, can indicate whether the reports are grounded in evidence or anecdote.

Boards and their committees usually meet with deans and some senior faculty members on a regular basis. Remembering to ask about particular reengineering initiatives will provide insights on whether the programs are being taken seriously. For example, deans who don't know much about the programs that impact their areas of cognizance are unlikely to be exercising effective leadership. The same is true for presidents and chief academic officers. Boards certainly need to avoid micromanagement, but pressing for answers to questions about particular initiatives will provide useful diagnostic information. Moreover, such questions will signal that talking the talk is not good enough.

*Implications for External Oversight Bodies*

Oversight bodies such as state higher education coordinating boards and accreditors differ in how they interact with universities, but each has its own way of getting attention. The recommendations of this book may well be of interest to such entities. An oversight body that is serious about promoting reengineering will request regular reports and direct its campus review teams to verify the information obtained.

The campus-wide capability-maturity ratings described in the second column of table 2.1 (presented earlier) can be particularly useful in this regard. As mentioned previously, the Hong Kong University Grants Committee (an oversight body) used this scale to gauge institutions' progress on the continuous improvement of teaching and learning quality.[27] The Committee was clear that how the results were achieved was a matter for the institutions themselves. The important thing was that education quality improvement was being taken seriously, that reasonable actions were being taken and assessed, and that progress was being made.

External oversight focuses on institutional performance, but this can only be ascertained by direct contact with departments and schools as well as the central administration. It's not necessary to examine all the operating units; the needed information can be obtained efficiently on a sampling basis. It's fairly easy to determine whether a particular unit is doing serious work on a given initiative. Respondents who are engaged in such work will talk the questioner's ear off about what they're doing and how it's working, whereas those who are not so engaged will soon lapse into generalities. Furthermore, all reengineering programs generate documents whose depth and scope are fairly easy to verify.

Oversight bodies will find it much simpler to work with capability-maturity assessments than to directly measure the quality or cost of teaching. While some wish for direct measures, in the end one can be reasonably sure that effective processes will lead to good—and well-measured—outcomes. (Adequate resources are required as well, but oversight bodies have no lack of experience in that domain.) I believe that the time will come when oversight bodies characterize institutions according to the capability and maturity of processes such as those discussed in this book and, when the processes are judged to be capable and mature, spend little time trying to duplicate the institutions' own performance measures and second-guessing their decisions.

# Chapter 3

# The New Scholarship of Teaching

Correcting the flaws in the academic business model will require significant changes in the way traditional universities conduct their teaching and learning activities. This won't be easy, all the more so because of the need to protect the essential characteristics of traditional universities. This chapter addresses the set of issues that deal with educational quality. (Cost is considered in chapter 4.) What is required, and called out by the chapter title, is a broader and deeper formulation of Ernest Boyer's "Scholarship of Teaching," introduced in chapter 1, which was promulgated a quarter century ago in his *Scholarship Reconsidered* and later elaborated in *Scholarship Assessed.*[1]

The familiar scholarship of discovery (research) develops new theories and facts: in other words, new ways of understanding the world. Such results often take the form of "abstract analytical knowledge"— powerful concepts but ones that can be difficult for students and other nonexperts to grasp. The scholarship of engagement applies research findings to real-world problems. In addition to producing practical results, such "active practice" brings the abstract analytical knowledge down to earth so broader audiences can understand it. The scholarship of integration provides "reflective observations" on both basic and applied research. In addition to their intrinsic value, such reflections can translate abstract, analytical, and highly specialized research reports into more accessible language and provide the context and perspective needed for broad understanding.

The scholarship of teaching should draw heavily on all of the other three kinds of scholarship, but because the scholarship of discovery looms so large in the academic mind, the emphasis has been disproportionately put on abstract analytical knowledge. A broadened scholarship of teaching would bring more reflective observation to the teaching agenda. It would place more emphasis on active practice, which is directly relevant to many fields and can provide contextual examples for others. Active practice also reflects what's called "concrete connected knowledge," which means more to many students than the abstract analytical knowledge of traditional research. Consideration of practice helps professors design teaching programs and connect their students' education to the real world. Last but not least, the new scholarship of teaching brings faculty incentives more into line with the needs of undergraduate education. The task of this chapter is to build on these ideas.

The following extension to the narrative introduced in chapter 2 will help set ideas as we embark on this task.

Extended discussion among the provost, the president, and other university officers, board members, and senior faculty had produced agreement that significant interventions were needed if the university was to advance its mission of teaching and learning. The questions were: "What should those interventions be?" and "How could they be accomplished?"

It was seductive to think that online courses and MOOCs could correct the flaws without any large-scale disruption of traditional academic work, but this idea had been rejected. First, it simply was not possible to achieve the substantial benefits of face-to-face education (a hallmark of traditional universities) in a purely online setting. Second, bypassing most of the faculty would ignore the wealth of talent, training, and experience that represented the university's comparative advantage— another hallmark. All agreed that potential magic bullets should be exploited to the extent possible, but that this should be done in a way that built on the university's human capital rather than marginalizing it.

The provost knew the needed victories would have to be achieved "in the trenches" by changing the core processes of teaching and learning. They would have to involve large numbers of individual professors as well as departmental hierarchies and faculty committees. "These are the people," he thought, "who are close enough to the action to make intelligent decisions and then follow through on implementing them without jeopardizing the university's basic strengths." Such change would not be effected easily or quickly. While it was necessary to start small, broad involvement and eventual buy-in by the majority of faculty would be essential.

The scale, duration, and importance of the interventions meant that improvement of teaching and learning effectiveness had to become a key results area for university planning. The lip service that had characterized previous initiatives to, say, comply with external requirements for student learning assessment would not do. Serious investments of time and attention by the university's leadership, as well as some dollars, would be required. The provost emphasized that the effort would start with him but that the active and visible support of the president and board also would be essential. He expected stakeholders both inside and outside the university to protest what they viewed as changes in the university's values: for example, deemphasis of research and erosion of academic freedom. Nothing could be further from the truth, but it would take much effort to handle the political fallout.

The program's goal would be to change the academic culture to put teaching and learning truly on a par with research in the university's operant value system. This would be done through sustained communications, backed up by new policies, procedures, tools, data, and incentive structures. It needed to be sufficient in scale, scope, and duration to ensure that the faculty would adopt the needed changes and take collective responsibility for sustaining them into the future.

The provost realized that not all his goals would be met. Despite the concerns of skeptics, however, he was optimistic about the fundamental integrity of the faculty, their willingness and ability to come to terms with the reality of the university's situation, and, most of all, that the changes he was proposing eventually would be viewed not only as palatable but also as being in their best interest.

## Conceptual Underpinnings

Content is king in university teaching. A corollary is that too few professors see anything very interesting about the processes by which content is delivered and made available to students. Talk about these processes and one is likely to get a big yawn. "Everyone knows," it is said, "that great teachers are born not made." Professors are not trained in how to improve teaching methods nor, for the most part, are they supplied with tools for doing so. Furthermore, university incentive systems do not make the improvement of teaching a high priority. Individuals and small groups of professors have innovated in the teaching process domain but seldom have they been able to interest colleagues in adopting and further developing their ideas.

But there are many reasons why content should share its kingly throne with the active consideration of teaching methods. Bob Zemsky's *Making Reform Work* summarizes some of these reasons in an aptly named chapter, "Were Learning to Matter."[2] Consider his quotation from David Kolb of Case Western Reserve University, for example: "Deep learning, learning for real comprehension, comes through a series of experience, reflection, abstraction, and active testing. These four cycle 'round and round' as we learn."[3] Reading and listening to professors talking is rarely the best way to activate the deep learning cycle. To use terms from the broader quality movement, such approaches are rarely "fit for purpose." For example, active learning is essential if material is not only to be remembered but readily recallable when needed for solving problems and illuminating other concepts.

Further, as noted earlier, the difficulty of measuring learning outcomes makes it hard to develop good intuition about what works by way of delivering content and what doesn't. We have a vicious cycle: it is difficult or impossible to improve learning quality in the absence of such intuition, and the intuition itself cannot improve without good learning metrics. Unfortunately, the metrics won't be improved as long as professors and faculty committees spend disproportionate time thinking about what should be taught as opposed to how learning should be delivered and measured.

Many studies show what happens when active learning is absent. For example, when beginning physics students were interviewed as they came out of class and asked what the lecture was about, they answered only in vague generalities. A similar study tested students fifteen minutes after the end of class by telling them a nonobvious fact contained in the lecture: only 10 percent could remember it.[4] The threshold problem with active learning, of course, is that it requires students to be motivated partners in the learning process. Engaging them effectively is a complex proposition—one that requires sustained attention to teaching and learning processes.

Differences in students' backgrounds and learning styles make the problem even more difficult. For example, students learn best from reading and listening when they already have information the brain can use to index the new material. They learn least when the material is disconnected from what they know or, worse, contradictory to prior beliefs. A good process will take students' prior beliefs into account and configure the learning tasks accordingly. Given the number of students taught, this requires what business calls "mass customization"—the use of technology to personalize the learning process. Designing such processes is difficult, but it's not beyond the capacity of today's professors if they approach it in the right way and with proper support.

The need to move beyond the teaching of discipline-based knowledge in discipline-oriented ways adds yet another element of complexity. The choice of content usually should not be motivated by disciplinary canons but rather by the skills and abilities that students will need in order to address problems in their chosen fields and in life. Discipline-trained faculty will not necessarily understand the kinds of emphases needed unless they spend time researching the matter, which again is a matter of process. Anyone who has taught mathematics and statistics to engineering, business, or social science students knows that the traditional theorem-proving methodology doesn't work. (Yet many math professors insist on doing this because it's how they learned.) What *does* work is to embed the concepts in problems that are interesting and understandable to students and then develop the problem-solving tools in a logical sequence of understandable steps.

Even then, it is important to understand how students will process the material being offered. Failure to do so can lead to the following problem reported by physics Nobelist Carl Wieman.[5] Students' problem-solving abilities were tested at the beginning and the end of an introductory physics course on the "novice versus expert" dimension described in table 3.1.[6] The teaching goal, and the faculty's expectation, was that the course would move students in the direction of novice to expert. The result was shocking: the majority of students behaved more like novices at the end of the course than they did at the beginning. Upon reflection, the reasons were not hard to see. The students had spent a semester memorizing information handed down by authority and then solving home and test problems in the most expedient way

| Table 3.1. Problem-solving by experts and novices | |
|---|---|
| Novice | Expert |
| Content: isolated pieces of information to be memorized. | Content: coherent structure of concepts. |
| Handed down by an authority. Unrelated to the real world. | Describes nature, established by experiment. |
| Problem-solving: pattern matching to memorized recipes. | Problem-solving: systematic concept-based strategies; widely applicable. |

possible—by matching them with patterns that they had seen recently in the textbook or in class. While the lecturers may have stressed structure and use of systematic concept-based strategies, the students' experiences did not run in that direction. It is indeed sobering that Wieman reports: "Nearly all intro physics courses lead to more novice-like behavior."

All this implies that the processes for teaching and learning should be designed as carefully as the curriculum, and that they should be subject to the same quality evaluations by faculty committees, administrators, and accreditors. Yet few professors seriously attempt such designs. Some have been heard to say that their job is to assign the right readings and say the right things clearly in class, and that if learning doesn't take place it's the students' fault. Granted that some students are, in fact, lazy or unmotivated, the problem more often stems from shortfalls in the delivery process.

This point was brought home forcibly by the demonstration of peer-assisted learning conducted by Harvard physicist Eric Mazur at this year's Aspen Forum for the Future of Higher Education. Mazur began by giving our group of about 125 nonphysicists a three-minute illustrated lecture on the thermal expansion of metals, then asked us to use our "clickers" (which had been handed out before the session) to answer a simple multiple-choice question on the material. The next step was the crucial one: find a neighbor who had made a different choice and talk with him or her for several minutes, then answer the same question a second time—which produced significantly more correct answers than in the first round. I know about active learning, but the demonstration was an epiphany nonetheless. Though I'm an engineer by training, I didn't know much about thermal expansion and got the first-round question wrong. The conversation with my neighbor (who got it right but didn't know why) led me to understand my error very quickly, and the correct logic and answer are now imprinted in my memory. Mazur describes the benefits of such "peer-assisted learning" as follows: "It continuously [and] actively engages the minds of the students, and it provides frequent and continuous feedback (to both the students and the instructor) about the level of understanding of the subject being discussed."[7]

There is a burgeoning literature on ways to engage students, achieve active learning, and more generally improve learning outcomes. It should be the rule rather than the exception for professors to know and exploit this literature. One may be tempted to conclude that the problems of teaching and learning are too complex to solve effectively, or that the solutions can't achieve large-scale deployment in traditional universities. I disagree. The evidence suggests that operationally meaningful solutions are possible if an institution starts small and then stays the course—provided faculty in sufficient numbers become engaged in the task.

The new scholarship of teaching will address these problems. This is a good time to be working on it. The problems are more widely recognized than even a few years ago, and technology is offering previously unimaginable possibilities that now are being seriously explored. Perhaps of equal importance, the needed conceptual base is being developed. This section describes four key building blocks: Kaizen (continuous improvement), systems thinking, service science, and learning science. I won't review the vast literature on technology because its application either is subsumed under these four building blocks or aims to replace, rather than reengineer, the differentiating elements of traditional university teaching.[8]

### Kaizen

The Japanese word "Kaizen" means "change for the better" (i.e., improvement). The improvements can occur episodically, as in course redesign, or continuously whereby "big results come from many small changes accumulated over time."[9] Continuous improvement is a centerpiece of the "quality movement" that helped transform American manufacturing during the 1980s. The Kaizen Institute describes continuous improvement as being based on these guiding principles:

1. "Good processes bring good results"
2. "Go see for yourself to grasp the current situation"
3. "Speak with data, manage by facts"
4. "Take action to contain and correct root causes of problems"
5. "Work as a team"
6. "Kaizen is everybody's business."[10]

Most people in traditional universities have assumed that Kaizen doesn't apply to academic operations. That's not the case, however, as we shall see.

How to exploit lessons from the quality movement in the improvement of teaching and learning was a key area of research at the National Center for Postsecondary Improvement (NCPI).[11] My staff and I worked with C. Jackson ("Jack") Grayson at the American Productivity and Quality Center (a cofounder of the Malcolm Baldrige National Quality Award), who was kind enough to include us in their briefings and open their files. Among other things, we encoded the large body of experience I had obtained by doing quality process reviews for the Hong Kong University Grants Committee into a set of faculty-friendly quality principles that are suitable for application to teaching and learning at the departmental and school levels. A slightly edited version of these principles appears in table 3.2. Readers will recognize their similarity in spirit with the bullet points listed previously, but we made no effort to achieve one-to-one correspondence.[12]

The principles were tested a few years later at the University of Missouri and the Tennessee Board of Regents (TBR), where the faculty we worked with found them to be both interesting and helpful. Missouri's Steve Graham collaborated on both projects, and Paula Myrick Short, then vice chancellor for Academic Affairs, served as both collaborator and client at TBR. Developed templates for applying the quality principles not only to teaching and learning methods but also to the articulation of educational goals, curricula, student assessment, and quality assurance can be found in our *Academic Quality Work: A Handbook for Improvement* (2007). (Application of similar principles to a department's research program can be found in the same reference.) I'll revisit

## Table 3.2. Principles for the continuous improvement of teaching

| Principle | Explanation |
|---|---|
| Define quality in terms of outcomes | • Defining quality in terms of outcomes brings the so-called "fitness for purpose" requirement, which lies at the core of all quality work, into the picture.<br>• Learning outcomes should pertain to what is or will become important for the department's students.<br>• Exemplary departments carefully determine their students' needs and then work to meet those needs. They know that student learning, not teaching per se, is what ultimately matters. |
| Focus on how things get done | • All activity is process, and teaching, learning, and assessment are activities. Therefore, departments should carefully analyze how teachers teach, how students learn, and how they all approach learning assessment.<br>• Departments should consult their discipline's pedagogical literature and collect data on what works well and what doesn't. They should stress active learning, exploit information technology, and not hesitate to experiment with new teaching and learning methods.<br>• Faculty should be quick to adopt their colleagues' successful innovations, which should become part of the department's modus operandi and form the baseline for future experimentation and improvement. |
| Work collaboratively | • Professors should demonstrate collegiality in teaching-related work, just as they do in research. For example, working in teams brings an array of talent to bear on difficult problems, disseminates insight, and allows members to hold one another accountable for team assignments.<br>• Collaboration makes the department a learning organization, not only for disciplinary content but also for education quality processes. It is ironic that although many professors routinely work together in research, they rarely do so in teaching-related tasks. |
| Base decisions on evidence | • Departments should monitor outcomes systematically; for example, by collecting data from students, graduates, and employers. Data on student preparation and learning styles can be helpful as well.<br>• The data should be analyzed carefully in light of disciplinary standards and the faculty's professional experience, and findings should be incorporated into the design of curricula, learning processes, and assessment methods. |
| Strive for coherence | • The concept of coherence, which was part of W. Edwards Deming's theory of profound knowledge, comes up again and again in discussions of academic reengineering.<br>• Departments should view learning through the lens of students' entire educational experience. Courses should build on one another to provide the desired depth and breadth. |

| Table 3.2. *continued* | |
| --- | --- |
| Principle | Explanation |
|  | • Students' portfolios of educational experiences should reflect coherence. For example, a mix of large lectures and small seminars produces better learning than a succession of medium-sized classes that consume the same amount of faculty time. |
| Learn from best practice | • Searching out best practice and adapting it to the local situation is called "benchmarking." (This is distinguishable from "benchmarks," which are performance metrics selected for comparison.)<br>• Faculty should identify and analyze good practice in comparable departments and institutions. They should compare good versus average or poor practices within their own departments, assess the causes of the differences, and seek ways to improve subpar performance.<br>• Studying how others achieve a goal provides insights into how to achieve it for oneself. The idea is not, as some skeptics seem to think, to force-fit others' work to the local situation. It is to think outside the box to gain stimulus and insight. |
| Make continuous improvement a priority | • Quality experts believe that every process always presents opportunities for incremental improvement; indeed continuous improvement, known as Kaizen in Japan, has become a cornerstone of the quality movement.<br>• Departments should strive to continuously improve teaching and learning. Although many professors will continue to emphasize research, enough discretionary time should be spent on quality work to maintain the impetus for improvement.<br>• Personnel committees should consider the results of quality improvement work, along with research and teaching performance, as important evidence for promotion and tenure. |

*Source*: Based on material in Massy, Graham, and Short, *Academic Quality Work*, 54–62.

the seven principles when I discuss "Organizing for Educational Improvement" near the end of this chapter.

### Systems Thinking

Application of systems thinking to traditional universities goes beyond continuous improvement to design new architectures for teaching and learning. The designer sets aside existing processes and tools (at least temporarily) to consider first principles, interesting analogues from other fields, and innovative applications of technology. Mostly the ideas are matters of common sense, supplemented by a few simple tools that fall under the broad heading of process flowcharting, but often ones the teachers haven't considered before.

Stanford University's recent experiment with "design thinking" represents an example of the systems approach. According to the *Chronicle of Higher Education*:

> Design thinking is an approach to problem-solving based on a few easy-to-grasp principles that sound obvious: 'Show Don't Tell,' 'Focus on Human Values,' 'Craft Clarity,' 'Embrace Experimentation,' 'Mindful of Process,' 'Bias toward Action,' and 'Radical Collaboration.' These seven points reduce to five modes—Emphasize, Define, Ideate, Prototype, Test—and three headings: Hear, Create, Deliver.
>
> Stanford president John Hennessy sees these principles as the core of a new model of education for undergraduates. Two such classes on design thinking already have been created: 'Designing Your Life,' which aims to help upperclassman think about the decisions that will shape their lives after graduating, and 'Designing Your Stanford,' which applies design thinking to helping first- and second-year students make the best choices about courses, majors, and extracurricular activities. Both are popular.[13]

Notice that the principles are action oriented and bear more than a passing similarity to the ones listed in table 3.2 for continuous quality improvement. What's particularly interesting is Stanford's use of the principles in shaping its undergraduate programs—a clear application of systems thinking.

"Flip teaching" (also known as "flipping the course" and "reverse instruction"), which has gained currency in recent years, provides a less exotic example of systems thinking. It starts with the separation of student engagement into "first exposure" and "deep engagement," in which students are introduced to materials and then engage in active learning through discussion, problem solving, and so forth. Many traditional courses achieve first exposure largely through lectures and leave deep engagement to TA-taught breakout sections. They use the most highly paid and experienced person—the faculty member—to deliver one-off, mostly one-way communication while the very challenging engagement activities are left to less experienced teaching assistants. Flip teaching achieves first exposure with technology supplemented by TAs, followed by engagement sessions taught by faculty. It's worth noting that the driving force for flip teaching is not economics, though there may be a salutary effect on cost, but rather effectiveness.

Some professors try flip teaching for a while and then revert to traditional lectures because it's easier to lecture than to sustain the kind of in-class interaction needed for deep engagement. This may be due to the approach's novelty and also, perhaps, by failure to find effective technology solutions for achieving good first exposure. These problems will subside over time. The root problem may be that it is, in fact, more demanding for faculty to engage students in deep learning experiences than simply to talk at them. However, the solution to this problem should not be to assign the active learning sessions to less experienced teachers.

Having too narrow a vision also may present a problem for flip teaching. Figure 3.1, which depicts a short module in a hypothetical beginning microeconomics course,[14] indicates how one's vision can be broadened by the application of flowcharting and a slightly enhanced way of conceptualizing the teaching problem. While simple, it embodies a number of ideas not normally included in traditional or even flipped courses.

- The boxes in the figure provide a detailed explication of "activities"— what teachers and students actually will do to achieve learning.
- The rows divide the activities into three engagement categories:
  - *Synchronous activities* represent the simultaneous effort of students and teachers, either face-to-face as in a conventional class or through telecommunications.
  - *Asynchronous activities: student* involve things like studying and paper writing, done alone or in groups but without real-time input from the teacher.
  - *Asynchronous activities: teacher* cover the preparation, grading, and other activities performed by professors and others while not in direct contact with students.
- The three phases in the learning process are called out by the boldface labels.[15] First exposure is when students encounter new information, concepts, or procedures. Deep engagement is where they analyze

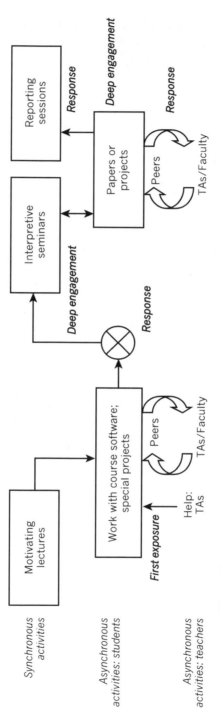

**Figure 3.1.** An enhanced teaching/learning architecture *Source:* Massy, *Honoring the Trust,* 132.

the material, synthesize it, use it to solve problems, and apply it to actual situations. Response is where the teacher provides feedback on students' attempts at synthesis, analysis, problem solving, or application. First exposure and deep engagement are at the core of flipped teaching, but response is not necessarily part of that design.

First exposure begins with the department's most articulate and charismatic professor delivering a short sequence of motivating lectures. (Being asked to give these lectures is considered to be an honor.) Then students work their way through a series of computer-based tutorials and simulations that introduce them to, say, supply-demand theory. The software operates asynchronously in student space, but TAs stand ready to help with procedures and clarify specific points where needed.

Moving to deep engagement, students advance to asynchronous work on special projects and eventually interpretive seminars, taught by faculty, once they have mastered the basic concepts. These provide opportunities to explore the learned material's implications and apply it to practical situations. Attendees are well prepared because they have passed the assessment algorithms embedded in the first-exposure software. (Special sections that combine remediation with interpretation cater to students who haven't achieved mastery.) Seminar instructors don't lecture on the first-exposure material, though they may offer enhancements and interpretations at teachable moments. Responses to student papers and project work take place mostly through instructor-mediated group activities, either in class or online. The seminars provide venues for individual reports, and larger groups may be convened to discuss team reports. Papers are submitted for student peer review, and students learn by critiquing one another's work. However, professors and TAs provide careful oversight and feedback.

The new architecture redefines the roles of students and faculty by making students more actively responsible for their own learning, but under close supervision by teachers. Active learning improves retention and leverages professorial and TA time. The architecture also provides an element of competency-based learning: that is, by advancing students from first-exposure to processing activities as soon as they are ready rather than holding back the best until the majority has mastered the material.

> **Learning Objects**
>
> Represent "intelligent agents" that, by embodying ideas in software, help teachers teach and students learn. Specifically, they
>
> 1. encapsulate *knowledge* in software by storing information in the form of text, formulas, pictures, data, etc.
> 2. provide *methods* to help students access the information and process it effectively.
> 3. generate *events* that stimulate student activity and ascertain learning progress or lack thereof.

The architecture also makes intensive use of online "learning objects"—software that combines content knowledge, interactive pedagogy, and student assessment as summarized in the sidebar above and discussed later in connection with Carnegie Mellon University's Open Learning Initiative. They allow students to learn more actively and receive better feedback without undermining the professor's role or losing the benefits of face-to-face interaction. Professors set learning goals, design the sequence of activities, select or develop the learning objects and other technology vehicles, monitor student progress, and provide special help when needed. Both the professor and the software offer content and insight to students at the time most conducive to learning, not in batch-processed doses. Professors see less dull and repetitive work and can interact with students in more satisfying ways. Last but not least, the use of learning objects will produce cost savings once professors have climbed the learning curve and development costs have been amortized. Because some of the course activity is embedded in preprogrammed learning, a smaller fraction remains as variable cost that must be replicated each time the course is given or a section class is added—thus opening the way for economies of scale.

*Service Science*

The emergent field of service science represents a very specific kind of systems thinking. It recognizes that to be fully effective, all service provision requires the sustained effort of receivers as well as suppliers—an idea called "value co-creation," or, more simply, "co-production."[16] Co-production offers powerful insights for teaching and learning, where it is widely acknowledged that students need to take proactive roles in their own education. It also applies to administrative and support service operations, where providers should work collaboratively with faculty to produce desired outcomes.

One lesson from value co-creation is that delivering a service requires the simultaneous joint effort of provider and user.[17] With products, on the other hand, value is "stored" in an artifact during the manufacturing process and then released later through the activities of users. The provider controls the process until the product has been produced to specification and delivered for sale. Not so with services. The provider designs the service delivery process and makes resources available, but no value is created until the user adds his or her own effort. Designers of MOOCs and other online learning systems need to keep this fact in mind. No matter how much value is stored in the software (e.g., in the form of lectures and written materials), its potential isn't realized until it is "released" by students.

Some service scientists say that users "drive" the value creation process because they initiate particular service instances and can exit from them at any time. That seems exaggerated when applied to higher education. While students do initiate and can exit from their overall educational experiences, learning activities over short timescales are indeed driven by instructors and software. There is a sense in which students drive the process when doing homework assignments and so forth, but too often they fail to do a good job. This brings home yet another point: that value co-creation requires not only well-designed processes and good resource support by providers but also motivation and a degree of know-how by users.

Another service science lesson is that providers should develop an "architecture of participation where actors connect and collaborate through a shared vision."[18] This requires a pervasive fabric of trust as well as a strategic approach by institutions that focuses on collaborating, sensing, responding, and learning from the journey users take through the service experience. Strategy is no longer engineered but is more of an emergent property of the collaborating, sensing, and learning enterprise. For higher education, this implies that the learning should be highly interactive yet subject to well-thought-out discipline.

Designing a good service process requires one to move beyond the representation of work as a "series of sequential steps where one component of the work concludes before the next begins." Service scientists use "practice diagrams" (i.e., flowcharts) to "show how work unfolds iteratively, cycling back-and-forth between components of the work until an eventual 'end state' is achieved."[19] Effective learning requires multiple feedback processes, where student interactions with teachers and technology allow the latter to tailor the experience to the student's emergent needs. It also is context specific,[20] as in the all-important "teachable moment."

Service scientists argue that providers, including those in higher education, must move beyond metrics defined around units of output (degrees, credit hours, etc.) to get at what really matters to users. This means developing an understanding of how students use their education and the kinds of satisfaction they derive from it. The fact that value in education is "unlocked" over an individual's lifetime complicates matters but does not negate the principle.

These lessons imply that service productivity and service quality are intimately linked.[21] It makes no sense to look at units of "output" without simultaneously looking at quality. Failure to do so can, in the words of one service science paper, "[t]rigger a set of self-reinforcing processes that lead to the persistent, continual erosion of service quality. . . . The positive feedbacks operate as vicious cycles that can drag an organization into a death spiral of declining quality, customer loss, budget cuts, higher work pressure, poor morale, higher employee attrition, and still lower quality."[22] There is some evidence that the combination of budget cuts and pressures to perform research may be having such an effect on undergraduate education at some schools.[23] Whether true or not, this danger is clear and present. The alternative is to create "quality pressure" by "becoming aware of the implications of poor service . . . and then, through training, incentives, measurement, and example, persuade [providers] that avoiding these costs is a priority."[24] In higher education, this translates to getting better learning measures and providing an impetus to act on them continuously and effectively.

The concepts of service science put a sharper edge on ideas already being discussed in some quarters of higher education. They may be a useful spur for thinking about change. Service science also offers a number of techniques that may be helpful. "Service blueprinting" is "[a] simple-to-learn process modeling approach in which potentially diverse groups within the organization consider how the process is delivering, and should deliver, its services. The outcome is a visual depiction or map of the service that highlights steps in the process, points of contact that take place between consumers and employees and among employees, and physical evidence of the quality of service"[25]—but without implying that service is a linear process. The architecture shown in figure 3.1 can be construed as such a blueprint. It represents a kind of systems thinking that is anchored on the student and his or her experiences as they emerge over time.

### Learning Science

Rooted in cognition, psychology, and other scientific disciplines, learning science is dramatically improving our understanding of how learning takes place—or fails to take place—and the ways in which teaching can be improved for maximum effectiveness. Examples of learning science can be found in James Zull's *The Art of Changing the Brain: Enriching the Practice of Teaching by Exploring the Biology of Learning.*[26] One of the important principles of learning science is that a student's prior knowledge matters. As Zull describes it: "[W]hen we speak of prior knowledge, we are speaking of something physical. It builds as brains physically change, and it is held in place by physical connections. We could say that prior knowledge is a thing!"[27] Given that prior knowledge has physical existence and demonstrable importance to learning, it behooves teachers to find out what it is for their students and then exploit this knowledge in the interest of learning.

Perhaps the longest-running effort to extend and apply the ideas of learning science began at Carnegie Mellon University about fifteen years ago. Collaborations of cognitive scientists, psychologists, and computer scientists led to an impressive set of principles for learning science and its applications to university teaching. Learning should be student centered, evidence based, and highly interactive, for example, and instructors need to acquire and use relevant knowledge about their students, organize and prioritize what is taught, and recognize and overcome their "expert blind spots." Many of the ideas are and were well known, though too often ignored in practice (e.g., meaningful engagement, goal-directed practice, and targeted feedback are necessary for deep learning). Others are more surprising (e.g., the way students organize knowledge is a major determinant of how they use it, prior knowledge can hinder as well as help learning, and students must learn to monitor, evaluate, and adjust their approaches if they are to become self-directed learners).

Carnegie Mellon University's Eberley Center for Teaching and Learning subsequently encapsulated these ideas into a set of "principles": for use in faculty training programs. The principles are sufficiently important; therefore, I have included them, in their entirety, as appendix A at the end of the book. It's hard to imagine a valid justification for course designers, or indeed for any university teacher, to remain ignorant of or indifferent to these principles and the enhancements to them that will evolve over time. One hopes that their mastery will become a staple of PhD programs and a prerequisite for all who teach in universities.

Breakthroughs in "learning analytics," defined as "the collection and analysis of data generated during the learning process in order to improve the quality of both learning and teaching,"[28] are rapidly expanding the knowledge base of learning science. These results stem from the application of sophisticated statistical models to the burgeoning databases that are created as by-products of computer-mediated teaching applications linked to student profiles and learning histories. Sooner or later, it will be possible to predict the value added of changes in teaching methods for particular groups of students, including, importantly, those who are at risk academically.

Learning science looms particularly large in the science, technology, engineering, and mathematics (STEM) fields, where it also is known as research-based instruction (RBI) and discipline-based education research (DBER). The National Research Council's Committee on the Status, Contributions, and Future Directions of Discipline-based Education Research recently published a synthesis of work to date.[29] The synthesis covers a "wide range of studies that includes basic and applied research . . . [that] combine expert knowledge of the science or engineering discipline, of the challenges of learning and teaching in that discipline, and of the science of learning and teaching generally."[30] The book contains many examples of DBER concepts and applications across all the major domains of science.

In addition to its description of scientific findings, the DBER report includes dozens, if not hundreds, of references on student learning assessment. Indeed, essentially all learning science studies include an assessment component because, without assessment, it is impossible to determine the efficacy of the experimental treatment. As discussed in the next section, the National Center for Academic Transformation (NCAT) also reports many examples of learning assessment—which is required as an integral part of its course redesign process. Many of NCAT's examples lie in the social science, humanities, and other non-technical fields. Finally, software learning objects such as those depicted in figure 3.1 include algorithms for student learning assessment.

Looking more broadly, education quality assessment should include a rigorous evaluation of whether an entity's teaching methods reflect learning science principles. The Teaching Practices Survey developed at the University of British Columbia is designed to "fully analyze the teaching practices used in any undergraduate mathematics and science course (except lab, project, and seminar courses), determine the extent of use of teaching practices that research has shown lead to improved learning, be quick and simple to complete while minimizing subjective judgments, allow meaningful widespread comparisons of the quality of teaching . . . , [and] identify specific opportunities for teaching improvement at the individual and departmental level[s]."[31] In a similar vein, the *Chronicle of Higher Education* recently reported on the College Education Project's methodology to "examine academic rigor and the quality of teaching in ways that conventional research tools, like student surveys, standardized tests, or faculty salary self-reports, often failed to adequately convey."[32]

The findings from learning science are not going unnoticed. The Association of American Universities (AAU) has launched a five-year initiative to "influence the STEM culture at AAU universities so they will use sustainable, student centered, evidence-based, active learning pedagogy in their classes, particularly at the first-year and sophomore levels."[33] The study will develop an analytical framework for assessing and improving STEM teaching quality and support projects at a number of AAU institutions. It will explore mechanisms for training, recognizing, and rewarding professors who want to improve the quality of STEM teaching, work with federal research agencies for recognizing, rewarding, and promoting such efforts, and develop effective means for sharing information.

Carnegie Mellon University's Simon Initiative Learning Engineering Ecosystem is another recent development in the learning science space. It defines "learning engineering" as, "bridging gaps between theory and practice, while improving both."[34] The approach emphasizes:

- building and leveraging cognitive models of expertise to inform the design of effective student-centered instructional materials,
- collecting rich data on student interactions and learning outcomes,
- data analysis via state-of-the-art machine learning and analytic methods,
- data-informed iterative improvement of the instructional materials, and
- leveraging these assets to derive fresh insights in learning science.[35]

The real news, however, is that the Simon initiative will "openly release its most effective learning engineering tools as a foundation for a large-scale, multi-institutional, open-source collaboration."[36] The tools, developed in collaboration with the Pittsburgh Science of Learning Center (PSLC) and others, constitute a suite of applications and services that will support a wide range of learning engineering innovations. Their release will dramatically advance the objectives of university reengineering.

## Illustrative Applications

We now turn to examples where the new scholarship of teaching has been applied successfully at traditional universities. The most venerable is known as course redesign. Invented some twenty years ago with the studio courses at Rensselaer Polytechnic Institute (RPI),[37] the idea has been widely utilized by Carol Twigg's National Center for Academic Transformation (NCAT), Carl Wieman's Science Education Initiative at the University of Colorado and the University of British Columbia, and Carnegie Mellon University's Open Learning Initiative (OLI). More recently, the new approach has been applied in the context of a new campus startup at the University of Minnesota–Rochester. Readers will note that most of the initiatives follow the paradigm described near the end of chapter 2.

## Course Redesign

As practiced by NCAT, course redesign is the "process of reengineering whole courses to achieve better learning outcomes at lower cost."[38] The model relies mainly on systems thinking and common sense, brought to bear through the medium of a predefined development template. It "analyzes instructional methods and identifies ways to boost active learning and efficiently leverage faculty, graduate students, and technology."[39] It's not about putting courses online or necessarily about applications of information technology—although blended IT applications almost always end up as part of the finished product.

Teams of departmental faculty and staff work with NCAT to see to the redesign. It is impossible to overstate the importance of such teamwork. The team members bring multiple talents and perspectives to bear on the redesign process. Further, collective responsibility is the best and perhaps the only way to get the changes rooted deeply in departmental thinking. Finally, participation in teams familiarizes more professors with the methods and benefits of redesign—hopefully to the point where they will adopt the methodology in additional courses.

The first step in redesign is to document the activities, costs, and outcomes of the course as it is currently taught. Participants become familiar with the idea of analyzing activities and the particulars of the status quo, and the analysis process elicits suggestions for how things might be done better. The team learns a lot simply by discussing these suggestions. Eventually, it settles on a proposed redesign and gets approval from departmental colleagues and administrators to implement it on a trial basis.

Every project requires rigorous evaluation of learning outcomes as measured by student performance and achievement. NCAT insists that proposed redesigns be compared with control groups. Quantitative comparisons typically rely on one or more of the following: comparison of common final exams, comparisons of common content items selected from exams, comparison of pre- and posttests, and comparison of student work using common rubrics. Other outcomes include increased course-completion rates, improved retention, better student attitudes toward the subject matter, increased student performance and downstream courses, and increased student satisfaction with the mode of instruction. National experts have provided consultation and oversight on the assessment procedures to make sure that the results are reliable and valid.[40] Cost comparisons also enter the redesign process. These rely on activity-based costing (ABC), which is discussed in chapter 4. Appendix B extends NCAT's spreadsheet-based tool for quantifying these costs to take more of the important factors explicitly into account.

NCAT conducted about 120 large-scale redesigns between 1999 and 2010: in research universities, comprehensive four-year institutions, liberal arts institutions, and community colleges. These included "16 courses in the humanities (developmental reading and writing, English composition, fine arts, history, music, Spanish, literature, and women's studies), 60 in quantitative subjects (developmental and college-level mathematics, statistics, and computing), 23 in the social sciences (political science, economics, psychology, and sociology), 15 in the natural sciences (anatomy and physiology, astronomy, biology, chemistry, and geology) and six in professional studies (accounting, business, education, engineering, and nursing)."[41] The findings showed that, "[o]n average, costs were reduced by 37% in redesigned courses with a range of 9% to 77%. Meanwhile, learning outcomes improved in 72% of the redesigns with the remaining 28% producing learning equivalent to traditional formats."[42] The focus has been primarily but not exclusively on large-enrollment, introductory courses in multiple disciplines, but there is no reason that the methodology can't also be used for smaller courses and individual modules within courses.

### Science Education Initiative

The Science Education Initiative (SEI) was an early, large-scale application of science-based principles to course redesign. It was implemented in the mid-2000s by physics Nobelist Carl Wieman and colleagues at the University of Colorado (CU) and the University of British Columbia (UBC). In addition to its emphasis on learning science, SEI is noteworthy because it was the first institution-wide effort to transform STEM teaching based on learning science principles, and because it provided innovators with a higher level of professional support than is typical with course redesign.

SEI began with a call for competitive proposals from departments to support widespread improvement in undergraduate education. The proffered grants were sufficient to fund the department's developmental efforts including, importantly, the hiring of science education specialists (SES) as discussed later. The funds proved sufficient to attract serious attention. The proposals had to address all core undergraduate courses, for both majors and nonmajors, so their preparation necessarily involved a collective discussion about teaching goals and practices. According to Wieman, "Typically this was the first time such a discussion had ever taken place in the department." Despite the department-wide reach, however, it was understood that actual transformation efforts would take place course by course, just as in NCAT's course redesign, "because the individual course is a more manageable and rewarding target for individual faculty members." The proposals also had to address "sustainability"—"that is, how the improved techniques, materials, and assessment data would be disseminated and reused."[43]

Wieman met personally with nearly every eligible department during the proposal-solicitation process, typically as part of a faculty meeting. His observations about these meetings are especially germane to achieving successful adoptions.

> The proportion of the department in attendance at the meeting and the guidance provided by the chair/head were good predictors of the overall interest of the department and of departmental leadership. These meetings also foreshadowed many of the issues that are played out throughout the SEI work.
>
> Despite some skepticism as to the possibility of making dramatic improvements in education, nearly everyone felt that student learning could and should be improved. But there was wide variation in the ideas about how to achieve that improvement. Departments that primarily discussed what *they* might do were more successful in their future efforts than those that focused on the deficiencies of the students or the educational system.
>
> Faculty frequently expressed concern that they might lose control of the courses they taught. More surprising was the very vocal opposition

of the few faculty members who prided themselves on being good teachers, and were recognized as such, but whose reputations were largely based on their ability to give captivating lectures rather than on any evidence of student learning.[44]

In the end, all but one of the eligible departments submitted proposals, some based on extensive faculty deliberations and others with the faculty's approval but without broad involvement or commitment. Five grants were awarded at CU and four at UBC. It is noteworthy that some faculty in the unsuccessful departments became interested in the process and resolved to carry its ideas forward when and where they could.

The SESs were mostly postdocs in the relevant scientific discipline. Success also required them to have "knowledge of educational and cognitive psychology research, proven teaching methods, and (most importantly) diplomatic skills." Some twenty-two were hired across the nine departments. In addition, a small central staff provided "training in a few key areas: learning research and science education, learning-goals development, clicker-question design, interpersonal communication, cognitive interviews of students, and designing and conducting rigorous assessments and research studies."[45] The departments hired the SESs, and, while they related to the central staff in a matrix arrangement, they were seen as valued resources by the departmental faculty.

The initiative is regarded as having been very successful. For example, only one of the seventy faculty members involved at UBC abandoned the program before completion, and forty-six of the fifty completers who taught other undergraduate courses applied the ideas learned to at least one of those courses.[46] According to Wieman et al., the model "demonstrates that it is possible to bring about large-scale change. Key elements of SEI are the focus on the department and a willingness to make a one-time investment to achieve change at scale. When this is done, teaching can be far more effective in that the faculty can find it more rewarding—a very encouraging sign for the future of science education."[47]

### Open Learning Initiative

Carnegie Mellon University's Open Learning Initiative (OLI) is a foundation-funded program to provide open educational resources.

The program implements learning science through the medium of software learning objects like intelligent tutoring systems, virtual laboratories, and simulations. The software provides students with frequent opportunities for assessment and feedback, and supports the kind of dynamic, flexible, and responsive instruction that characterizes learning science. From its inception in 2001, the goal was to integrate "[Carnegie Mellon University]'s expertise in cognitive tutoring into whole courses that would stand on their own and enact instruction."[48] The resulting courses have been made available to, and used by, faculty at a wide variety of institutions.

OLI course development engages faculty domain experts from multiple institutions, students, learning science researchers, human-computer interaction experts, and software engineers in the development and improvement of learning environments. The team begins by creating a parameterized skill model that establishes the relationships between learning objectives, the skills associated with each objective, the tasks needed to manifest the skill, and metrics for assessing task proficiency. (In this context, "skill" stands for all relevant elements of the content domain.) Each learning objective may have multiple component skills, each skill may contribute to one or more objectives, each task may contribute to more than one skill, and each skill may be assessed by one or more steps in the task. The OLI tutorials and other materials assist students during the problem-solving process, and the embedded assessments collect data for purposes of ongoing continuous improvement and basic research as well as student evaluation.

Stanford's Candace Thille, who headed the OLI program for a time, has studied the dissemination and implementation of OLI technology.[49] The dissemination she looked at involved asking senior institutional administrators to invite faculty to a workshop to learn about the technology and consider using it in a course or participating in an evaluation. Some participants had not heard of OLI but expressed a general interest in using technology. Others had heard about OLI and had specific reasons for considering adoption: for example, because of the individualized feedback that could be provided to students and instructors. While recognizing that a few workshop hours were insufficient to develop deep knowledge about OLI, the organizers felt that by the end of the workshops the faculty had a sufficient understanding to make a decision about whether to participate. "The most common words faculty used to describe OLI were 'technology,' 'feedback loop', 'data,' and 'scientific,' which were in fact appropriate descriptors. Many faculty reported that the decision to participate was an 'easy' one."[50]

Thille conducted follow-up interviews with faculty who had signed up for the project. The interviews elicited mostly favorable comments, which were consistent with the benefits discussed throughout this chapter. However, two apprehensions of general importance did come to light. One concerned the question of "fit": the alignment of the OLI course goals with those of the instructor. The reaction generally was favorable, but a number of respondents expressed doubts: for example, "The way the information is conveyed, I think *with some modification*, would be a good fit for my course." OLI courses carry an open license that does not prohibit modification, but the technology itself is "locked down," which makes it difficult to do so. (That situation may be changing, however.) At root, of course, lurks the "complexity of balancing faculty desire for individual control and the commitment to science-based, data-driven design."[51] Thille argues that there is a "sweet spot here: the OLI technology needs to provide just the right combination of well-designed structure, support, and flexibility . . . [s]o that faculty members feel [that] they are the instructors and that the OLI environment supports them . . . [m]uch like a very good teaching assistant." She argues that at the end of the day, what's needed is to "[s]witch from a purely individual, intuitive approach to an evidence-based collaborative approach for course development, delivery, assessment, and research."[52]

The amount of time taken to learn and implement the technology was the second important concern. Significant time commitments were needed to plan the use of OLI for classroom transformation, and additional time was required for learning to use the tools effectively and making mid-course corrections. This does not include the time required later for analyzing data generated by the OLI tools and effecting continuous improvement. In Thille's words, "In this study, time is cited as a, if not *the*, primary barrier to implementing innovations. Administrators who would like their faculty to experiment with new practices must provide sufficient time and resources for faculty to engage in the innovation."[53] I noted earlier that most faculty are extremely busy—hence this finding cannot be overemphasized.

## Two "Outside the Box" Proposals

The materials in this chapter demonstrate that teaching processes and metrics can be substantially improved and that effective approaches exist for achieving and monitoring adoption. In time, these approaches can be expected to transform teaching and learning in traditional universities. I now want to offer two proposals for accelerating this process and also, in the fullness of time, for helping to solve the problems of market inefficiency and weak quality assurance discussed in chapter 2. I am aware that these proposals represent what Suzanne Walsh of the Bill and Melinda Gates Foundation calls "unchallenged solutions"— ideas that, though logically argued and perhaps strongly advocated, have not met the test of experience. That can't be helped at this stage, but I do believe that they are worth serious consideration.

### Departmental Teaching Improvement Portfolios

The idea is very simple: to capture the emergent experience gained by departments during their improvement efforts and make it widely available to others inside and outside the institution. The data in the portfolio would cover course design and redesign activities, together with the evidence that led to the design choices and the results obtained from implementation. Because compilation would be a collective departmental responsibility, most, if not all, faculty would be expected to contribute and learn about others' contributions. The fundamental objective would be to develop information and human capital that can be used by everyone, currently and in the future, to further the cause of student learning. This is happening now through the normal academic processes of conference attendance and publication, but the systematic collection of data at the department level would connect the dots much more quickly.

These portfolios are analogous to the student learning portfolios being used to assess learner performance in some institutions and majors. Preparing such a portfolio requires the student to assemble, review, assimilate, and integrate many otherwise disparate information elements—hopefully in ways that make the whole greater than the sum of the parts. The result becomes part of the student's record, so both the student and the professor can use it to identify gaps and areas that need improvement and later assess progress in filling the gaps.

In our context, the portfolio development tasks can be expected to spur knowledge transfer across faculty members, including new hires, and eventually to help change the department's culture. A subset of the information, with privacy-sensitive data removed, would be made available for sharing both inside and outside the university. Such transparency would spur the further testing and adoption of successful ideas, and also facilitate meta-research. A transparent portfolio also would provide a wealth of information for satisfying externally based compliance requirements: if nothing else, the university could demonstrate the extent to which it is applying the new scholarship of teaching. Just imagine the difference between the resulting evidence-based presentations with drill-downs in response to questions and the unsupportable rhetoric now often provided to oversight bodies.

But while process-related evidence would be extremely valuable, it won't satisfy the demand for, in Ewell's words as quoted in chapter 2, "[r]eporting actual learning outcomes in comparable or benchmark forms." The answer is, as mentioned, that evidence-based improvement requires an effective measurement component. The resulting metrics would become an important part of the departmental teaching portfolio. This would stimulate proposals for comparable metrics that fit particular situations. Professional integrity and competition eventually could motivate departments to adopt these metrics where they are applicable—an outcome that would be facilitated by institutions' efforts to meet compliance pressures. Results from applying the metrics would be included in the portfolios and eventually benchmarked through further meta-research.

Oversight bodies want quality information sooner rather than later, but it's counterproductive to push for standardized tests and other hoped-for magic bullets that, as discussed in chapter 2, may well never become available. Conversely, I have never visited an academic department where it isn't possible to get valid local measures of student learning—provided the efforts needed to develop them are forthcoming. The portfolio framework could spur such development in ways that also contribute to improvement and thus meet the needs of both institutions and regulators.

*Generally Accepted Learning Assessment Principles*

The shortfalls in learning metrics and the resulting adverse effects on market efficiency call out for what might be described as "generally accepted learning assessment principles" (GALAPs). These principles would encapsulate best practice on how to evaluate learning and communicate the results inside and outside the university. The development task will require understanding, for different kinds of learning situations, about the kinds of data that provide meaningful information and those that don't.

The nature of "evidence about learning" is well summarized in Peter Ewell's paper for the Western Association of Schools and Colleges (WASC), a regional accreditor. His main arguments are listed in the following paragraph.

Evidence is different from things such as "information," "data," or "fact" in at least five subtle but important ways:

1. Evidence is *intentional and purposeful*; it is advanced to address deliberately posed questions that are important to both institutions and their stakeholders.
2. Evidence always entails *interpretation and reflection*; it does not "speak for itself."
3. Good evidence is *integrated and holistic*; it does not consist merely of a list of unrelated "facts."
4. What counts as evidence can be both *quantitative and qualitative*; it is not just confined to numbers.
5. Good evidence can be either *direct or indirect*; it does not always require obtrusive data gathering that uses specially designed instruments.

Evidence should:

1. Cover knowledge and skills taught throughout the program's curriculum.
2. Involve multiple judgments of student performance.
3. Provide information on multiple dimensions of student performance.
4. Involve more than surveys and self-reports of competence and growth by students.
5. Be relevant, verifiable, representative, cumulative, and actionable.[54]

Embodying these ideas in a set of GALAP principles would be a major step forward—more productive, in my opinion, than a continued search for the holy grail of one-size-fits-all standardized tests.

Experience with generally accepted accounting principles (GAAP) indicates how a well-developed GALAP statement could improve market efficiency and help satisfy the compliance requirements imposed by regulators. The essential concept is that, under GAAP, one can be confident that data mean what they are asserted to mean. The definitions are reasonably precise, for example, and issues like the timing of revenue and expense, and hence profit recognition, have been taken into account. GAAP allows considerable flexibility in how firms report their data, but the principles are specific enough to circumscribe discretion in auditable ways. With well-articulated and accepted learning assessment principles, it would be difficult to publish results based mainly on spin and wishful thinking—or no results at all, for that matter. Once concrete, relevant, and verifiable evidence about learning enters the public domain, higher education's many rating and evaluation services could be counted upon to find new ways of analyzing and interpreting it—just as analogous entities do for financial data.

## Organizing for Improvement

Quality doesn't just happen. The fundamental message of Deming and other quality pioneers is that sustaining, assuring, and improving quality requires systematic effort. How to organize faculty activities so that the needed "systematic effort" is applied to quality improvement is the subject of this section. My basic proposition is that the classic list of faculty activities—teaching, research, and service—be expanded to include such efforts. I have called this "academic quality work" (AQW).[55] (Service and its close cousin departmental administration represent additional activities.) AQW shifts the scholarship of teaching from the mainly self-generated and self-fulfilled concern of individual professors to include departments' collective responsibility for educational improvement. Defining it explicitly and organizing to do it systematically can help offset the effects of unmonitored joint production that were discussed in chapter 2. Universities should adjust their faculty workload expectations to carve out time for AQW. This might be done by adjusting teaching loads or encouraging faculty who are less effective in traditional research and scholarship (or who care strongly about quality or just want to do something different) to engage in quality work. Finally, it is extremely important that AQW be recognized in faculty reward systems.

It's useful to distinguish such work from the tasks required to actually produce the good or service in question. My book with Steve Graham and Paula Myrick Short defined AQW as "organized activities dedicated to improving and assuring education and research quality. They systematize the university's approach to quality instead of leaving it mainly to self-initiated and -monitored individual effort. They provide what higher education quality pioneers David Dill and Frans van Vught[56] call 'a framework for quality management in higher education . . . drawn from insights in Deming's approach, but grounded in the context of academic operations.' "[57]

The definition covers research as well as teaching. Research is covered in the aforementioned volume but will not be discussed here. The previous sections of this chapter illustrated some content areas of AQW. Now we turn to the process of getting it embedded in departmental routines.

AQW is at once familiar and foreign to most professors. It's familiar in that most, if not all, professors desire to improve their teaching. They practice the scholarship of teaching to some extent. What's foreign is the notion that educational improvement activities should be systematic rather than situational, that they should go beyond curriculum and personal teaching prowess, and that departments bear collective responsibility for quality assurance. U.S. accreditors have promoted many elements of AQW in recent years, but the idea of organized, comprehensive, and systematic "quality work" has yet to take hold.

How can departments systematize their approach to quality? I believe that there are two overarching tasks. The first is to follow generalizable principles of good practice whose value has been demonstrated in nonacademic settings if not already in academe. This chapter has presented a significant number of such principles, beginning with those set forth in table 3.2. The second requirement is to address *all* of the areas of activity necessary for effective teaching and learning, and to do so on a regular basis. Comprehensive and regular coverage is important to ensure that good work in one area is not negated by shortfalls elsewhere or complaisance that leads to backsliding.

*Domains of Academic Quality Work*

Table 3.3 presents the domains of AQW as Graham, Short, and I believe it should be applied in teaching, together with the defining question that should be asked in each domain. (Additional questions about each teaching domain, and a full set of questions on research, can be found in our book.[58]) A department that can honestly answer all five questions in the affirmative is likely to do a better job of teaching than one that can't. This can provide an effective motivation for improvement. And, as will be mentioned shortly, it also provides indirect evidence about teaching performance—evidence that is not now obtainable from other sources given the shortfalls in student assessment methodologies. The domains emerged from hands-on experience in Hong Kong and were refined by similar experience in Missouri and Tennessee. Professors were asked repeatedly whether the five domains are relevant and whether anything has been omitted, and the answers came out overwhelmingly favorable. Furthermore, it generally was agreed that an explicit listing of the five domains is important for departmental quality improvement. While curriculum receives a great deal of attention, for example, the matter of learning objectives usually is implicit or grounded in disciplinary canons rather than student needs and

| Table 3.3. Domains of academic quality work | |
| --- | --- |
| Domain | Questions to be asked |
| Learning objectives | What knowledge, skills, abilities, and values should the students acquire from their educational experience? |
| Curriculum | Does the curriculum truly deliver the learning objectives? |
| Teaching methods | Is teaching at the state of the art in terms of active learning, use of technology, etc., given the learning objectives? |
| Learning assessment | Do groups of faculty systematically collect evidence on student learning and use it to improve teaching quality? |
| Quality assurance | Can departments assure themselves that work on the first four domains is of high quality and being delivered as intended? |

wants. Our respondents also corroborated the view, expressed in this and earlier chapters, that teaching methods and learning assessment receive far too little systematic attention. The inclusion of quality assurance elicited much discussion, but in the end most who participated in our projects agreed that departments do bear a major responsibility for ensuring that teaching and teaching assessment are being carried forward as planned, and thus that they need to give the matter systematic attention.

### Changing Departmental Behavior

What can a provost or dean do to introduce faculty to AQW and then get it embedded in departmental routines? Chapter 2 has already presented the answer: in figure 2.4, "The Improvement Cycle," and its associated discussion. Indeed, that material came originally from my colleagues and my work on the implementation of AQW. The first step is to convene a series of voluntary workshops as indicated by the "explain" callout in the figure, to introduce and process the AQW domains and principles and why they are important. The workshops should be designed to encourage a few "innovator" departments to step forward to conduct pilot implementations. We had no trouble getting volunteers in Missouri and Tennessee, and the same was true in the project by Carl Wieman that was described earlier. One then works with the pilot departments to complete and embed the improvement cycle, and in subsequent years with additional departments to propagate the AQW concept across the campus.

Self-review and peer review emerged as key elements of the improvement cycle.[59] The first step in an AQW initiative is for the department to organize a task force to conduct the self-review. A tenured faculty member should chair the task force, which should reach out to professors and others as widely as possible. The charge is to reflect on how the AQW principles are currently being applied to the five AQW domains, thus answering the questions in table 3.3 (and Massy, Graham, and Short's *Academic Quality Work*) and producing a short report to provide a basis for peer review. The peer review should be scheduled at the beginning of the process, usually near then end of the current academic year, so that the task force has a definite deadline to work with. Subsequent reviews should be conducted at three-to-five-year intervals, but the AQW task force or an equivalent should remain in being in order to maintain momentum as discussed in chapter 2.

Although primarily intended to improve practice, peer review of departmental attention to the AQW principles also can be used to mark progress toward educational quality improvement. For example, the reviewers might note a lack of attention to outcomes, inadequate use of facts, lack of coherence, or indifference to best practice. Or one might see great collegiality, strong focus on teaching and learning, effective learning assessment, and commitment to continuous improvement. Few who reflect seriously about teaching and learning quality have difficulty distinguishing between the good, the bad, and the ugly when it comes to the application of these principles. Likewise, it isn't difficult to discern whether the principles are being applied in all the focal areas of academic quality work. Data like these apply the capability maturity scale (CM) that was discussed in chapter 2. Provosts and deans will do well to maintain a scorecard of departmental CM results for use in prioritizing further interventions and as performance metrics for the overall education quality program.

My experience in Hong Kong and Tennessee contradicts the often-heard assertion that one cannot combine formative and summative evaluations in the same peer-review process. [60] As mentioned, a degree of summative evaluation is required to provide good formative feedback. Further, the reviews rely on panelists' direct judgments about knowledge of and involvement with AQW (informed but not dominated by the self-study reports)—these judgments are not affected much by efforts to spin the department's performance. One can learn very quickly whether a respondent is engaged with the relevant activities, for example. If so, he or she will be able to provide thick descriptions of what is being done, why, and what the results are; if not, the conversation will soon sputter into vague generalities.

Let me close with an anecdote that comes out of my work in Hong Kong.[61] Our review panels probed the extent of quality work at the university, school, and departmental levels. The latter proved to be the most important, because it is only at the grassroots level that one can determine what actually is happening. (University-level policy statements and committee reports can be made to sound good regardless of performance on the ground.) Our approach was to have two-or three-person teams visit a few sample departments in each of the key schools on campus and then talk with the cognizant deans. The first round of reviews served mainly to introduce the concepts of academic quality work and its associated domains and principles: the necessary first step in the adoption process. The second round, conducted five years later, showed that the ideas had been taken up in some schools and departments on each campus but not in others.

Perhaps the most telling lessons were learned when we talked with school deans about differences in performance among their departments. Deans who had bought into the program usually knew about the variation and were eager to talk with us about how they could bring the poor performers closer to the better ones. Those who were sympathetic but less engaged were not aware but happy to engage in discussion about the variations and the strategies they might use to improve matters. The worst responses came from deans who, while perhaps vaguely aware of differences in quality work among their departments, claimed that it was not their responsibility to do anything about it. It was as if these deans felt that their job was to hire as many of the best professors as possible and then turn them loose to "do their thing." A few even cited academic freedom as a reason for not intervening to improve quality—a view we categorically rejected in our reports to senior university leaders and the public. By this time, I shouldn't have to point out that school deans must play a key role in reengineering and that negative attitudes will jeopardize the success of any reengineering program.

# Chapter 4

# The Cost of Teaching

Costs loom large in today's discussions of higher education. They are a major part of the reengineering story. The innovations discussed in chapter 3 addressed teaching effectiveness but not cost or margin. This chapter looks at teaching activities from the standpoint of cost and, importantly, cost containment. It develops the principles needed to quantify and cost out the activities associated with teaching—and the revenues and margins associated with particular courses and programs. Focusing on activities as well as cost allows us to mitigate the tendency, justly feared by many faculty, to sacrifice quality in the interest of saving money.

The following narrative, motivated by a real situation, illustrates what can happen when costs are driven downward without careful consideration of quality.[1]

> The English department at a New England university had, over most of a decade, lost a third of its regular faculty lines to budget cuts despite enrollment increases. It responded by boosting teaching loads and class size, cutting some required seminars from the curriculum and staffing more than half its sections with low-cost adjuncts hired on the casual payroll. Fewer papers were assigned (this was an English department!), and most examinations were shifted from essays to multiple choice or short-answer questions that could be graded more easily. Scholarship came essentially to a halt, and some of the best professors decamped for other institutions. Like other departments facing similar problems, this one had lobbied the central administration to save its faculty lines but had not been successful—so each year, the remaining faculty mem-

bers simply hunkered down and made do with what they had been allocated.

Administrators benchmarked departmental productivity against student credit hours per faculty FTE (SCH/FFTE) using data published by the University of Delaware.[2] Not surprisingly, the English department looked good on this measure. Some concern was expressed about equity—whether "faculty were working too hard"—but the data didn't alert the dean or provost that there might be a quality-of-education issue. The problem, of course, was that true performance (the amount of *learning* per dollar expended) plummeted even as SCH/FFTE showed handsome improvements.

While the department's ability to assess learning outcomes was still at an early stage, the chair felt the changes in departmental activity suggested strongly that the necessary conditions for teaching effectiveness were not being met. It seemed obvious that the budget-driven work-arounds were eroding teaching and learning quality, yet the department had been unable to convince anyone that more resources were needed despite the university's financial problems.

Such scenarios are repeated again and again in today's traditional colleges and universities. The problem occurs at every level, not just in departments. Deans and provosts worry about quality but often lack convincing evidence that more resources are needed. They are right to wonder about whether existing resources are being used effectively, but there comes a point where it's obvious that overly stringent budgets preclude effective learning no matter how good the teaching may be.

What's necessary is to marshal the data universities do have in order to provide early warning that budget cuts may be undermining quality. I will describe a model for accomplishing this objective. Because the model is based on detailed analyses of teaching activities, it can be used for benchmarking and cost containment as well as for productivity improvement. It also can be used for planning and resource allocation at the departmental and higher university levels. Using the model for these manifestly academic purposes will go a long way toward reversing the dissociation of teaching effectiveness from cost that was discussed in chapter 2.

## Alternative Approaches

The well-known mantra "if you can't measure something you can't improve it" definitely applies to teaching cost. But how should these costs be measured? There are many ways to look at teaching cost. It's important that decision-makers in universities know which ones will help them make good decisions and which are likely to be misleading. This section describes five different approaches to cost measurement and comes down firmly in favor of the last one, activity-based costing (ABC), for most planning and management purposes.

### Single-Factor Productivity Ratios

Single-factor productivity ratios such as student credit hours per full-time faculty FTE (SCH/FFTE) often are used to measure a department's teaching productivity. "Single factor" means that a single output (SCH) appears in the numerator and a single input (FFTE) appears in the denominator of the fraction. Such measures reflect the fact that productivity should be defined in terms of physical quantities: for example, as in output per man-hour.[3]

The English department narrative showed how a single-factor productivity ratio can produce misleading results when used without reference to other information. Figure 4.1 illustrates the problem. The department's SCH/FFTE ratio was above its benchmark, but did this indicate high productivity, as the university seemed to think? Or did it reflect low-quality, weak research and unsustainable workload as argued by the department chair? The fact is, there's no way to tell without a detailed investigation at ground level—which in this case turned out to show quality degradation.

The second problem with single-factor ratios is measurement of a single input and output. In fact, there are many inputs and many outputs, and while simplifications are acceptable in some circumstances, one should be careful about what's being lost. Teaching inputs involve adjunct faculty, support staff, materials and supplies, and plant and equipment as well as regular faculty. While the regular faculty input may have been dominant in the past, this is becoming less and less true. In addition to adjunct usage, modern teaching increasingly involves

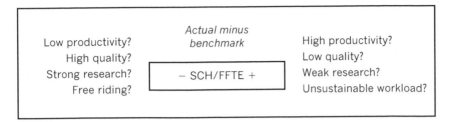

**Figure 4.1.** Ambiguity in the interpretation of a single-factor productivity ratio

technology—with its attendant requirements for support staff, equipment, and so forth. Using SCH/FFTE in situations where professors have substituted information technology for faculty face-to-face teaching will produce grossly misleading results. The fact that many departments produce both teaching and research further complicates the use of single-factor productivity ratios. Research-intensive departments may be expected to have lower SCH/FFTE ratios than teaching-intensive departments, other things being equal.

Some circumstances favor the use of single-factor productivity ratios: for example, when broad comparisons are called for and it's not practical to look at fine structure. The results can help a dean or provost to focus investigative resources or an oversight body to ask provocative questions. (The Delaware ratios are very useful for such purposes.) However, strong health warnings should be provided whenever using single-factor ratios. Statistics that deviate from the norms should be examined using disaggregate data to determine what's really happening. In other words, using single-factor ratios for benchmarking and accountability should be considered as the first step of any analysis, not the only one. A similar caveat applies to the two ratios that are discussed next.

### Cost-per-Unit Ratios

Ratios like cost per student credit hour (cost/SCH) go some way toward solving the single-factor problem. They take account of all the inputs, each weighted by its unit cost. (Economists have shown that, under most circumstances, unit cost is the best weighting that can be used.) Unfortunately, however, cost-per-unit ratios also suffer from the problem of ambiguity (shown in figure 4.1). One can't know, for example, whether a reduction in cost/SCH implies a gain in productivity or an erosion of education quality and research.

Cost ratios suffer from two other difficulties that make them less desirable than productivity ratios for many purposes. The first arises because inputs of lesser quality generally come at a lower price: for example, teachers on the casual payroll usually cost less per contact hour then do regular faculty. Substitution of lower-cost for higher-cost inputs will reduce output quality in this case. Members of the National Research Council (NRC) Panel on the Measurement of Productivity in Higher Education were very concerned lest the use of cost ratios trigger a "race to the bottom," where universities compete on finding the cheapest teaching resources.[4] Most of us felt this to be a clear and present danger in today's traditional higher education.

A second problem concerns variation of input prices over time and across geographic areas. Universities in high-wage areas can be expected to cost more, other things being equal, than those in low-wage areas. It would be a mistake to tag the former as being less productive than the latter, yet this is what happens when cost ratios are applied without regard to price differentials. The same is true when prices change over time. Secular trends in the relative costs of people and information technology will produce a distorted view of productivity change when cost ratios are the only measure. I'm not saying that cost-per-unit ratios never should be used—only that they should be used with due regard to their limitations.

### Multifactor Productivity Ratios

The aforementioned NRC panel proposed a teaching productivity measure that surmounts many—but definitely not all—of the problems described previously.[5] Its multifactor productivity index handles multiple inputs and outputs, and uses information about prices in what most economists believe to be the best possible way. (It does not solve the quality problem, however.) The Lumina Foundation, a panel sponsor, has demonstrated that the index can be approximated from IPEDS data in a meaningful way and is developing a web-based demonstration tool for use by states and the federal government.

The panel emphasized that "productivity" is defined as the ratio of physical outputs to physical inputs, *where both have been adjusted for quality changes.* ("Cheapening" the product does not represent productivity improvement.) But, as noted in chapter 2, the panel was unable to recommend a method for making quality adjustments. Having evaluated the options, it found no alternative to proposing a ratio of unadjusted output changes to unadjusted input changes.[6] The need to add higher education to the nation's portfolio of productivity measures trumped concerns about its possible misuse within the sector. However, the index should not be allowed to stand by itself: the panel recommended strongly that "[e]ffective and transparent quality assurance systems should be maintained to ensure that output quality does not trigger a race for the bottom."[7] It went on to suggest that peer-review processes such as the ones in Tennessee and Hong Kong (described in chapter 3) be used to ensure that teaching and learning remain robust.

The NRC panel concluded that enrollment alone is an inadequate measure of educational output because it does not recognize the importance of degree completion. (Where applicable, attainment of certificates or other completion milestones can be included along with degrees.) The panel's proposed measure is:

*adjusted credit hours = credit hours + (sheepskin effect × completions).*

The "sheepskin effect" represents the additional value that credit hours have when they are accumulated and organized into a completed degree. Based on studies of the effect of earned credits and degrees on salaries, we concluded that, for undergraduate degrees, a value equal to a year's worth of credits provides a reasonable approximation.

The index uses three input variables: the quantity of labor, the amount of nonlabor expenditure, and the rental value of capital utilized in the educational production process. Each input is described by (i) physical quantities or surrogates for quantity and (ii) expenditures. The physical quantity of labor is represented by FTEs, and deflated dollars are used as surrogates for nonlabor expenditures and capital. These three quantity figures are aggregated using undeflated dollar expenditures as weights: a method that, though perhaps counterintuitive, has been proven as optimally fit for purpose. Importantly, the index tracks the rates of change of the input and output variables rather than the variables themselves—which alleviates the problem described earlier as encouraging a race to the bottom. It does not mitigate the quality problem, however.

Further description of the NRC index is beyond the scope of this book. Interested readers should consult the panel's report or two journal articles by its authors that discuss the method in nontechnical terms.[8] For present purposes, it's enough to say that, while the NRC's aggregate productivity index should prove useful for state oversight bodies and university systems as well as for federal statistical agencies, the requirements for productivity evaluation within universities require one to get closer to the action—to examine the activities that actually produce teaching and learning.

### Top-Down Cost Allocation

Getting closer to the action requires drilling down to lower levels of aggregation than those typically used in the productivity and cost ratios (e.g., to the level of individual courses), yet such information is not tracked in university accounting systems. For example, when NACUBO's Scott Pattison asked university officials how much it cost them per capita to educate an undergraduate versus a graduate student, they couldn't answer the question.[9] When such data are available, they usually come from top-down cost allocation. This method pushes costing downward, but, like the three measures considered earlier, it sheds little light on what's really happening in the department and no light at all on educational quality.

Figure 4.2 shows how top-down allocation to the course level works for a department in a university devoted mainly to teaching.[10] (Costing in research universities will be discussed in chapter 5.) The box at the top of the diagram, the "cost pool" for instruction, is the most detailed breakdown available in the university's accounting system. What's desired is to allocate the cost pool among the department's various courses. We might wish that the general ledger tracked cost on a course-by-course basis, but this isn't likely to be practical anytime soon. Hence one must identify an "allocation driver," such as student credit hours (SCH), shown by the leftward arrow, that *is* available for individual courses and is believed to correlate reasonably well with cost.

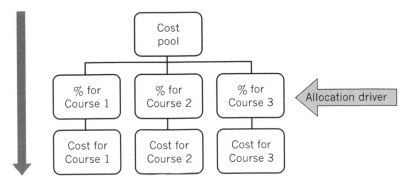

**Figure 4.2.** Top-down cost allocations to courses

The calculations themselves are straightforward: divide each course's SCH by the department's total SCH and allocate overall instruction cost according to the resulting percentages. The downward arrow at the left of the figure emphasizes that the calculations move in a top-down direction. The search for drivers that are appropriate for particular circumstances lies at the core of the traditional cost accounting professional's expertise.

Top-down cost allocation is widely used in universities for purposes of pricing and in determining margins across schools and departments. For example, the allocation of overhead expenditures to grants and contracts is the starting point for government negotiations on the indirect cost rate. Similar calculations inform tuition setting, where administrators want to know whether the full costs of education are being recovered. Overhead allocations also help administrators understand which organizational units are contributing to the bottom line and which are losing money. It's worth noting that these overhead allocations may be based on more sophisticated drivers than student credit hours, as used in the example.

Unfortunately, top-down cost allocation is not very helpful for containing the cost of teaching. Dartmouth professor Jack K. Shank puts the proposition more colorfully when he says that, when applied to management problems such as this one, such methods are "at best useless and at worst dysfunctional and misleading."[11] This is because they don't consider the specific activities involved in teaching and learning. Per-course costs calculated according to figure 4.2 always come out being proportional to SCH, without regard to class size, instructor type, whether the class is a lecture or lab, or uses of information technology. Hence they cannot support productivity-related analytics.

My experience suggests that professors and others within schools and departments understand these shortfalls at an intuitive level—and that this is one reason for their lack of interest in the subject of cost accounting. They may understand its relevance for overhead calculations and for learning about the university's areas of financial strength and weakness, but, as these matters are, for the most part, out of their control, they are happy to leave cost accounting to the financial people. Unfortunately, however, this perpetuates the disassociation between effectiveness and cost discussed earlier.

### Activity-Based Costing (ABC)

The fifth and last approach to activity and cost modeling, what I call "course-based ABC," is the one that really works. This bottom-up analysis contains information about teaching activities that is of intrinsic interest to faculty members—data that do reflect what actually happens during the teaching process with enough detail to identify possible inefficiencies and opportunities for improvement. Top-down cost-allocation models don't provide the requisite information, but course-based ABC models do. Happily, such models are beginning to attract attention. The University of California's Maria Anguiano recently advocated the use of course-based ABC in a pathbreaking policy paper for the Bill and Melinda Gates Foundation.[12] This chapter describes course-based ABC as it is applied to individual classes, departments, degree programs, and the campus as a whole.

The need to understand costs at the activity level is by no means unique to universities: in fact, Texas Instruments developed a general ABC model in the late 1970s based on antecedents that can be traced back to accountants in England in the 1890s.[13] The resulting ABC model analyzes the process used to produce a product or service and estimates the cost of each process activity. Then, the activity-level costs are added up to provide an estimate of total process cost. This bottom-up methodology literally turns top-down allocation on its head. It starts with concepts and data that are grounded in reality as seen by people who do the work—in our case departmental faculty and staff—and then uses simple rules to bring these data together to produce the desired cost estimates.

Figure 4.3 summarizes the bottom-up methodology. The cost figures for individual courses are shown near the top of the diagram. The procedure for calculating these costs uses the four basic variables. Additional details on the variables and calculation engine for course-based ABC can be found in appendix B.

Variables for Course-Based ABC
- *Activities*: what's actually done to produce teaching and learning. For example, Activity 1 might refer to contact sessions, Activity 2 to out-of-class teacher involvement with students, and Activity 3 to special student projects. Figure 4.3 shows activities only for Course 2; the other courses also have their lists of activities (which may differ from those for Course 2).
- *Volume drivers*: the system's throughput: for example, the student credit hours for each course. Volume drivers are determined outside the ABC model as indicated by their darker shading.
- *Resources*: the resources used in performing the activities: it might be that Resource 1 is faculty time, Resource 2 is the time of laboratory assistants, Resource 3 is facilities usage, and so forth.
- *Unit costs*: the cost per hour or similar unit for a given resource: for example, Unit cost 1 is the cost of faculty time. The unit costs also are estimated outside the ABC model.

Appendix B describes how each activity's resource usage is determined by its volume driver: for example, how many units of each resource will be required to produce a given number of credit hours. These results are rolled up, as indicated by the arrow at the left of the figure, to get the cost of courses and, eventually, the department's overall instruction cost. The model covers two basic kinds of activities: (i) those that are directly proportional to enrollment (e.g., grading) and (ii) those that depend on intermediate variables such as class size and duration. For example, a class that meets three times a week for one hour requires three faculty contact hours and three facilities hours per section, with the number of sections being determined by the acceptable class

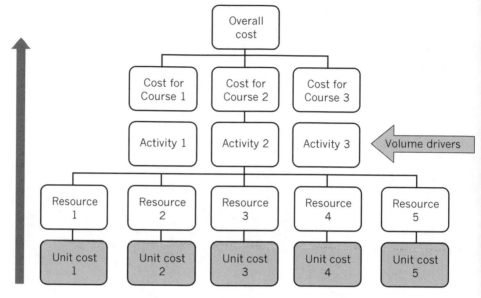

**Figure 4.3.** Bottom-up ("course-based") ABC

size. Bob Zemsky and I introduced such a model at an EDUCOM workshop some twenty years ago, and variations have been used many times by the National Center for Academic Transformation, among others.[14]

The variables will be familiar to department chairs and others responsible for setting teaching schedules and loads. Such people must balance class sizes with the number of sections offered, which, along with the number of available faculty, determines average teaching load. Extending the model to differentiate among different kinds of faculty adds another element of decision-making: namely, the number of sections taught by adjunct as opposed to regular faculty. Building the model around variables that are meaningful for decision-making goes a long way toward establishing its relevance. For example, it provides a quick way of calculating the consequences of different strategies for allocating a department's resources. Once the model is being used for these purposes, it's only a small step to bring cost measurement into the picture. Finally, it's worth noting that any single-factor productivity or cost ratio is easily calculated from the course-based ABC model.

Course-based ABC is very important for the reengineering of traditional universities. It satisfies the criteria for analyzing what economists call the "teaching production function" by getting to the heart of the relationship between resource utilization and output. While it's true that the quality of output is not measured, certain variables with plausible relationships to quality are measured: for example, as when too few small classes, overworking of faculty, and overuse of casual-payroll adjuncts degrade the quality of learning. No model can substitute for detailed knowledge of facts on the ground, but the course-based ABC model provides fine-structure insight about where to dig for facts as well as a basis for benchmarking and trend analysis. The "faculty-friendly activity and cost model" that lies at the core of this chapter builds on the course-based ABC model described in appendix B.

## Design of Teaching Systems

Course redesign (described in chapter 3) provided an original impetus for course-based ABC because the redesign process required that cost be considered side by side with quality. Redesign templates such as the one shown in appendix B focus on activity and cost analysis for single courses, where faculty are integrally familiar with what they and the students are expected to do. They break a course down into its most elemental components, the individual activities that generate student learning. Such breakdowns are feasible and desirable during course design or redesign because faculty must consider the fine structures of alternative teaching activities. It turns out, however, that courses represent only one level in a more complex design continuum.

Table 4.1 depicts the four levels that are important for the design of teaching systems. I've been focusing on the micro level, the design of individual courses and modules within courses. Chapter 3 was about the nano level, the design of individual learning activities and, where applicable, of software "learning objects." It described how new concepts and information about learning effectiveness can be used to transform our understanding of how nano objects should be designed and organized into modules and courses. The emphasis in chapter 3 was on learning quality, but cost issues were never far from the surface. A good cost-containment strategy will address the trade-offs between effectiveness and cost at both the nano- and micro-design levels.

| Table 4.1. Design levels for teaching activities | |
| --- | --- |
| Design level | Examples |
| Macro | All courses<br>Curricular "portfolio" design |
| Mezzanine | Groups of courses<br>Trends and benchmarks |
| Micro | Individual courses<br>Module and course design |
| Nano | Individual learning activities<br>Learning object design |

Course design involves creating interlocking combinations of teaching activities. The process has become familiar on many campuses, and it surely will become more important as the reengineering of teaching and learning gains momentum. It also will become more complicated as professors focus on modules, each of which may involve different cost-quality trade-offs, rather than whole courses considered as monoliths. How to envision and manage many such modules can be quite complex. This suggests the need for a computer-aided course design (CACD) tool to help visualize how the various activities might fit together and track resource usage and cost for the various alternatives. My design concept for such a tool is presented in appendix C. Today's software tools make it possible to create such a tool without much effort—perhaps even as a student project in computer science.

Moving now to the top of the figure, macro design involves assembling courses into curricula that meet the learning objectives of a major, general education, or other program. One such objective is for the curriculum to reflect what Robert Zemsky calls "structure and coherence," which, unfortunately, is too often honored in the breach.[15] Another is that the design should go beyond definitions of subject matter to include the profile of experiences to which students are exposed in the curriculum: what I have called "course attribute portfolios." To accomplish this, one needs the mezzanine level of design—so named because it lies midway between the micro and macro levels.

## Mezzanine-Level Design

Mezzanine-level design involves assembling courses into categories that reflect various teaching methods. A goal of the course category taxonomy should do three things:

1. summarize teaching activities in ways that are more interpretable than looking at the data for individual courses,
2. enable inferences about learning quality to the maximum extent possible given the underlying data, and
3. permit inferences about the learning environments experienced by students as they pursue their programs.

The following discussion assumes that data similar to those obtained from the aforementioned course-based design template are available for all courses. While this certainly is not practical using the labor-intensive design methods discussed so far, I soon demonstrate that extracting a core level of data from a university's central data systems is entirely feasible. The course category taxonomy organizes the data for all the courses in a department or major in a way that facilitates achievement of the three goals.

The taxonomy that's shown in figure 4.4 illustrates the approach I've found most useful. One can think of it as a tree structure with branches truncated in cases where no courses exist. The column showing branches for the primary section (indicated by the label at the bottom of the diagram) distinguishes among three common teaching approaches. Additional approaches involving, say, case discussions, flipped classrooms, problem-based learning, hybrid technology applications, and online delivery easily could be added. The next column refers to primary section size, which distinguishes among small, medium, large, and very large classes. The last two columns refer to types and sizes of secondary sections: the breakouts and labs often associated with large primary sections. Notice that "none" is included as an option for each type and that the size categories are different than those for the primary sections.

The tree can be further stratified by course level. My work generally used lower-division undergraduate, upper-division undergraduate, and

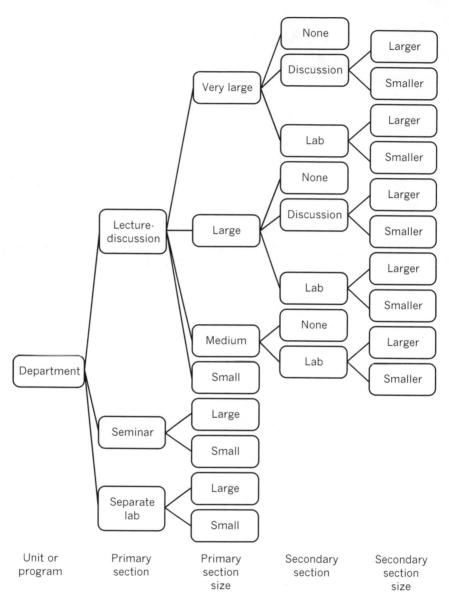

| Unit or program | Primary section | Primary section size | Secondary section | Secondary section size |
|---|---|---|---|---|

**Figure 4.4.** Illustrative teaching categories

graduate courses as identified by the first digit of the course number. One also can differentiate according to whether a course is required for one or more majors or as a prerequisite for other courses. The main limitations here are whether sample sizes at the end nodes of the tree are large enough to be meaningful and whether the resulting reports contain more categories than users can assimilate.

The taxonomy can be used to make inferences about learning quality. It's well known that large, lecture-discussion classes without breakouts are an ineffective way to deliver content that requires a high degree of interaction. (This was the problem cited in the English department narrative.) Indeed, some universities have instituted freshman seminar programs to ensure that all entering undergraduates get at least one intensive student-teacher exposure early in their college experience. The advent of online teaching makes the explicit consideration of such trade-offs even more important.

### Course Attribute Portfolios

The taxonomy enables a powerful method for looking at teaching and learning in universities: the course attribute portfolio. Most faculty are familiar with what might be called a course content portfolio—the requirements for a program or degree. The course attribute portfolio idea carries this a step further to include the array of course attributes to which the student is exposed. As mentioned, *how* learning is presented can make a big difference; hence it's sensible to consider the incidence of alternative methods when designing and evaluating curricula. The course attribute portfolio furthers the departmental teaching portfolio idea discussed in chapter 3, albeit at a more aggregate level and with a cruder set of attributes than envisioned there.

The concept is analogous to the one used in modern endowment investing, which is depicted in table 4.2 and elaborated in the sidebar (see p. 128).[16] Once again, the mezzanine concept, here represented by a taxonomy of asset classes rather than courses, represented the critical breakthrough. Asset classes are characterized by attributes such as expected returns, risk profiles, and correlations (i.e., the degree to which the asset classes move together or separately). Invention of the mezzanine concept in the 1970s enabled a division of labor between an investor's strategy development, now formulated in terms of asset classes,

| Table 4.2. Design levels for endowment investment | |
|---|---|
| Design level | Examples |
| Macro | Investment portfolio (e.g., for an endowment fund) |
| Mezzanine | Asset classes (e.g., stocks versus bonds; see sidebar) |
| Micro | Investment vehicles (e.g., a mutual fund or asset manager) |
| Nano | Individual securities (e.g., General Electric stock, T-bill) |

### Asset Classes for Investment Management

"Asset classes" represent groupings of vehicles that have fairly similar risk and return characteristics. Typical asset classes are defined in terms of: (i) domestic, international, and emerging markets; (ii) large capitalization, small capitalization, venture capital, and "private" equities; (iii) long- and short-term fixed income; and, for composite vehicles such as mutual funds, (iv) whether the investment style is active or passive, judgmental or formula based, etc.

A thriving industry of consultants now exists for determining class characteristics and assigning stocks, bonds, and other vehicles to the classes. Selecting the vehicles to represent each class comes later, and, in most cases, this choice is regarded as being less important than the asset-class allocations themselves.

and the detailed technical decisions about individual stocks and bonds made by hands-on investment managers.

Without the mezzanine layer, traditional investors had to make decisions about individual securities. They had to choose from thousands of options, many with inconsistent or incomplete data. They used simplistic rules of thumb that considered relatively few alternatives. Most neither knew about nor felt any urgency about getting better data and analysis tools. Like most faculty in today's traditional universities, they believed that they could make good decisions based on gut feel, past practice, and the occasional insight or tip. However, studies showed that this incurred huge opportunity losses.

The asset class construct opened the way for better understanding of investment options, trade-offs between risk and return, and portfolio strategy. Eventually, this yielded comprehensive datasets and powerful analytical tools for decision-making and performance monitoring. It's often said that only three things are important in the construction of modern investment portfolios: asset-class mix, asset-class mix, and asset-class mix. The selection of managers and individual securities does matter, of course, but shifts in asset-class mix affect results to a degree that swamps the other factors. Now, some thirty years on, fiduciary investors are expected to use these data and tools. To ignore asset-class mix is regarded as imprudent, if not potentially illegal.

The portfolio idea certainly applies to the design of teaching programs. Consider the so-called "barbell strategy" for class sizes that was developed some twenty years ago by Richard Light at the Harvard Graduate School of Education.[17] For many subject areas, once class size reaches a threshold that makes interaction difficult, additional increments don't greatly degrade learning quality. This means that additional small seminars, which maximize interaction, can be "paid for" by increasing the size of lecture courses, without serious quality degradation. The trick is to ensure that all students get a balanced exposure to the range of teaching methods—that some don't get a lean diet of lectures while others get a rich menu of seminars. This requires looking at teaching methods as well as content in portfolio terms.

The use of capstone seminars by many departments provides another example. Seminars are not only small, but when taught most effectively they differ qualitatively from conventional classes because students are encouraged to carry the main load. The case method and problem-based learning (PBL) instructional styles also differ qualitatively from conventional classes and thus merit explicit consideration in the portfolio. The advent of new technology opens a plethora of additional new

styles. As mentioned, my prototype "teaching method taxonomy" (presented in figure 4.4) will need to be expanded as these and similar approaches become available.

The distribution of courses among taxonomic categories should be
considered explicitly in curricular design, right along with subject matter content. This wasn't so important when the available approaches to
teaching were limited, but those days are past. The need will become
even greater when, as recently proposed by MIT, curricular design is
addressed in terms of "modules" rather than whole courses.[18] This will
vastly increase the number of ways teaching method options can be
combined. And just as in the investment field, this will make mezzanine-
level portfolio analysis a necessary condition for good decision-making.
The time may come when failure to consider course attribute portfolios
will be viewed as imprudent, or at least competitively disadvantageous.

### An Example of Portfolio Usage

The following "thought experiment" illustrates how an academic
department can use the course attribute portfolio. (This is just one example of the many possible applications: I provide a more detailed treatment shortly.) The experiment is a counterfactual projection of how the
English department narrative presented earlier might have come out
differently if course attribute data had been available. Table 4.3 shows
one of the many reports that could come from such an analysis. The
italic and boldface figures indicate exceptions: in other words, that the

**Table 4.3. Section counts in English classes**

|  | 2007 | 2008 | 2009 | 2010 | 2011 | 2012 |
|---|---|---|---|---|---|---|
| Activities (sections per year) | | | | | | |
| Lecture-discussion classes | | | | | | |
| Large | 31 | 32 | 35 | *38* | **42** | **45** |
| Medium | 55 | 54 | 57 | 56 | 53 | 50 |
| Small | 45 | 45 | 44 | 43 | 44 | 43 |
| In-major seminars (all) | 16 | 14 | *12* | **9** | 7 | **6** |
| Resources | | | | | | |
| Percent adjunct | 25% | 27% | 30% | 35% | *41%* | **53%** |
| Faculty teaching load | 5.1 | 5.2 | 5.3 | 5.4 | *5.6* | **5.8** |

*Note*: Boldface text indicates that data in the cell are in the "unacceptable region," and
italic text indicates that data in the cell are in the "warning region."

department's statistics were outside the range that would be expected based on normal variation (exact definitions are provided later).

The malaise faced by the English department had become apparent by the end of 2012. The reduced number of in-major seminars and medium-sized lecture-discussion courses coupled with a proliferation of large classes suggested reductions in active learning and, therefore, education quality. Interestingly, the number of specialty seminars remained constant as faculty fought to retain these easy teaching assignments in the face of heavier overall workloads. (There was nothing wrong with the seminars per se, but the dean didn't think they represented the highest and best use of faculty time from the school's point of view.) Other concerns were the upward trends in faculty teaching load and adjunct percentages.

Comparing the departmental data trends with experience across the university convinced the provost that the chair's concerns had some validity. He asked the dean to look into the matter further. It did not take long to confirm the concerns set forth in the original narrative and to find that English was indeed in a downward quality spiral.

The data triggered a new budget conversation. This wasn't an easy conversation, to be sure, because the university still faced the financial difficulties that had forced it to cut budgets in the first place. In the end, though, the provost authorized some additional faculty lines on an emergency basis. He also made clear that this was a stopgap solution to give the department space to make needed changes and that the extra lines might well have to be withdrawn when some anticipated faculty retirements came to fruition.

The benefits that would accrue from changing the budget conversation speak for themselves. Universities must "do what they have to do" to live within their means, but it's better for everyone if the decisions are based on meaningful evidence. Aggregate ratios of the kind discussed early in this chapter are ambiguous to the point of failing the "meaningful evidence" test described in chapter 3. However, disaggregating to the activity level can, if done carefully, allow at least some of the needed inferences to be made. Putting the resulting body of evidence in the hands of departments, deans, and provosts can at least partially substitute rationality for guesswork and political jockeying.

Departments also must "do what they have to do" to cope with financial limits. Analysis of the fine structure of teaching activities can help here, too, as indicated in this extension of the English department thought experiment.

> The temporary nature of the provost's allocation meant that the department must learn "do more with less"—that is, to maintain or even improve its education quality with a smaller long-term budget commitment. With help from the institutional research office, faculty in the department began exploring their options in light of data from a predictive version of the course-based ABC model.
>
> The first step was to redesign freshman English along the lines made familiar by NCAT (discussed in chapter 3). But while the improvements were significant, it was clear that they couldn't solve the quality and cost problem by themselves. After some deliberation and use of the model to test alternatives, the department decided on a mixed strategy that included restoration of required capstone seminars for majors while limiting specialty seminars, modest decreases in adjunct usage and increases in average teaching load, and use of a "barbell" strategy (discussed earlier) to ensure that nonmajors as well as majors got a course attribute portfolio that included small as well as large classes.
>
> No one thought that the solution was ideal, but it was the best they could do given the resource constraints—and certainly far better than anything they had been able to imagine previously. All agreed that using the model both drove home the necessity for action and enabled them to come up with an acceptable compromise solution.

## Modeling from University Transactional Data

Cost-containment above the level of course-by-course redesign would benefit greatly from the availability of ABC data for all the courses that are required for a degree program. Yet the template given in appendix B relies on data provided by faculty who are intimately familiar with the course in question. This approach cannot be scaled to the mezzanine- and macro-levels of teaching activity design. This problem motivated me to embark on a research project to see how much of the needed data can be extracted from a university's whole suite of transactional data systems (not just the accounting system)—the project I report on in this section.

It proved possible to combine readily available transactional data with reasonable business rules to produce a model that can achieve the goals described earlier. This depends upon what might be called "big data": that is, information from multiple and complex sources that must be brought together for purposes of costing. That's not quite the definition of "big data" as used in other contexts, but it does convey the idea that things can be done now that were difficult or impossible with the IT applications of just a few years ago. Perhaps a better term would be "big enough data" to run the models. Universities have just seen the tip of the iceberg for big-data applications. Once learning software objects of the kind discussed in chapter 3 become widely used, campuses will be awash in data—which is bound to revolutionize our understanding of student learning and how to analyze it.

Provision of a campus-wide model based on transactions data offers several major advantages. First, the analysis can be initiated by the central administration and then provided to schools and departments as a planning and budgeting aid. In contrast, the protocols of appendix B must be initiated and carried forward almost entirely by faculty. Second, my experience using the model indicates that department and program chairs will find the information useful—which is a prerequisite for adoption. (I present the evidence for this assertion shortly.) Third, the model provides information that is directly applicable, and extremely valuable, for the financial planning and budgeting models to be discussed in the next chapter. There is no other way to obtain this kind of information.

The following quotation from Maria Anguiano's Gates Foundation paper describes why course-based activity analysis is an essential element of resource allocation:

> While cost-per-course information is a starting point, it is not enough. In order to improve performance, institutions must also capture information on the educational activities performed within each course. Only with costs bucketed into meaningful course [activity categories] do institutions have the knowledge necessary to

improve academic productivity. With costs calculated by relevant activity, course delivery transforms from being a black box fixed total dollar amount, to being broken up into its component parts and therefore something that can be redesigned and improved. With this information, all departments, deans, and faculty are given the tools they need to calculate the cost effect of any changes and innovations in their course delivery, something that has only been accomplished as one-off exercises at institutions in the past.[19]

Maria was referring to the teaching activity and costing models being discussed here. Her views reflect Bill Gates's well-publicized observation at the 2014 NACUBO Annual Meeting: "Technology is taking things that used to be separate and bringing them together."[20]

### The Prototype Model

My work on a prototype model began a decade or so ago as I was experimenting with a new software package, Quantrix Modeler,[21] which offers considerable promise for the development of small planning and budgeting models. Thinking about the relation of such models to course-based ABC led to a discussion paper on the subject and then a proposal to the Lumina Foundation for a pilot test.[22] The proposal was accepted, and the test was performed in 2012 and 2013 at a large public research university's flagship campus with help from the National Center for Higher Education Management Systems (NCHEMS). We implemented the model in three departments that had volunteered to participate: chemistry, mathematics, and psychology. The central administration (which had volunteered the campus's participation) provided enthusiastic support and access to data. Implementation required simplification of the appendix B model and development of prototype procedures for data extraction. While my prototype is no longer in the main line of model development, the lessons learned advanced the state of the art. Representatives from the nonprofit Public Agenda organization participated in our meetings in order to provide Lumina with an independent review of faculty reactions.

The strategy behind the campus-wide, course-based ABC model is simple: (i) describe the demand for teaching as a function of course enrollments; (ii) describe the supply of teaching as a function of faculty

---

### The Fundamental Equations

Demand for Teaching

$$nS = ENR / ACS$$

Supply of Teaching

$$nS = FAC_{FTE} \cdot ATL + OT_S$$

Demand Equals Supply

$$\rightarrow EFR = ACS / ATL(1 - frOT)$$

Cost of Teaching

$$Cost = C_{FAC,T} FAC_{FTE} / ATL + C_{OT,S} OT_S$$

Definitions

$nS$ = number of class sections
$ENR$ = enrollment
$FAC_{FTE}$ = regular faculty FTE
$OT_S$ = sections by "other teachers"
$ACS$ = average class size
$ATL$ = average teaching load
$frOT$ = OT sections/all sections
$EFR$ = enrollment/faculty FTE
$C_{FAC,T}$ = unit cost for faculty
$C_{OT,S}$ = unit cost for other teaching

---

FTE's, teaching loads, and the number of sections taught by adjuncts; and (iii) set supply equal to demand. To model the direct cost of teacher time, just multiply faculty FTEs and adjunct usage by their respective compensation rates. The equations for doing this are shown in the sidebar (above).[23] They apply separately to the course's collection of primary sections and also to collections of secondary sections such as breakouts and labs. The actual model (illustrated in the sidebar) also takes account of course type, course level, and faculty rank, but the basic ideas are the same.

The equations are "structural" in the sense of representing behavior in terms of causal relations among operationally meaningful policy variables: in our case, ACS, ATL, and fOT. This contrasts with the single-factor models discussed earlier: ratios such as student credit hours per faculty FTE (SCH/FFTE).[24] (My structural model uses the policy variables to calculate an overall EFR, which is a close cousin of SCH/FFTE.) As mentioned previously, nonstructural models do not pretend to capture the causal relations between policy variables and outcomes.[25]

Another well-known advantage of structural models is their ability to incorporate "latent variables"—variables that are not measured directly but which can be inferred from the ones that are measured. "Educational quality" is the key latent variable in our case. Quality can't be measured directly, but it can, to some extent, be inferred from the three policy variables. The English department narrative illustrated this kind of inference. It also showed how the inability of single-factor productivity ratios to support inferences about quality makes uncritical usage of them a dangerous proposition. Results presented shortly provide more illustrations of how the prototype structural model supports quality-related inferences.

### Data Extraction

Most university timetabling, student registration, and HR systems now contain the data needed to populate the aforementioned model. Our pilot university was no exception. The data included class frequency, duration, section count, instruction mode, enrollment, and instructor name or job classification. (Individual salaries were not needed—only the job classification.) We modeled the fall, winter, and spring semesters for the 2007–2011 academic years, stratified according to course level: lower division, upper division, and graduate based on the first digit of the course number.

The timetabling database gave us meeting days, starting time, ending time, and room number for each primary and secondary section. These data represent the key breakthrough needed to extend course-based ABC from a few redesign instances to a campus-wide IT system, thus freeing universities from the much less powerful top-down allocation schemes described earlier in this chapter. The database also listed an instructor name for each primary section, which we used to determine job classification and thus average compensation (for the classification, not the individual). We ended up using "full professor," "associate professor," "assistant professor," and a catchall called "other teaching staff," which consisted mainly of paid adjuncts. It was not possible to associate names with secondary sections (e.g., labs and breakouts), so we arbitrarily assigned those to the "other staff" category—which in this case consisted mainly of teaching assistants. These data allowed us to match resources to unit costs and thus complete the ABC paradigm. These definitions served us well in the pilot, but many variations are possible.

The resulting data provided everything needed to calculate the ABC model for student contact activities and their costs. The system also contained data for calculating certain performance indicators. For example, we linked classroom room numbers to a room size file that, together with enrollment, yielded percent capacity utilization. The system logged enrollment on the twelfth day of the semester and just prior to the examination period. This enabled us to calculate attrition during the semester. Finally, at the request of a department chair, the model calculated the percentage of classes in each course category that started before 9 a.m. ("percent early"). Eventually, it may become possible to track data for the percentage of students who fail the course and the number who are denied entry. (The latter requires a registration system that tracks the number of enrollment requests that are denied because the course is full.) The Holy Grail of performance indicators is to include information on learning effectiveness, but this will have to wait until more courses use "before and after" methods to assess learning in their relevant knowledge domains. If and when this is accomplished, it will be easy to add the data to the course-based ABC model.

As mentioned, our pilot campus's data system included the assignment of teachers to primary class sections. These data were not always accurate: for example, when assignments were changed at the last minute or listed as "to be announced." However, they were sufficient for approximating the course-by-course distributions of teacher types as in the English department narrative. Such data allow the model to track the number of sections taught by each person in each course category—which in turn allows the linkage of faculty effort to section type, class size, enrollment, and the performance indicators. We did not originally display the workload detail because of fears that it might be unduly sensitive. However, one of the department chairs asked to see these results and found them very interesting.

*Dashboards and Exception Reporting*

Decision support models include dashboards and exception reporting. The prototype's dashboard included reports on each department's activity and performance indicators, arrayed by year, semester, course level, course category, and instructor type. The Quantrix software provides great flexibility in how the reports are organized, stratified, and so forth, and whether they are presented in terms of raw numbers or percentages, or in tabular or graphic form. This capability has proved invaluable for working with the inevitably complex data on teaching activity.

The model also featured a multilevel exception-reporting scheme. The scheme's parameters are defined in figure 4.5. They can be approximated by statistical analysis of the historical data and then refined judgmentally, if desired.[26]

- *Target*, what is judged to be the most appropriate value for the variable in question, based on experience, analysis, or benchmarking.
- *Normal Range*, "low normal" (LN) to "high normal" (HN), where everything is going well. It's desirable to show whether the variable is above or below its target, but using a range instead of a single value recognizes that the data are bound to shift by small amounts from year to year and that these small shifts aren't likely to be important.
- *Unacceptability Thresholds*, "low critical" (LC) and "high critical" (HC), which signal serious problems that need to be addressed lest quality or productivity fall below tolerable levels.

A variable is considered normal (e.g., colored green on the dashboard) if it is between LN and HN, in a warning region (yellow) if it is between LC and LN or HN and HC, and unacceptable (red) if it is below LC or above HC. The warning region is depicted by italics and the unacceptable region with boldface and italics in presentations without color.

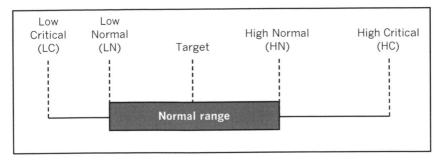

**Figure 4.5.** Normal range and acceptability thresholds

*Sample Results*

As mentioned previously, the model was prototyped in three depart-ments at a large public research university campus. The following sam-ple results for chemistry, taken from the materials used in our final presentation, illustrate the kinds of insights that can be obtained. (Readers who aren't interested in this level of detail can scan the mate-rial without loss of continuity.) While only a few interesting combina-tions of variables and stratifications are shown here, the model's inter-active interface could call up almost any combination.

ACTIVITY ANALYSIS

Table 4.4 presents an overview of the department's courses for 2011. On offer were 173 courses taught in 275 primary sections (this was a big department). The sections met for an average of four hours per week with an average class size of 80.5 students, which represented an aver-age 57.9 percent of room capacity.

Almost half the sections were taught by "other staff" (i.e., not by reg-ular faculty), which was considered large but not surprising given the department's tight budget. The average student attrition rate was just under 6 percent. No values for capacity utilization, other staff usage, or attrition were in the critical zone, though a number were in the warn-ing zone.

But while interesting, these totals obscure certain patterns that have implications for departmental planning and further model development. The number of class preparations per taught section (*teachers ÷ sections*) varies considerably by instruction mode and class size, for example.

## Table 4.4. Overview of course attributes

| Instruction mode | Class size | No. of courses | No. of teachers | No. of sections | Hours per week | Average class size | Average capacity utilization | "Other staff" sections | Average attrition |
|---|---|---|---|---|---|---|---|---|---|
| All modes and sizes | | 173 | NA | 275 | 4.0 | 80.5 | 57.9% | 49.8% | 5.8% |
| With breakout | Very large | 5 | 8 | 9 | 4.0 | 405.1 | 86.9% | 55.6% | 5.3% |
| | Large | 15 | 15 | 23 | 4.7 | 201.4 | 75.3% | 65.2% | 5.0% |
| | Medium | 12 | 9 | 14 | 2.4 | 86.1 | 60.6% | 71.4% | 6.6% |
| | Small | 27 | 30 | 33 | 3.0 | 22.4 | 38.0% | 36.4% | 4.9% |
| Lecture | Very large | 7 | 7 | 7 | 4.1 | 380.3 | 82.4% | 28.6% | 6.3% |
| | Large | 15 | 16 | 22 | 6.6 | 191.2 | 61.9% | 63.6% | 7.7% |
| | Medium | 24 | 25 | 25 | 6.5 | 87.2 | 51.9% | 48.0% | 7.2% |
| | Small | 47 | 81 | 89 | 4.8 | 21.1 | 25.4% | 43.8% | 4.3% |
| Lab | Medium | 6 | 4 | 36 | 4.0 | 15.8 | 91.6% | 63.9% | 1.8% |
| | Small | 3 | 3 | 4 | 4.0 | 7.5 | 56.6% | 100.0% | 3.3% |
| Seminar | Very large | 2 | 3 | 3 | 1.0 | 82.0 | 67.0% | 33.3% | 0.4% |
| | Large | 2 | 2 | 2 | 2.0 | 29.5 | 19.7% | 0.0% | 0.0% |
| | Medium | 3 | 3 | 3 | 2.0 | 14.3 | 11.7% | 0.0% | 0.0% |
| | Small | 5 | 5 | 5 | 2.8 | 9.2 | 7.4% | 0.0% | 0.0% |

*Note:* Italic text indicates the data in the cell are in the "warning region."

Table 4.5. Time trends for percentage of lecture courses

| Course level | Instruction mode | Class size | 2007 | 2008 | 2009 | 2010 | 2011 |
|---|---|---|---|---|---|---|---|
| UG lower division | Lecture | Very large | 0.7% | *2.9%* | *1.8%* | **5.0%** | **5.1%** |
| | | Large | 14.1% | **9.2%** | *10.3%* | 9.9% | *12.3%* |
| | | Medium | 10.7% | *8.6%* | *8.5%* | 8.5% | *10.1%* |
| | | Small | 8.7% | 30.5% | 32.1% | *34.0%* | *31.9%* |
| | | All sizes | 34.2% | 51.1% | 52.7% | *57.4%* | *59.4%* |
| UG upper division | Lecture | Very large | 1.5% | 1.5% | *0.0%* | *0.0%* | *0.0%* |
| | | Large | 4.5% | 4.5% | 6.3% | **7.5%** | 5.3% |
| | | Medium | 13.6% | 11.9% | *12.7%* | *11.3%* | **10.5%** |
| | | Small | 16.7% | 20.9% | 20.3% | 21.3% | 17.9% |
| | | All sizes | 36.4% | 38.8% | 39.2% | 40.0% | 33.7% |
| Graduate | Lecture | Medium | 0.0% | **0.0%** | **0.0%** | 1.9% | 2.4% |
| | | Small | 63.2% | *59.3%* | 69.2% | 69.2% | 66.7% |
| | | All sizes | 63.2% | *59.3%* | 69.2% | 71.2% | 69.0% |

*Note*: Boldface text indicates that data in the cell are in the "unacceptable region," and italic text indicates that data in the cell are in the "warning region."

The patterns hold up for the years prior to 2011 (not shown), which suggests that the department should take them seriously. The eighty-two-person average class size for two very large seminars may indicate a coding problem that the department might wish to correct to avoid misrepresenting its instructional style to prospective students. Moving on across the table, average capacity utilization is highest for the larger classes and surprisingly low for most seminars and other small classes. The percentage of sections taught by "other staff" seems surprisingly high, but, given that, the pattern is more or less what one would expect. Drilling down into the data does not disclose any additional patterns, but the university may wish to consider whether such low proportions of teaching by regular faculty are consistent with its educational promises to undergraduates. Finally, average attrition shows a pattern that I address shortly.

Table 4.5 presents time series for the percentage of lecture courses by course-level and class-size category. As might be expected, there are relatively more lectures in lower-division than in upper-division undergraduate courses. Perhaps more interesting is the trend toward large and very large lower-division classes, and indeed toward lower-division lectures generally. Most of the figures for 2010 and 2011 are in the

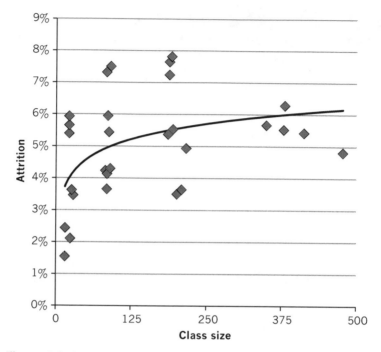

**Figure 4.6.** Class size versus attrition for undergraduate lecture courses

warning zone and a few are critical. (The three critical values for 2008 and 2009 are on the low side.) Moreover, the percentage of lower-division classes with breakout sections (not shown) dropped steadily from 48 percent in 2008 to 40 percent in 2011, whereas the one for upper-division courses remained steady. These results suggest the kind of problem described in the English department narrative, especially for lower-division undergraduates.

The scatter diagram in figure 4.6 hints at a relationship between class size and student attrition. The points display average attrition in the class-size categories for lower- and upper-division lecture courses in the four years covered by the dataset. (The three bounded categories show up as distinct columns of points, and the open-ended "very large" category produces the cluster at the right of the diagram.) The diagram suggests that average attrition may rise with class size at the lower end of the size range and then flatten out as classes get large enough to preclude frequent interaction with the professor. No such pattern emerges for graduate courses, seminars, or labs at any level—perhaps because the range of class sizes is so small. The results are noisy and certainly not definitive, but they illustrate what may be obtainable from the model as the number of data points increases.

## TEACHING LOADS

The model also can help department chairs understand the distribution of teaching loads. For example, the spark lines in figure 4.7 provide instant visualization of how loads vary across instructors. Each bar shows the number of sections taught by a given instructor during 2011. Two things pop out from the figure: (i) there is much variation in the amount of teaching done by faculty, and (ii) the vast majority of "other staff" teach only one or two sections during the year. Neither of these is necessarily problematic, but they may suggest needed actions or further analysis. Several follow-ups come to mind. One could determine whether loads of more than, say, five sections include summer teaching and whether any are due to assignment changes that weren't entered into the database. The smaller, regular faculty loads could be adjusted for sponsored research activity (whether subject to an academic-year buy-out or not). The department also might consider how the spreading of teaching responsibility across so many "other staff" members affects quality and quality assurance. Once again, "big data" makes many data points available over time and across course categories, which facilitates evidence-based decision-making.

## TOTAL, AVERAGE, AND INCREMENTAL COST

Last but not least comes the question of costs. These results are illustrated in table 4.6, for the teachers responsible for classroom contact. "Total cost" is simply the buildup, for both primary and secondary sections, of *resource utilization × unit cost* in the ABC model. "Cost per enrollment" and "cost per section" were calculated as *total cost ÷ (enrollment × sections)*. The results may seem low, but the prototype did not include materials and supplies, TAs not responsible for sections, graders and technicians, or facilities and equipment. (These can be allocated using standard cost-accounting methods, and they are included

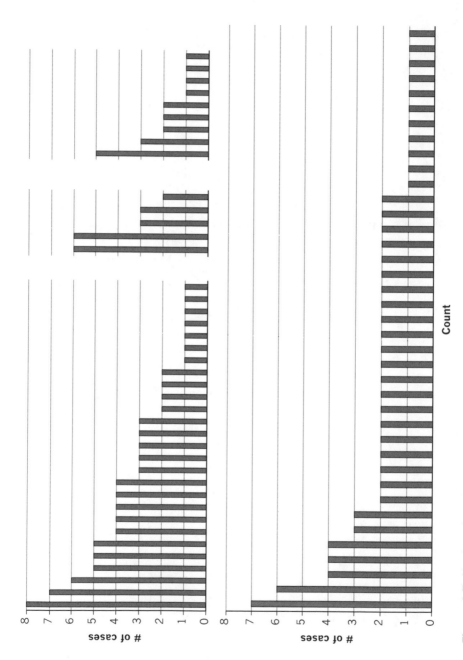

**Figure 4.7.** Number of sections taught for (clockwise from upper left): full professors, associate professors, assistant professors, and other teaching staff

## Table 4.6. Direct costs for classroom teachers

| Instruction mode | Class size | Total cost | Cost per section | Average cost per enrollment | Slack as % of enrollment | Incremental cost (10% change) |
|---|---|---|---|---|---|---|
| All modes and sizes | | $5,485,195 | $14,275 | $471 | | |
| With breakout | Very large | $95,803 | $10,645 | $26 | 3.7% | $24 |
| | Large | $244,829 | $10,645 | $53 | 3.3% | $25 |
| | Medium | $106,336 | $7,595 | $88 | 2.2% | $87 |
| | Small | $519,547 | $15,744 | $704 | 7.0% | $100 |
| | All sizes | $966,514 | $13,283 | $103 | | |
| Lecture | Very large | $172,633 | $24,662 | $65 | 2.8% | $93 |
| | Large | $752,019 | $34,183 | $179 | 1.2% | $187 |
| | Medium | $840,280 | $33,611 | $385 | 2.8% | $201 |
| | Small | $2,011,660 | $22,603 | $1,071 | 3.6% | $163 |
| | All sizes | $3,776,592 | $26,410 | $346 | | |
| Lab | Medium | $533,061 | $14,807 | $940 | 2.5% | $421 |
| | Small | $23,454 | $5,864 | $782 | 26.7% | $37 |
| | All sizes | $556,516 | $13,913 | $932 | | |
| Seminar | Very large | $18,708 | $6,236 | $76 | 3.7% | $189 |
| | Large | $34,483 | $17,242 | $584 | 1.7% | $3,233 |
| | Medium | $43,303 | $14,434 | $1,007 | 2.3% | $2,966 |
| | Small | $89,079 | $17,816 | $1,937 | 4.3% | $2,247 |
| | All sizes | $185,573 | $14,275 | $471 | | |

in the operational model described later.) It is, of course, possible to stratify by course level, drill down to section type, and display the time series for years and semesters.

The last two columns of the table present quantities that will help planners consider the effects of enrollment fluctuation. "Slack as percent of enrollment" represents unused capacity—the amount by which enrollment could increase without violating the department's quality standards as embodied in the exception reporting parameters. Defining the available slack is important because accommodating a few students in a section with excess capacity incurs per-student costs such as grading but no additional cost for classroom contact. The slack values shown in the table assume, for purposes of demonstration only, that enrollment is allowed to increase to 1.5 standard deviations above its current level. The standard deviation was calculated from the course category's historical data. This is equivalent to the midpoint of the warning range (see figure 4.5) used for exception reporting in earlier tables.[27]

The stair-steps of figure 4.8 show the extra sections that will be required for enrollment increases greater than the available slack. Each one of these incurs the cost per section shown in table 4.6. The resulting cost per incremental student can be quite large: for example, adding just one student to a small seminar that is filled to capacity incurs the category's full $17,816 per-section cost. (A department might relax its capacity constraint in this case, but the principle is clear.) Adding successive students generates smaller average per-student incremental costs until all sections, including the new one, have been filled. Therefore, the incremental cost per enrollment shown in the last column of table 4–6 is a blend of: (i) the costless students that fill in the available slack, and (ii) the sometimes-expensive students in any newly required sections.

Calculating the incremental cost requires an assumption about how many extra students are expected to enroll. There are many plausible assumptions, but the best one is to represent the extra students by a probability distribution. The "exponential distribution," shown by the declining curve superimposed on the stair-steps in figure 4.8, is a good candidate. My procedure, detailed in appendix D, calculates the weighted average of the steps (depicted by the large arrow in the figure) using the areas under the curve as weights. Dividing the result by the exponen-

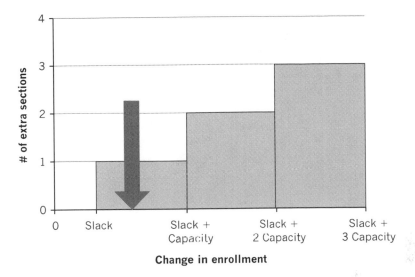

**Figure 4.8.** Calculation of expected incremental cost per enrollment

tial distribution's mean yields the expected incremental cost per enrollment. The incremental cost figures in the last column are based on an expected 10 percent change in student numbers.[28] The blending of high- and low-cost incremental students produces results that can be more or less than average cost, depending on the amount of slack in relation to average class size. Increasing expected enrollment causes incremental cost to move toward the lowest possible value for average cost—which will be less than the earlier value if there had originally been slack in the system.

### Departmental Reaction

The project began by holding initial meetings with the three volunteer departments, in which we explained what the model could do and the data that would be needed. In the words of the external reviewer, "They were less than fully successful" in that the "reception from the chairs was polite but not overwhelmingly enthusiastic." His later interviews elicited responses that ranged from "mild interest to active skepticism." Further, "two chairs thought they would learn nothing from the tool [i.e., the model] that they either didn't already know or could do anything about. One [of these] thought that he could use it to prove points to others. The third chair, in his first year, was more interested and thought he might even learn something for himself."[29]

We returned to campus some months later with the populated model and met with two of the three participating chairs. According to the reviewer:

> Our reception was very different from what we saw on our last visit. After our initial review of what the tool could do, they were extremely engaged and said they now saw how this could help them. Within a few minutes of demonstrating the prototype (which still had incomplete data), the chairs were asking questions and finding information that was surprisingly interesting to them. One chair was so tantalized by the tool that he returned for a second session, bringing with him two other department members who handle departmental scheduling.[30]

> The chair who returned for the follow-up session described how he had been skeptical about the model until a few days before the meeting, when he received a memo from an associate dean asking that he eliminate many if not most of his low-enrollment courses. The reason was a combination of budget stringency and concerns about course proliferation and declining class sizes. The juxtaposition of this letter and our reported results produced an epiphany: whatever the outcome of the discussions that would eventually ensue, they would be better if he came armed with detailed course-level data that were available to and understood by everyone concerned.

Our external reviewer went on to generalize these thoughts:

> What makes the tool so potentially valuable is that it rapidly provides answers to questions that are extremely important and yet are very difficult to answer in practical terms. As I can testify given my own experience as a recovering department chair, there is a serious hole in the existing portfolio of available metrics, as follows:
>
> • From a practical point of view, many of the most important decisions that impact productivity and the student experience are made at the department level, in assigning courses of different sizes with different types of instructors for different categories of students.

- Although all of the data necessary to analyze the impact of these decisions exist in various university systems, there is no easy way either for a department to access the information or for deans or other administrators to analyze and compare how departments are deploying their resources to meet the needs of students.

The tool, however, puts the ability to ask and answer these questions right at the fingertips of the people who are actually making or reviewing the decisions. The general idea is that it provides a way to look at [the information discussed earlier]. All of these factors can be analyzed against one another and over time with a few keystrokes. The tool also flags any values that are significantly different from their average over the years covered in the dataset.[31]

The experience on this campus supports my hypothesis that putting teaching activity data in the hands of faculty will be both worthwhile and well received—at least by some. And because much of the advantage arises from comparing results over time and across departments, it is desirable to model all the departments that comprise at least the undergraduate core of the university.

## Extending the Model across the Campus

With the prototype successfully completed and demonstrated, my next concerns were: (i) how to extend the model to cover the whole range of university activity, and (ii) how to scale the model from a few departments to the whole campus. The first uses methodology that is standard in university cost accounting, but I'll briefly describe it so as to present a complete picture. (Some readers may wish to skip this subsection.) Answering the second question led to some serendipitous developments that are discussed in the following section.

### University Cost Allocations

A university's cost model should cover all of the academic and non-academic operating units included in a campus's "education and general" sector. (Auxiliaries such as athletics, housing, and food services also need to be modeled but not necessarily as part of the main university.) Users of activity and cost data also are interested in revenues and margin, so the model should track these along with the other variables.

Because the teaching activity model is rooted at the micro level, it allows the calculation of revenue and margin for departments and even individual courses.

Figure 4.9 presents a high-level map of the university's data structure. (Specifics depend on the general ledger and perhaps other factors.) Part A, starting with the shaded box near the top of the figure, divides the campus into two broad sectors: direct academic operations and support services and administration. The direct category consists of two subsectors: departments (including separately organized teaching programs), which branch into teaching, research, and administration, and deans' offices and other school-level activities. Moving on, the support services and administration branch is subdivided into academic support and other support, and then by organizational unit. The unit structure generally follows the university's general ledger, although this is not entirely necessary.

Because the model is to be used for decision-making rather than historical accounting, each unit's line items of revenue and expense should be divided into fixed and variable components. Most revenue is variable (e.g., dependent on enrollments and tuition rates). The idea of fixed revenue, which consists of items that don't vary with activity in the short run, may not be as familiar, but the actual items are not mysterious. They include block-grant subsidies from government, investment returns, donations, depreciation, and debt service.[32]

Drivers for the cost-side variable items are the same as those used in top-down allocation (e.g., enrollment, staff FTEs, and facilities square footage). However, it has not been common to divide overhead cost into its fixed and variable components—which is important for internal decision-making but not for financial reporting. Making this distinction is not as hard as it might seem. As Stanford's CFO, for example, I approximated the split simply by classifying general ledger accounts: for example, the president's office and the HR unit that negotiated benefits contracts were designated as fixed-cost units and the HR section that counseled employees was classified as varying with staff FTEs. The scheme designated about two-thirds of the university's overall administrative and support services cost as variable, though the fraction was not uniform across operating units. Another approach, which is used by the Pilbara Group in its predictive model (to be discussed shortly), is

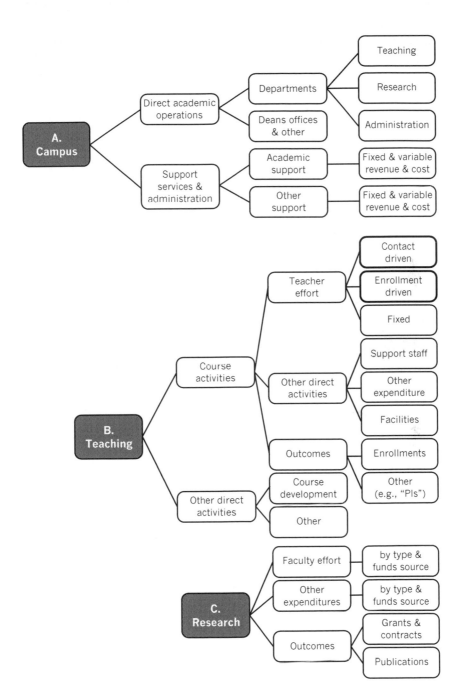

**Figure 4.9.** A university's data structure

to estimate the fixed and variable components through regression analysis.

Part B of the figure depicts the teaching component of departmental activity and part C depicts the research component. The branches for course activities were described in previous sections, and the contact-driven subbranches were detailed earlier in this section. (Both branching points are called out with heavy borders.) Data for direct in-class contact can be obtained from timetabling systems. Other data, including the enrollment-driven and fixed-effort components of faculty effort, can be approximated using rules of thumb, also known as "business rules," of the kind described in appendix B.

There are many ways to characterize research, but the one I've used most often simply tracks faculty effort and other expenditures by activity type and funds source, as well as available outcomes measures. Getting grants and contracts is very important for many schools, so it has been listed as an outcome, even though the money also is an input to the research process. Publications are not the only outcome of the research process, so other variables should be considered when available.

Getting "other expenditures" for research usually is straightforward because the accounting system codes most such expenditures as "organized research," but this is not true for faculty effort. Time charged to sponsored projects is readily discernable, but, as mentioned earlier, "departmental research" appears on the books as "instruction." One can get a brisk argument about whether this is appropriate from the standpoint of historical analysis, but including it in a predictive model would overstate the incremental costs of changing teaching activities and adding or deleting courses. While some might argue that departmental research always should be a fixed add-on to faculty cost per hour,[33] I prefer to model it in terms of teaching load—which is a policy variable in its own right that we shall see *is* included in the predictive model.

It might make sense to include departmental research along with course development in the "other direct activities" branch for teaching, but even this logic breaks down when faculty spend substantial unfunded time on sponsored projects that don't directly relate to most teaching.[34] Therefore, I believe the right approach is to split faculty effort into its instructional and research components, where the latter includes departmental research as approximated by a business rule, at the outset of the analysis.[35]

### The Pilbara Model

I mentioned earlier that development of my teaching activity and cost model beyond the prototype stage would require substantial commitments of time and capital. Approaching the end of my career, I was not in a position to take on this kind of project. At the same time, however, I very much wanted to see the concepts reduced to practice and to facilitate their adoption by traditional colleges and universities.

The breakthrough came as I was teaching in an Australian master's degree program at the University of Melbourne's L. H. Martin Institute. Professor Leo Goedegebuure, the Institute's director, sought my advice about whether an ABC model developed recently by the Pilbara Group might tie into the subject matter. I hadn't heard about the model, but, after study, my answer was emphatically "yes!" The model took an accountant's point of view, but its data structures were similar to mine, and, crucially, it used timetabling data to reach down to the course level. The model already was being applied at more than a dozen campuses in Australia, and the company had aspirations for extending this to American universities.

The Martin Institute decided to work with Pilbara personnel to use the model as a key exercise in its Leading Universities program for prospective vice chancellors, in which I was slated to give lectures on my research. This experience demonstrated that my concepts could be combined with Pilbara's ABC model to produce a comprehensive and powerful teaching activity and cost model that could be implemented on a "build once, use many times" basis for a campus with only a few months of effort.

This is not the place to describe the Pilbara Group's methods in any detail,[36] but a few comments about their key attributes will be helpful. The model implements course taxonomies—including the one illustrated in figure 4.4. It can track the allocation structure in figure 4.9 or indeed any structure supported by a campus's transaction systems. It can be used for both historical and predictive analysis, as will be discussed in the next section. Both versions separate prices and quantities and can track the fixed and variable components of revenue and cost, if desired. (Regression-based estimates of fixed and variable costs are included in the predictive model.) The model calculates these variables, plus margin, for every department and course or, for nonacademic operations, to the level of the lowest organizational subunit identified in the general ledger. It allocates overheads to direct cost objectives according to user-specified drivers. Where applicable, the calculations employ business rules that can be tailored to a campus's particular requirements. Finally, the model's user interface provides seamless roll-ups and drill-downs, and displays a wide variety of easily customizable tables and graphics.

Having gotten to know the Pilbara executives through the Martin Institute, the next question was whether they could and would generalize their model to include the factors identified in my research as being important for academics as well as financial people. They were quick to agree. In addition to my own representations, a talk at the July 2013 NACUBO meeting by the CFO at the University of Sydney (an Australian Pilbara Group campus) produced feedback that emphasized the importance of appealing to academics.[37] This underscored the fact that, to be accepted in the United States, the model had to bridge the gap between financial and academic officers.

The Pilbara model proved capable of handling all the variables needed to implement my research results. Its current version produces all the reports presented earlier in this chapter, right down to the level of primary and secondary sections by size category and course level, which are expressed in terms of appropriate business rules. It also includes the noncontact activity variables included in the course-based ABC model as described in appendix B. A number of Pilbara clients have customized its predictive model to provide seamless interconnection with their financial planning and budgeting systems. My efforts to work upward from micro-level course-based ABC models had intersected perfectly with their efforts to work downward, with the connecting point being the course timetabling system. It should also be noted that the information in this chapter is sufficient to allow a university to build its own teaching activity and cost model if desired.[38]

Only one data issue emerged as potentially problematic. As implemented at American universities, my research had relied on the availability of data linking instructor names, or at least job descriptions, to the teaching of individual sections within courses. I had found in Australia, however, that such data aren't commonly available—and thus was not surprised to learn that Pilbara Group's model obtains the needed linkages using business rules instead of direct observation. Their model can handle observed linkages if the data are available, but the default is to distribute pools of faculty expense to courses through top-down allocation. The top-down method might seem inconsistent with the basic tenets of course-based ABC, but the day is saved by using contact hours (obtained from the timetabling data) as the allocation driver. Indeed, this was one of the Pilbara model's original breakthroughs.

But while allocating resource pools based on contact hours works well for many purposes, I remain convinced that direct linkage of resources to activities is the method of choice. One cannot track adjunct faculty usage by course type without direct data linkages, for example, nor can one accurately compare teaching methods that differ markedly in, say, the seniority of staff required to teach a given number of contact hours. These issues will become more important with the advent of new teaching methods. Given the advantages of direct linkage, it would be a good thing for campuses to revise their data systems to provide the needed linkages if they do not already do so.

## Areas of Application

There are two reasons for caring about historical data from the teaching activity and cost model. The first is simply to report on the campus's current situation (e.g., to meet external accountability requirements). The second reason, and for purposes of this book the more important one, is to inform planning and budgeting decisions. The model's greatest usefulness will be as an aid for decision-makers at the departmental, decanal, and provostial levels—people on the firing line who are charged with containing cost with minimal adverse impact on quality. This offers a serendipitous benefit because the greatest impetus for improving and maintaining models and data comes from their usefulness to people at the local level—who must be relied upon to provide feedback and/or verify the data.

*Departmental Planning*

Departmental planning revolves around resource allocation. Chairs and program directors need to allocate the resources they have in ways that best balance the needs of students with those driven by other departmental objectives—research and scholarship, for example. Sometimes, they also must make the case for more faculty and other resources, as in the English department narrative. Viewing the department's historical data can help greatly in performing these tasks.

The ability to predict future trends can be even more helpful, particularly when the predictions depend on the department's own actions. One way to handle this is by doing "what-if analyses" on various choice options. The activity analysis and costing model is well suited to what-if analysis because it's based on structural variables that actually are used in departmental planning.

Suppose, for example, that a department wants to project the impact of expected enrollment increases on class sizes, teaching loads, and adjunct utilization. A properly configured course-based model makes this fairly easy: simply enter the enrollment projection and a few decision-making assumptions and observe the result. The question is "what decision-making assumptions?" Prediction in this situation requires one to assume values for two of the three policy variables in the sidebar (see p. 135): for example, with enrollment and faculty size given, teaching loads and the use of nonfaculty teachers determine section counts and thus class sizes. Additional assumptions about the distribution of sections among course categories and of effort across resource types (including adjuncts) also are needed to solve the full model. Decision-makers can explore a range of possible choices in order to determine the one that best meets their objectives.

This is a classic problem, and a variety of methods have been developed for dealing with it. The simplest (but least effective) method is simply to test alternative choices until one seems acceptable or there is no time to look further. This is called "satisficing" (a concept discussed in chapter 2) because it accepts a minimally acceptable solution rather than demanding a really good one.[39] It's what most people do most of the time. However, it leaves much to be desired in complex situations such as departmental resource planning, where the number of variables and the range of alternatives are both large.

A second approach is to develop policy-based "decision rules" (which go into the model as "business rules") for adjusting the variables in light of different circumstances. For example, one might accept increases in class size within the "normal range" for exception reporting (shown in figure 4.5), then increase adjunct use up to its policy maximum, and then increase teaching loads to handle any remaining problems. (This is more or less what departmental planners actually do in practice.) It's easy to build such rules into the model. The problem is that the rules can be complicated and time consuming to develop, and even then may not anticipate all contingencies. Errors or omissions in formulating the rules can produce anomalous results.

A third approach is to develop statistical decision rules based on what this or similar departments have done in the past. Analysts might estimate regression equations that relate average class size and resource usage to enrollment, for example, and then embed these as business rules in the model. This approach has much to recommend it, particularly in planning at the program, school, and campus levels. As mentioned, it has been implemented in the Pilbara Group's predictive model.

I have prototyped a fourth, even more powerful, approach that lies ready to be developed. It will allow planners to work with individual decision variables instead of statistical generalizations. There is a very powerful way of doing this. Its technical name is "optimization," but I prefer to call it "smart what-if" analysis. Doing smart what-ifs means having the computer search the space of possible choices to find *the* one that's demonstrably best in terms of prespecified policy criteria. The data needed to do this analysis are the same as for exception reporting (i.e., the policy targets and acceptability thresholds for each planning variable). Classroom capacity constraints can be added if desired. A brief description of my prototype is given in appendix F.

Smart what-if analysis represents the way of the future for many areas of decision-making. It may seem like a stretch for departments that have yet to fully embrace big data, but the capability of today's software makes it possible to embed optimization tools seamlessly in a predictive teaching activity and cost model. Anyone who uses such a model to do ordinary what-ifs should be able to "graduate" to a suitably embedded optimization model without much difficulty. I trust that the software needed to make this happen will be developed in the near future.

*Degree Program Analysis*

So far, I've been discussing teaching activity and costing models as applied to data organized by "supplier" departments, or the units that do the teaching. There is another way of looking at the data, however: through the eyes of students as they take courses to satisfy the requirements for degrees, majors, and subprograms such as general education. This can be accomplished by configuring the model to look at course profiles for programs instead of those offered by a given department.[40]

The reconfigured teaching activity and cost model can analyze differences in students' exposure to course categories, class sizes, and regular versus adjunct faculty as they pursue their academic awards. The "barbell strategy" for curricular design discussed earlier provides an example of how such results might be used. The model also can determine whether particular patterns of courses are associated with high attrition, failing grades, and other factors that increase time to degree and dropout rates. Such information will be interesting for curriculum designers and faculty members generally, as well as for academic administrators.

Perhaps more importantly, the model can estimate the costs, revenues, and margins for any program listed in the university's catalogue. By what factor do costs for students studying science exceed those for students pursuing business degrees, for example? What is tuition revenue net of financial aid for different programs? Which programs are making and losing money? These and similar questions now are looming large for the central administrations of traditional universities and for some deans and department chairs as well. I'm not suggesting that such financial questions should dominate university planning, but the data are absolutely essential for good decision-making. Chapter 5 discusses the integration of these results into financial planning and budgeting models, and how to balance data on program margins with mission-related considerations.

The so-called "elective" and "dropout" problems have greatly complicated institutional researchers' efforts to analyze the aforementioned issues. The teaching activity and cost model can handle electives by averaging data for courses actually taken by students in each degree program: for example, the low-cost courses taken by some students are averaged with high-cost ones taken by others to get results for the program as a whole. (Alternatively, the analysis could include only required courses as specified in the catalog.) Students who drop out of programs can be handled in a similar way: by including only the courses taken by completing students or by including the ones taken by all students, including dropouts.[41]

Performing these analyses for groups of students who have been identified by the admissions office as, say, "academically disadvantaged" will allow the analysis of course profiles (including numbers of courses taken), costs, revenues, and margins by student segment—a subject I'll explore more deeply in the next section. As in so many other data analysis situations, the ability to get information at a highly granular level (in our case, individual student registrations cross-referenced with course profiles) allows one to study important relationships on a regular basis.

### Student Segment Analysis

"Who gets to graduate?" is of increasing importance for colleges and universities. A recent *New York Times Magazine* article described it this way: "Here's a basic truth about American colleges: rich kids complete their degrees; poor and working-class kids usually don't."[42] The article goes on to describe a new experiment at the University of Texas that illustrates the kinds of things a campus can do to improve the situation. The teaching activity and cost model can help campuses implement Texas-style intervention on a routine basis.

The key lies in the model's ability to track groups of students through courses. The *NYT* article recounts how David Laude, a UT-Austin chemistry professor who later went into the administration to work on graduation rate issues, initiated the program. Laude

[c]ombed through the records of every student in his freshman chemistry class and identified about fifty who possessed two of the [previously defined] 'adversity indicators' common among students who failed the course in the past: low SATs, low family income, less-educated parents.

He invited them all to apply to a new program, which he would later give the august-sounding name 'Texas Interdisciplinary Plan,' or TIP. Students in TIP were placed in their own, smaller section of chemistry 301.

The TIP students got "identical material, identical lectures, identical tests" as compared to the standard five-hundred-student chemistry class, but there was a two-hundred-point difference in average SAT scores between the two sections. The lectures were supplemented by, for example, two hours each week of extra instruction, special advisors, and peer mentors—and repeated reinforcement that the TIP students "[w]eren't sub-par students who needed help; they were part of a community of high-achieving scholars." The results were very gratifying.

Even Laude was surprised by how effectively TIP worked. 'When I started giving them the tests, they got the same grades as the larger section,' he said. 'And when the course is over, this group of students who were two hundred points lower on the SAT had exactly the same grades as the students in the larger section.' The impact went beyond Chemistry 301. This cohort of students who, statistically, were on track to fail returned for their sophomore year at rates above average for the university as a whole, and three years later they had graduation rates that were also above the U.T. average.

The availability of a segmented campus-wide teaching activity model would greatly facilitate such initiatives. The model can track dropout and failure rates by course category (which includes class size as a criterion) for every student segment, major, and teaching department. Identifying outliers on these variables will flag the kinds of students Professor Laude had to obtain manually by "combing through the records."

Many universities already have mounted initiatives for identifying and helping academically disadvantaged students. For example, they may have created special sections for introductory courses—sections, as in the *Times* article, that have reduced class sizes and perhaps include special learning resources. My prototyping experience suggests that these special sections are identifiable in a university's timetabling system: for example, by special registration requirements. If so, the model's data extraction routines can be programmed to give them a special course designator (e.g., History 10s), to put them in separate course categories for purposes of activity and cost analysis. The predictive model might also simulate the creation of special sections, with supplementary resources, for identified at-risk segments and determine how much such initiatives would cost. While no single solution to the graduation rate problem should be viewed as a panacea, it's exciting to imagine the difference that the aforementioned approach would make if deployed on a large scale.

Use of the activity analysis and costing model for such purposes will be greatly facilitated if the system can easily look up the course category for each course in the curriculum (e.g., to determine that, say, History 10 falls into the "lower division large lecture" category). Good systems architecture will create the needed lookup table when courses are assigned to categories in the first place. Then, the analysis proceeds in three steps: (i) identify a group of students with the target segmentation criteria, (ii) list the courses taken by these students, and (iii) accumulate the desired data for these courses. Data might include the number of courses taken in each department and course category, the frequency distributions of class sizes and faculty types to which the student has been exposed, and the cost of the courses. How soon and how often students with particular race, ethnicity, and academic aptitude characteristics take particular patterns of courses provides just one example of the information obtainable from this kind of analysis.

In closing, let me note that the ability to use student segment data as described previously will stimulate efforts to develop more effective segmentation criteria. Today's criteria come largely from enrollment management people, who focus on getting students (including disadvantaged ones) into the university. The availability of rich databases on student performance after matriculation, coupled with the motivation to use such data to improve graduation rates for low-performing groups, will allow researchers to develop segmentation criteria that focus explicitly on graduation rates.

### School, Campus, and System Resource Allocation

The teaching activity and cost models will help people at the top levels of university administration determine budget allocations in times of plenty and places to cut in times of financial stringency. Financial models for assisting in these determinations have become commonplace, but the ability to get data about activities, revenues, costs, and margins at the department and program level has not. Chapter 5 describes the uses of these data in some detail, so I'll illustrate the possibilities with just two examples.

The first is to use the model for benchmarking—what many schools do now with single-factor productivity and cost ratios, only much better. Suppose a university system or consortium of campuses agreed on a common course type taxonomy and other key business rules. Comparability of course categories would make it possible to share a wide variety of data on teaching activities, and this plus a consistent treatment of research would allow effective sharing of teaching costs—thus producing the familiar benefits of benchmarking while mitigating some of its downsides.

I mentioned earlier that the University of Melbourne's Leading Universities program for prospective vice chancellors used the Pilbara model as a simulation exercise. The simulation was a key element of the third and final week of the program. Participants were divided into groups and given a case, "Australia University," then asked to prepare a strategic plan—including financial projections based on the model. This proved to be interesting enough, but the experience got richer when we threw two unexpected events into the exercise: a sharp drop in international student demand due to some widely publicized social problems in the local area and a decision by the Australian government to cut per-student funding for some subject areas.

The groups' first steps were to simulate the university's financial performance using the new enrollment and revenue estimates—a task made possible by the model's granularity to the level of faculty ("school" in U.S. parlance), department, and student type. The next step, given the shocks' serious impact on the bottom line, was to look for ways to economize. The groups experimented with what might be called the "usual suspects" of this chapter (e.g., mix of class types, class sizes, teaching loads, and teacher types), all of which were included in the model. In addition, because of the model's granularity and campus-wide scope, they could search for situations where essentially the same subject was taught in multiple departments. When cuts informed by these results proved insufficient, they turned to closing a program or even a whole campus ("Australia University" had a main campus and several smaller ones). These larger questions also could be explored by using the model—provided that assumptions were made about whether the "displaced" students could be retained and, if so, in what programs and what administrative and support service costs would be saved by closing a campus. Like all elements of the simulation, the benefit accrued not so much by finding specific numbers but in the sometimes-heated discussions about strategies, behavioral assumptions, and expected outcomes elicited by experience with a rich model.[43]

# Chapter 5

# Financial Planning and Budgeting

Financial planning and budgeting (FP&B) rank high on the list of university leaders' responsibilities. Nearly everything a university does depends on resources, and it's the job of the administration to find and allocate the unrestricted funds needed to do the job. Universities have been improving their approaches to resource allocation over the years, but conceptual and technological advances now make it possible to do much better. This chapter addresses three major problems that bedevil financial planners and budgeters: the need for a comprehensive financial planning framework, a budget decision support system, and a good model for making the trade-offs between mission and money that were described in chapter 2. The need is illustrated by the following extension of our hypothetical narrative.

> The provost was considering next year's financial planning and budgeting cycle. He and the president had become increasingly uneasy about the process during the past few years. The individual decisions may have been well informed and thoughtful, but they were having more and more trouble seeing the forest as opposed to the individual trees. This didn't matter so much when resources were plentiful, but the new era of budget stringency put a big premium on making decisions in a strategic way. The alternative was never-ending rounds of firefighting, as one problem after another demanded attention. The provost wanted to work with his staff, the CFO, and the people in IT to develop a more coherent system for supporting the planning and budgeting process, but what should the system look like?
>
> The university was awash in data, but it was hard to figure out what it all meant. Was it possible to do a better job of envisioning informa-

tion about the campus's complex operations and how they fit together across organizational units and over time—to get at least a rough view of the whole in addition to detailed views of the individual pieces? How should the university differentiate among the different kinds of "investment opportunities" to be confronted in the budget process: for example, those that would generate or sustain value in the short run versus those aiming to generate value in the future? (The university viewed all program-related expenditures as "investments" for creating value, whether they related to plant and equipment or current operations.) How should "financial sustainability" be defined, and what steps should be taken to achieve it?

The provost and his staff did not look forward to being inundated with the year's hundreds of requests for general funds, each backed up with extensive documentation laced with assertions of "ineluctable need" but no mention of school and departmental restricted and designated funds balances that seemed to grow inexorably over time. (They were willing to embrace responsibility center management to some degree but were concerned about diluting their ability to steer the institution.) And, given the uncertainties about financial sustainability, it was not clear how much money should be made available for allocation in the current cycle.

Yet another concern was about how to balance mission-related priorities, defined in subjective terms, with the hard quantitative data on revenues, costs, and margins. Arguments had raged in prior years about whether, when the chips were down, academic considerations should trump financial ones or vice versa. Sometimes, it seemed like the deans and faculty were on one side of the argument and the CFO, backed by many trustees, were on the other. Surely, there must be a middle ground. But what could it be?

The concepts and models presented in this chapter allow the university to be viewed in holistic terms. No integrated decision support systems for financial planning and budgeting exist at the present time, but one can be constructed given recent improvements in data availability, software, and computing power. Most of the elements to be described here have been applied in practice somewhere, but they have not been brought together into a single system. The closest I came was about a decade ago at the National University of Singapore (NUS), where I worked with Ajith Prasad (senior director for the Office of Resource Planning and himself a modeling expert) to build a prototype model that has informed and motivated the university's financial planning to the present day. The material to be presented updates and extends that work.

### Envisioning University Information

Strong actors operating in a decentralized environment are one of the things that characterize universities. The resulting decentralization of decision-making requires the university's FP&B information to be widely shared—certainly among senior academic and financial officers and trustees but also among deans and, given our traditions of shared governance, among faculty as well. But this introduces yet another problem. Universities are complex organizations, so the amount information is voluminous and easily overwhelming to busy people. What's required is that institutions have a well-thought-out strategy for envisioning and sharing FP&B information: one that presents the needed data in ways that are both coherent and engaging.

Edmund Tufte coined the phrase "envisioning information" as "work at the intersection of image, word, number, art"—with the objective of seeing the whole. "The instruments are those of writing and typography, of managing large datasets and statistical analysis, of line and layout and color,"[1] which are used to overcome the limitations of flat displays and bring data to life. In the present context, that means using the power of IT to allow the vast amount of university FP&B data to be seen as a Gestalt—to show enough at any one time to draw meaningful conclusions but not so much as to overwhelm while at the same time inviting users to dig deeper to answer questions and pursue new ideas.

Campus financial planning and budgeting models mostly consist of disconnected spreadsheets. One of their many shortcomings is that they turn off people who aren't already committed to understanding the connection between finance and academics. Another is a tendency to encourage static thinking: for example, as Tufte describes in his iconic criticism of PowerPoint.[2] The complex nature of campus internal economies require that data be "envisioned" in deep, dynamic, and engaging ways—including by those who know much more about the university's mission than they do about costs, revenues, and margins. The following sections describe the kinds of features I have in mind. Some are included in today's models, and I hope the others will be incorporated in the not-too-distant future.

Stanford recognized this problem decades ago, during my tenure in the central administration. Each year, it publishes its *Stanford University Budget Plan*, which includes all anticipated operating revenue and expense for the next year as well as a capital budget that is set in the context of a multiyear capital plan.[3] The idea is to provide a single integrated source of information about the university's plans, budgets, and finance for use by trustees, academic and financial officers, and faculty. The book, which came to 130 pages in 2014/15, includes sections for each of the university's schools and significant administrative and support operations. Each section considers "programmatic directions" and an overview of the "consolidated budget"—that is, all revenues and expenditures regardless of whether they are restricted or unrestricted. Where applicable, the programmatic directions include priorities for school and organizational growth, connections to other schools and communities, and important initiatives related to facilities and infrastructure. Detailed backup information, including the multiyear forecasts that inform the planning effort, are available online to people within the university. My goal now is to take these ideas to the next level, in a way that fully exploits the power of today's technology.

The discussion is aimed at policymakers rather than experts in financial planning and budgeting. By necessity, it gets into certain technical areas, but I don't dwell on those details. The objective is to outline a system that will be accessible to academic leaders, where the technical detail has been worked out by experts and then hidden "under the hood." Bridging the gap between academic and financial staff requires that provosts, deans, department chairs, and others be able to exercise "self-service" in working through different views of financial data—because that's the only way they can truly assimilate the information.

Today's advanced budget systems can do a good job in helping experts assimilate the financial information, but they do not meet the self-service needs of nonexperts. They also tend to be rather inflexible: difficult to adapt to changes in the university's information environment, the needs of users, and improvements in the state of the art of modeling. The decision support system envisioned in this chapter consists of "loosely coupled" modular building blocks. Discussion of the software is beyond our scope, but it's important to recognize that the requirements go well beyond spreadsheets and even the relational database and reporting software typically used in university information systems. For example, the state of the art is moving toward "common message models" (CMMs) that permit modules to be interconnected like Legos with communications being handled by routing "messages" through a common "switchboard." This allows the application to evolve over time by plugging in new modules in an efficient and controlled manner with minimal risk of breaking the system.[4]

### Multiple Views

Envisioning FP&B information requires multiple views of the data. Figure 5.1 maps the three main views discussed in this book, each of which enables its own set of insights. Axes with heavy lines depict "activities," "sources of funds," "uses of funds," and "margins" and "funds balances"—the constructs around which FP&B is traditionally organized. Axes with dotted lines depict "mission," "market," and "margins"—the functional representation called out by the subtitle of this book. ("Margins" falls into both categories, so it has a heavy dotted line.) Data for different "Organizational units and programs" can be viewed by traversing a third axis, represented by the center label in the figure. They include academic departments, schools, support service units, and a central resource allocation unit ("CENTRAL") to be discussed later. Programs refer to sets of activities within (or sometimes among) units: for example, degree and research programs. A fourth way of viewing the data, in terms of time periods, is implicit in the aforementioned discussion because each variable must be tracked over appropriate historical and planning periods.

"Activities" appear at the top of the diagram because they are the engines that drive the university forward. Activities are powered through "uses of funds," which appears at the three o'clock position. "Mission" appears between "activities" and "uses of funds" because both can be viewed as value indicators: the former directly and the latter as surrogates for activities that are too small and varied to be described explicitly. "Sources of funds" (nine o'clock) are strongly influenced by "market"

**Figure 5.1.** Views of the data

behavior, which is why the two appear close together. Similarly, "funds balances" appears next to "margin" because the latter is a strong driver of changes in balance sheets. While not precise, the juxtapositions do suggest the causal structure behind the FP&B constructs.

Understanding a university is like blind people describing an elephant: one "sees" a trunk, one a tail, one a leg, and so on. The challenge is to keep data for all the dimensions in mind at once. The solution requires a FP&B system that provides:

- *Dashboards* that give "summary views of the whole" for the various FP&B entities and datasets;
- *Navigational tools* that allow users to transit seamlessly among the various views described earlier and drill down to get detailed reports for any area; and
- *Robust models* that forecast market behavior and predict how alternative planning assumptions will affect the university's future performance.

Imagine that you're responsible for university-level FP&B. You and your staff need to envision information for all the operating units. Some of the information will be obtainable only by drilling down to lower-level units, so you'll be authorized to look at everything—except for special "private spaces" where deans and others are developing plans for later submission. You can, with certain exceptions, enter planning assumptions for any organizational level and, if you wish, specify that they be propagated to lower levels. You know that lower-level data have been rolled up in accordance with prespecified business rules—

including the consolidation of financial information among organizational units when applicable.

Other decision-makers need access to more constrained sets of FP&B data, but the basic requirements are the same. School-level planners access information and enter data only for their schools and departments, for example. Financial specialists must access campus-wide information but may be authorized to enter inputs for information only for their areas of responsibility.

### Dashboards and Navigation

Getting a comprehensive view of activities, resources, and financial performance is not easy. Universities are too complicated for an organizational unit's data to be presented in a single display, and even if the technical barriers could be surmounted, the large mass of material would make assimilation impossible. Multiple displays are needed so that the data can be viewed at different depths, in different ways (e.g., as tables or graphics), from different vantage points, and where applicable for different entities. Each display should tell a coherent story with respect to its domain; in the language of management science, each should be "complete on important issues." Finally, seamless navigation among the displays allows users to integrate the stories without system-induced distractions.

These requirements make the design of a comprehensive FP&B dashboard—or, rather, a system of dashboards—a high priority for traditional universities. The remainder of this section sketches what such a system might look like. I focus on how it should look to the user, but readers should keep in mind that what goes on "under the hood" also is critically important. In particular, all the data should emanate from a single underlying structure, and rollups should follow consistent business rules. Failures of consistency make the university's internal economy seem more complex than it really is. They are distracting and, therefore, detrimental to the cause of envisioning information.

Figure 5.2 illustrates the design of the top-level dashboard for a typical academic unit (e.g., a school or department). The solid-line axes pertain to variables the university controls directly—what I will call "primary planning variables" (PPVs) because they represent the main content of FP&B processes.[5] The dashed lines denote "supplementary

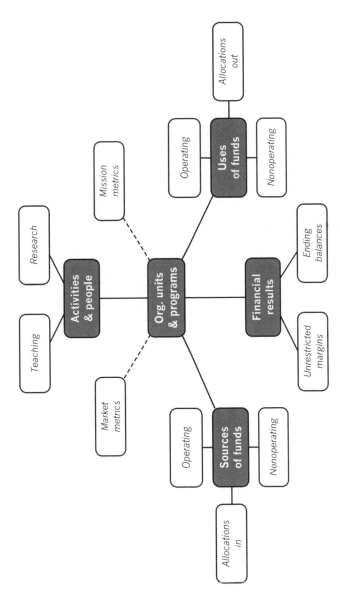

**Figure 5.2.** The top-level FP&B dashboard

planning variables" (SPVs); these describe outcomes that while dependent upon the primary planning variables are materially different in some important sense. (Readers may note that figure 5.1's "margins" and "funds balances" now have been brought together under the rubric "financial results.") Suggested variables for the first level of detail in each PPV category are shown in the outer boxes.

The kinds of variables that might populate the PPV categories are shown in table 5.1. The list is based on one currently used by Stanford University, though I have changed some details to reflect usage in this chapter. My goal is to describe the proposed dashboard in enough detail to demonstrate the approach and also to permit implementation by

**Table 5.1. Illustrative dashboard variables**

| Activities and people | | |
|---|---|---|
| *Headcounts* | *Teaching* | *Research* |
| Faculty | Credit hours | % Research-active faculty |
| Other teaching staff | Average teaching load | % Faculty with G & C |
| Nonteaching staff | % Adjunct | Publications |
| Students | Cost per credit hour | Citations |
| Uses of funds | | |
| *Operating* | *Allocations out* | *Nonoperating* |
| Academic compensation | For operations | To designated reserves |
| Other compensation | For special purposes | Debt service |
| Other operating expense | To capital budgets | Other nonoperating exp. |
| Facilities-related cost | Other allocations | Transfers (net) |
| Charged overheads | | |
| Sources of funds | | |
| *Operating* | *Allocations in* | *Nonoperating* |
| Tuition and fees | For operations: internal | Current gifts |
| (Student financial aid) | For operations: external | Endowment spending |
| Research (gross) | Special purpose: internal | Other nonoperating inc. |
| Self-supporting programs | Special purpose: external | Use of reserves (net) |
| Other operating revenue | ("Return" of revenue) | |
| Financial results | | |
| *Unrestricted margins* | Ending funds balances | |
| (Surpluses or deficits) | Current funds | Other funds |
| Direct | Unrestricted | Endowment |
| Burdened | Restricted | Other financial |

those with the requisite skill sets. However, some readers may wish to skip the variable-by-variable discussion.

The table 5.1 is divided into four panels, each of which correspond to one of the four solid-line axes in figure 5.2.

- Activities and people
  - *Teaching:* the four variables were discussed extensively in connection with ABC, and the drilldowns could include all the variables considered there.
  - *Research:* the listed variables will be familiar to most research universities; many drilldowns come readily to mind.
- Uses of funds
  - *Operating* expense: the cost of operating the entity being considered (e.g., a school or department). Facilities-related cost has been separated from other operating expenses because the former is less discretionary than the latter. Overheads charged on a current basis (e.g., through an overhead rate) are included because they are directly associated with operations. As discussed previously, further detail should be obtainable by drilling down on a particular variable.
  - *Allocations out:* discretionary transfers to other units (usually but not necessarily further down in the organizational hierarchy), capital budgets, and special program-related purposes like incentives and special projects. CENTRAL allocations to support schools and support service units, and similar allocations from schools to academic departments (mainly in responsibility center management), fall into this category.
  - *Nonoperating* expense: transfers to designated reserves (e.g., self-insurance), debt service, and items not accounted for elsewhere.
- Sources of funds
  - *Operating* revenues: money that is earned or made available for use by the unit during the year. Tuition and fees are important funds sources for most departments, but they need to be linked to student financial aid because the latter discounts the price received by the institution. (Financial aid is not shown as an operating expense because it's not an "activity" that consumes resources.)

Research is gross of indirect cost, but self-supporting programs may be gross or net of their direct expenses depending on how they are organized. (Auxiliaries and service centers may be treated on a net basis, for example.) Drill-downs should include the ability to get student revenue by market segment and student level as well as research revenue by sponsoring organization.

- ○ *Allocations in:* money the unit receives from other entities to support its expenditures. Operating allocations from CENTRAL or a school as well as state grants based on enrollments fall under the operations rubric. Internal or external special allocations might be for incentives or earmarked projects (other than research). "Return" of revenue (shown as a negative number) consists of money earned by the unit, usually from tuition and research projects, that flows to CENTRAL under revenue sharing, revenue center management (RCM) "tax," indirect cost, and similar formulas. While not an "Allocation in," positioning the figure in this column allows one to quickly determine whether the entity is a net gainer or loser in terms of allocations.
- ○ *Nonoperating* income: funds available, other than from operations and allocations in, to fund the unit's obligations. The first three items are self-explanatory. Use of reserves is identified separately because this is not a sustainable funds source. All reserves are covered (the figure will be negative if additions exceed withdrawals), but individual items must be obtained by drilling down.

- Financial results
  - ○ *Unrestricted margins (surplus or deficit):* the "bottom line" as generally considered in resource allocation. "Direct" margin is simply the unit's unrestricted cash flow. "Burdened" margin adds in allocated overheads (i.e., overheads not charged to units on a current basis). The circumstances in which burdened and unburdened margins should be used are discussed in chapter 4.
  - ○ *Ending balances:* the unit's current unrestricted and restricted funds, endowments, and other financial assets (all noncurrent funds except, e.g., money actually invested in buildings).

The variables are intended for decision-making, not financial reporting. They don't follow standard fund accounting or GAAP definitions, but they must be reconcilable to them. One example is in the treatment of transfers, where internal allocations and returned revenue are shown as "allocations out" and "allocations in," respectively. Applying standard accounting rules would consolidate out these variables and obscure information that is vital for FP&B decision-making.

The dashboards should use icons and graphics to the maximum extent possible, because this provides the greatest leverage for envisioning information. They should be configured so that clicking drills down to the detail for the selected item. For example, right-clicking anywhere on the dashboard might produce an organization chart showing all the organizational units the user is authorized to access. Selecting a unit would display that unit's data for the screen that currently is being viewed. Right-clicking within a unit might display a list of that unit's programs, where selecting an item would access whatever reports are available for the unit. Graphics should be used liberally. Standardized reports should be provided to reduce the cognitive load for users who don't work with the system every day, and advanced users should also be able to specify custom charts and reports.

The ability to save the results of what-if analyses should be another feature of the system. Planners need to test the sensitivity of many ideas and assumptions, browse through them multiple times during the planning process, and eventually submit their choices to the system's "production" file. Users with appropriate privileges should be able to enter all required data in situ—on or close to the screen(s) where results will be displayed—in order to minimize cognitive load and the possibly of error.[6]

### The Time Dimension

A comprehensive FP&B dashboard system will allow users to analyze past events and envision alternative futures. The system should be able to access a detailed history for every variable (e.g., as described in appendix B for the "Activities and people" variables). It also should allow users to project the variables into the future based on external events and, where applicable, the university's policy decisions. (Forecasting the *market* dimension of figure 5.1 requires consideration of pricing policies, for example.) And because decision-makers want to test a variety of alternative policies, the system should support "what-if" analysis and allow for comparing multiple planning scenarios—all presented in context of the unit's historical record.

Viewing the model's time dimension in terms of three distinct periods will facilitate the construction and interpretation of predictive models.

- *History* data describe actual data on past performance. Examples of how they can be used to diagnose problems and set planning priorities were discussed in chapter 4. These data provide context and, when conditions are favorable, can be used to project simple trends. Five years is about the minimum time period needed for extrapolation. Longer series may be useful in some situations, but one must be sure that circumstances haven't changed enough to destroy comparability.
- *Current* data are used to determine the "planning base" needed to project the future. These data are at once historical and predictive, because the current year's actuals aren't yet known and thus must be projected to year-end based on the budget and any emergent variances. Hence considerable thought is required to cast current-year data into a form suitable for forecasting.
- *Forecast* data represent the future the model aims to predict. Forecasts of market behavior depend on assumptions about the behavior of customers and suppliers, those related to the mission require predictions about the university's own activities and outcomes, and financial forecasts depend on both. I've found that five-year forecasts work well in most situations. It's hard to gauge financial sustainability using much less than five years, and going further out involves ever-greater uncertainty.

Making and interpreting forecasts requires one to distinguish between "controllable" and "uncontrollable" variables. The former fall within the purview of campus decision-makers, whereas the latter should be viewed as exogenous. Typical controllable variables include tuition, salary pools, and funding allocations. Typical uncontrollables are inflation, competitive tuition and salary rates, government appropriations, and cost rise on utilities and other purchased items. Failure to understand the difference between what's controllable and what's not always leads to trouble.

## Coherent Financial Planning

Financial planning and budgeting are key drivers of university performance. They empower the academic and other activities that deliver on the institutional and user value propositions ("mission" and "market") described back in chapter 2. Coherent financial planning enables the university to consider its options over time and, importantly, to consider the trade-offs between supporting current value-creating activities and investing in activities that will enhance value in the future. The next section, "Coherent Resource Allocation," describes how the university can consider its current array of options in a seamless way. Failure to achieve coherence in either domain invites fragmentation, which many commentators believe to be the bane of the modern university.

The report of the Kellogg Commission, at the turn of the millennium, expressed concern that "the *uni*-versity [would] become an institutionally fragmented aggregation of departments." It argued that the shared responsibilities associated with governance can, and should, "connect the fragmented pieces into a coherent whole."[7] Former SUNY president Joseph Burke carried this idea further in *Fixing the Fragmented University*, which offers a number of "means and methods" for achieving coherence.[8] University of Michigan president Jim Duderstadt's "Fixing the Fragmented University: A View from the Bridge" argues that decentralization in universities allows them to function as "loosely coupled adaptive systems," but that while this can facilitate adaptation to changing environments, it also inhibits their response to the broader requirements of their mission.[9] My "Using the Budget to Fight Fragmentation" holds that, while governance factors are important, the strongest immediate antidotes to fragmentation revolve around financial planning and budgeting.[10]

### Different Kinds of Investments

Traditionally, financial planning and budgeting has focused on unrestricted current funds—the ones directly controlled by the central administration. But that's not the whole story. Capital funds also need to be allocated, and expenditures from a good many restricted funds should be considered as well. The following list differentiates between the support of current activities and making investments (also a kind of "activity") in projects that will pay off in the future. The items are presented in order of increasing lag time between an authorization to spend and initiation of the stream of benefits (i.e., in terms of the proximity of cause and effect).

- Support current activities in current ways (e.g., teach students, perform research, and supply support services).
- Invest in process development and improvement (e.g., redesign courses as described in chapter 3).
- Invest in organizational and market development (e.g., develop new academic programs).
- Invest in human resources (e.g., hire faculty to provide new academic leadership and train staff in new skills).
- Invest in facilities and major equipment (e.g., plan and construct a new building).

These are the "levers" that budgeters push and pull as they try to maximize mission attainment. The investments become increasingly strategic as one goes down the list. The challenge is to go beyond supporting current activities in current ways, to "steer the institution" by choosing portfolios of new activities and longer-term investments.

University leaders steer by investing unrestricted funds in various activities and capital projects as well as by influencing the acquisition and expenditure of restricted funds. Doing a good job requires full knowledge of flows and balances for both the restricted and unrestricted funds. This requires comprehensive and effective financial planning. Because such planning is not as easy as it sounds, many universities concentrate mainly on their unrestricted funds. Unfortunately, such a focus exacerbates the fragmentation problem.

Steering requires one to look ahead for three to five years—or longer if disruptive events are looming on the horizon. Failure to do so means that the university is trapped in a reactive mode: responding to events rather than anticipating and trying to mitigate or exploit them. Not looking ahead virtually guarantees that most of the emphasis will be on current operations performed in current ways. The university will lurch toward each set of budget authorizations without enough forward thinking about future needs and possibilities.

Market variables and other uncontrollables do not move in linear and predictable ways. Shifting trends, corrections, and random perturbations occur all the time, and while some are welcome, others can be quite painful. All universities must contend with fluctuations in student demand and government funding, for example, and endowed universities also must deal with the ups and downs of the capital markets. Market rates for salaries and other inputs are yet another source of disruptive change.

Universities must adjust their financial plans in response to "real" externally driven changes, but it's hard to distinguish what's real and what's just a passing blip. Moving too quickly puts the institution's activities at risk, whereas moving too slowly will lead to even worse corrections in the future. But while this problem cannot be eliminated, it is possible to manage it. The first step is to recognize that all future years are not the same when it comes to uncertainty.

Best practice in planning suggests that one should distinguish between the first, middle, and last years of the forecast period. The progression is shown in figure 5.3. Looking first to the controllable variables, the first year is the one for which the budget is being prepared. The task here is to make the decisions that drive immediate actions—decisions that are not easy to undo. The middle years involve plans rather than decisions; plans are important for providing context, but they can be revised as necessary.

One's ability to anticipate desirable values for the controllable variables declines dramatically as one moves toward the end of the planning period. This can be reflected by showing the last year in the forecast period as being different than the others. In effect, this "terminal year" sums up what's expected to happen beyond the point where detailed plans are likely to be meaningful. And because statements about these future controllables are not based on detailed forecasts, one should view them not as budget decisions but rather as policies that place only broad limits on anticipated future decisions. The result is a multiyear rolling plan that is detailed and specific for the upcoming budget year, detailed but tentative for the middle years, and broadly indicative for the terminal year.

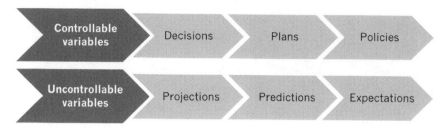

**Figure 5.3.** First, middle, and late years of the forecast period

Turning now to the uncontrollables, the first-year projections often can assume the persistence of currently observable conditions. The middle-year forecasts require predictions based on analyses of market conditions and other exogenous factors, predictions that are usually less precise than their persistence-based cousins. The terminal-year forecasts, which I call "expectations," usually must rely on long-term trends or even informed guesswork.

The aforementioned discussion replicates the familiar pattern of weather forecasting. Tomorrow's forecasts are obtained by adjusting current conditions for well-understood, short-term effects. Forecasts up to ten days or so are rooted in current conditions but also depend on less-than-well-understood elements of atmospheric behavior. Forecasts further out are based on climatic factors not tightly linked to current conditions. The climate models are subject to considerable uncertainty, so people ask why they should be used for important decisions. The reason might be described thusly: "Direct observation of future events would be far better than reliance on any imperfect model, but, unfortunately, such observations are not available at the present time."

Uncontrollable fluctuations pose more problems for traditional universities than in most for-profit businesses. There are two reasons for this. First, it takes a good deal of time to adjust the size of most teaching and research programs. Lead times for hiring regular faculty can easily be a year or more, for example, and many serve on multiyear contracts or even with tenure. (Universities "flex" their workforces with adjunct faculty, but, as I argued in chapter 4, too much reliance on adjuncts can be problematic.) The fabric of academic programs can be hurt badly by precipitous reductions—as we used to say at Stanford, "It takes years to build an excellent department, but that excellence can be destroyed in a year or two." Second, profits serve as a kind of financial buffer for business firms, in the sense that profits not earned need not be paid out to shareholders. Public corporations take a hit in their stock price, but by itself this does not lead to cash-flow problems. Conversely, universities tend to spend a substantial fraction of what firms earn as profits: as noted, these expenditure flows are hard to change in the short run.

### Financial Sustainability

The search for financial sustainability is of great importance to universities. This means developing resource allocation protocols that avoid "start-stop" budgeting to the maximum extent possible. Understanding future trends and modeling their quantitative implications is essential, but all such predictions are subject to error. Managing the resulting perturbations requires decision rules for minimizing the possibility of unexpected financial shortfalls and taking account of how uncertainty tends to increase over time. Some of the rules are rather technical, so some readers may wish to focus mainly on the principles discussed in this and the following subsections.

Sustainability decision rules were developed and implemented at Stanford beginning in the 1970s, under the rubric of "long-run financial equilibrium" (LRFE). Equilibrium requires that three conditions be fulfilled. First, income must equal expense after taking account of all needed transfers and other adjustments (i.e., there is no significant surplus or deficit). The second is less familiar: the growth rate of income needs to be approximately equal to the growth rate of expense. This helps what is in balance to stay in balance. The third is that there are no hidden liabilities: that all significant obligations are taken into account. Consistent failure to observe these conditions dramatically raises the likelihood of financial difficulty—and the greater the divergence, the more vexing the problem. One might think this is obvious, but it's easy to find examples where campuses have willfully or inadvertently ignored one or more of the three conditions and have ended up regretting it.

These conditions are analogous to flying a light airplane. You want the plane to maintain its altitude, so the first requirement is to point the nose horizontal to the ground ("budget balance"). But that isn't enough.

You also want the plane to have proper "trim," so that the nose is neither too heavy nor too light. Failure to maintain trim means that you
have to constantly fight the controls. A moment of inattention will cause
the nose to fall into a dive or rise into a stall. This is equivalent to maintaining "trim" for income and expense. Unexpected perturbations will
push the budget out of balance from time to time, but the problem is
not hard to correct if prompt adjustments are made. The final condition
is that the airplane be well maintained ("no hidden liabilities"), so that
the engine doesn't cut out or the control system fail.

Implementation of the two conditions depends on distinguishing between plans and policies as discussed in connection with figure 5.3. To
review briefly, plans are detailed roadmaps to guide future action. They
are informed by predictions—hopefully fairly accurate ones—that are
based on structural analyses to the extent possible. Conversely, policies
are based on broad-gauge expectations that provide only general guidance about the future. The Stanford model took these expectations as
reflecting a "long-term steady state," which the university had decided
to consider when setting long-term pricing and spending policies.[11]

The fact that equilibrium is a long-run concept means that the conditions for budget and growth-rate quality must apply in the steady
state. It would be good if they also applied for earlier years in the planning period, but that often is not practical. Such a requirement would
force each year's budget to fully reflect all perturbations of income and
expense that had occurred during the previous year. Most universities
would not tolerate such large degrees of variation, especially when some
of them might be reversed before long.

The answer is to "smooth" the year-to-year fluctuations by moving
only part of the distance toward financial equilibrium each year—
treating the planning period as a time for "transition to equilibrium."
The FP&B system should permit deficits during the planning period
while converging to equilibrium in the steady state. Surpluses and deficits are posted to reserves or endowment and thus reflected in future
income so that it's harder to achieve equilibrium if big deficits have been
incurred along the way.

Figure 5.4 illustrates the transition to equilibrium for salary
increases—which, as everyone knows, are subject to a plethora of perturbations. The university wants to match the market average for a

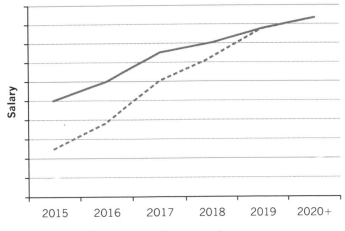

**Figure 5.4.** Closing a salary gap

group of jobs (e.g., faculty in a given field), for which the actual (2015) and forecasted values are shown by a solid line. The campus's current average salary is shown by the 2015 value of the dashed line. Whether the discrepancy between actual and market was due to unexpected market movements or institutional inattention doesn't matter for present purposes; what does matter is that the gap is too large to be closed in a single year. Instead, the university plans to close the gap in stages as shown by the progression of the dashed line after 2015.

- *Market analysis* has predicted that competitive salaries will grow as indicated for 2016 through 2019, but similar predictions are not available for 2020 and beyond. Hence the last point in the figure (2020+) is simply the expected growth of productivity in the economy, which experts believe is a meaningful long-term indicator of salary growth.
- The *equilibrium decision rule* says that the university should close a certain fraction of the gap between actual and projected market salaries during each year of the planning period and that the gap should vanish in the steady state. The chart uses a figure of 25 percent: one-quarter of the length of the planning period. (At Stanford, we tended to frontload the adjustment so that the gap could be closed quickly.) This brings salaries to parity at the end of 2019, after which the model projects them as growing at the same rate as the market.

The same logic can be used for any uncontrollable variable. This kind of "crawling peg" system ensures that market-based perturbations are not ignored in planning while at the same time avoiding the effects of statistically unusual events.

Unsustainable growth in academic program expenditures is a special but very important case of disequilibrium. Expanding programs in response to short-term market upticks, and starting new ones on soft money for that matter, incur future liabilities that may be difficult to manage. Spending from endowments at a level that fails to maintain their purchasing power is another classic problem (e.g., when too large a spending rate causes the real value of an endowed chair to decline while the faculty salary it supports increases steadily). There is a large literature on sustainable endowment spending, much of which is underpinned by my concept of long-run financial equilibrium, and putting a good set of decision rules into one's FP&B model will help decisionmakers avoid these pitfalls.[12]

Strategies for transitioning toward target levels for balance sheet items like operating and capital reserves also can be built into the model. (Too many universities ignore their balance sheets when developing operating budgets.) Hidden deferred maintenance liabilities, which arise when the funded growth of maintenance expense is below the rate that's truly needed, also should be included (e.g., by doing engineering studies of maintenance requirements). These and other applications are discussed in my book with David Hopkins and in the subsequent literature.[13]

### *Mitigating Financial Risk*

The transition-to-equilibrium approach manages risk by adjusting particular expenditures in light of known gaps and expected future changes. Now we address the general question of risk (i.e., for managing the many small uncertainties that can mushroom into big problems if not managed properly). This takes us into the domain of financial rather than budget analysis: the "F" in FP&B. The financial domain underscores the importance of strong CFO participation in the university's resource allocation processes—even though, as repeatedly emphasized in this book, the university's mission-related judgments should be driven primarily by academics.

The structures needed for managing financial risk already are included in our FP&B paradigm. The main structures are the operating reserves of the academic units and central administration. They act as "surge tanks" for the surpluses and deficits incurred at various organizational levels. Another is the separation of income streams into "part of the budget base" and "one-time": the former being money the university expects to be sustained over time and the latter being short term in nature. The separation is a good idea, but it must be viewed as an imperfect mechanism for mitigating risk because the categorization is somewhat arbitrary and even the budget base is a moving target until the end of the fiscal year. Stanford designed its "conditional budget," where base-funding commitments are withheld until late in the budget year (when the revenue picture would be more clear), to deal with this problem. This provided only a partial fix, however, and it does not appear to have caught on with other universities.[14]

But just how large should the surge tanks be? This question is of great importance to the management of university balance sheets and to the entities that lend them money. To answer it, one must quantify the degree of volatility in university income and expenditure streams as well as the effect of this volatility on the institution's multiple "bottom lines." Generations of financial researchers have studied such questions in the context of stock-market volatility, but it has received relatively little attention in nonprofits such as traditional universities.

Detailed discussion of volatility is beyond the scope of this book, but a few brief comments are in order. David Hopkins and I introduced the topic in our 1981 *Planning Models for Colleges and Universities*. We followed this with a number of papers that applied management science tools such as dynamic optimization under uncertainty to the problem of university budget planning.[15] The techniques were complicated, however, and they didn't turn out to be practical given the data and computational facilities of the time. What did prove practical was work by financial researchers on the volatility of endowment returns and its implications for LRFE-related decision rules on sustainable spending from endowment.[16] That work now is part of the standard university financial management canon.

The arguments given earlier suggest that quantification of uncertainty for the operating budget, as well as for the endowment, should be viewed as an important element of comprehensive FP&B models. Models that don't consider uncertainty can give misleading results due to what's called the "flaw of averages"—the tendency of "plans based on average assumptions to be wrong on average."[17] I demonstrated a comprehensive Monte Carlo model of university income and spending in a 2008 paper titled "Capital Structure and Risk Management," presented at the Lehman Brothers–sponsored Forum for Higher Education Finance. To quote briefly from that paper: "Items in the operating budget can be as volatile as the returns from some asset classes, and the fluctuations for the various items may well be correlated with each other and with the asset-class returns. . . . How should we think about the operating portfolio, both in and of itself and in relation to investment strategy? How might major changes in operating-item volatility be mitigated by countervailing changes in other operating items and/or asset allocations?"[18]

Lehman Brothers partner John Augustine describes the approach as "using the endowment [and by extension other balance sheet investments] to hedge operational risk" and "a helpful corrective in line with current capital market and rating agency guidelines, which now focus far more on the importance of operating matters [such as] annual debt service-to-budget ratios than on the more traditional debt-to-asset ratios."[19] Former MIT and Caltech executive vice president John Curry (now with Deloitte Consulting) believes that this kind of analysis will enable decision-makers to "don operating budget 'conceptual lenses' to look at the balance sheet from that perspective. Why is that important? Well, for one reason, it's through the operating budget that the real business of colleges and universities gets done" and, therefore, where the consequences of risk get felt.[20]

## Coherent Resource Allocation

Poorly managed universities develop their annual budgets without sufficient thought to the broader ramifications of what they're doing. Spending authority is allocated, and tuition and salary rates are set, because these things have to be done—but too often the decisions are made on an incremental basis using inchoate goals, opaque logic, and incomplete evidence. Decisions made this way almost guarantee fragmentation. In contrast, a good budgeting system will emphasize coherence across organizational units and programs as well as over time.

## Table 5.2. Seven major goals of budgeting

1. To steer the institution by investing general funds in new activities and programs and/or disinvesting from current ones.
2. To leverage restricted funds in support of high-priority budget needs.
3. To stimulate the growth of general and restricted fund revenue by encouraging entrepreneurship and fund-raising through decentralization and other means.
4. To provide support for special projects, like startup and reengineering initiatives, that will improve the university's performance over the long run.
5. To reward and provide incentives for good performance in all areas, especially in those that align with the university's strategic plans.
6. To maintain financial sustainability.
7. To quantify and mitigate financial risk: e.g., by managing the timing of expenditures and optimizing contingency reserves.

*Source*: Adapted from Massy, "Using the Budget to Fight Fragmentation and Improve Quality."

The "Seven Major Goals of Budgeting," listed in table 5.2, present some important desiderata for coherent resource allocation. The first goal, discussed earlier, is to steer the institution by controlling the expenditure of general funds. The second extends the steering concept to include restricted funds, and the third seeks to grow the budget by expanding the availability of both kinds of funds. The fourth goal speaks to special projects that are outside the mainstream budget but nevertheless important, and the fifth goal speaks to rewards and incentives related to performance in all areas. Finally, the sixth and seventh goals address financial sustainability and risk management as discussed previously.

### All Funds Budgeting

Most academic programs rely on multiple funding sources—not simply the "unrestricted current" ("general") funds that are budgeted by the central administration. University accounting systems segregate *funds sources* neatly into general funds and other funds, but *funds uses* for an academic or other mission-critical program can involve both kinds of sources. Looking only at the unrestricted current component of a program's funding may give only a partial picture, and looking at a unit's budget requests without considering its restricted funds and operating reserves is equally myopic. The solution to this problem has come to be called "all funds budgeting," which we began to use at Stanford during the 1980s.

All funds budgeting evaluates requests for general fund increments in light of the unit's restricted funds availability and operating reserves. I will include "designated funds," which are like restricted funds except that their "restrictions" were imposed by previous administrations and trustees rather than donors under the "restricted funds" rubric because the actions that set them up represent promises that should be kept. (These actions can be reversed if things get bad enough, of course.) Including restricted funds in the main budget process gives the general funds allocators a complete picture of the requested activities and their costs. Looking at all funds is essential if one is considering a degree or other academic program, but it's important for line-item allocations as well. Failure to do so may invite a "shell game" where, for example, "ineluctable need" for the item is claimed when the unit could fund some or all of it from its own sources. Adroit provosts and deans negotiate cost-sharing agreements in situations like this. In addition to stretching scarce general funds, such agreements provide litmus tests of the requester's priorities.

But what about the objection that because restricted funds actually are *restricted* in terms of purpose, they cannot be called forth at the behest of the central administration? This certainly is true, but all degrees of restriction are not the same. Some funds are only "lightly restricted" in that the fund "controller" (the person with spending authority) can exercise considerable discretion over their use—as with funds restricted to a school or broad area of research, for example. Likewise, restricted funds for library acquisitions, student financial aid, and certain endowed chairs supplement or substitute for general funds allocated for the same purpose. The challenge is to understand each fund's degree of restriction and make this information available to decision-makers at appropriate levels in a timely way. Meeting donor intent always should be the overriding requirement, but this does not mean restricted funds can never be used in support of mainstream university priorities.

Stanford developed the system shown in table 5.3 as a way of meeting the restricted fund challenge. Beginning a decade or so ago, the university's budget office worked with accounting, legal, development, and operating-unit staff to classify each of its funds according to a scheme like the following.[21] (The two columns are read separately.)

| Table 5.3. Scheme for classifying funds | |
| --- | --- |
| Levels of restriction | Levels of control |
| Unrestricted | University |
| Moderately restricted | School |
| Highly restricted | Department |
| Currently unusable | Program or institute |
| Pending designation | Faculty/PI |

- *Level of Restriction.* Unrestricted funds are available to the university's budget process, and moderately restricted funds are at least potentially available. Highly restricted funds contain covenants that preclude general use, although some may happen to align with mainstream objectives. Funds not currently usable for current expenditures and those that are pending designation can't be considered in budgeting, though they might become available in the future.
- *Level of Control.* Describes where the fund controller resides in the university's organizational hierarchy. The range runs from the central university (e.g., the president, the provost, and the budget office) to a school or department, to a program or institute, or even to individual faculty members.

Stanford has thousands of restricted funds, so it was necessary to involve a significant number of people in the classification process. This was accomplished over a period of years by developing a set of anchored criteria and training participants on how to use them. Audits are performed on a sampling basis to ensure that new funds are being classified correctly, and "close calls" are subject to further review if and when a fund is being considered for expenditure.

Use of the classifications begins by matching applicable budget requests with the array of restricted funds controlled by the originating person or unit. Then the level of restriction for each such fund determines whether it's a candidate for cost sharing. The process, which is applied to funds balances as well as current gifts and grants, informs negotiations about whether to use the particular fund. Perhaps more important, deans, chairs, and other budget item proposers are encouraged to explore their restricted funds before making proposals to the central administration. The resulting cultural as well as operational shift goes a long way toward relieving the problem, encountered in many universities, that the central administration is starved for general funds while restricted fund balances grow in the operating units.

One exception to the all-funds requirement should be noted, however. Auxiliaries such as housing and food service, hospitals and clinics, the university press, and perhaps intercollegiate athletics can be handled separately, with only their overhead allocations, purchases of services, and surpluses or deficits entering the university's main FP&B calculations. (The unit's expected margin contribution or subsidy must be approved by the university, of course.) Such separate treatment is equivalent to what's called "equity accounting" for the unconsolidated subsidiaries of for-profit organizations.

### Separating Tuition Decisions from Allocations

The ability of universities to respond to public concerns about tuition growth depends critically on how their financial planning and budgeting process is organized. Unfortunately, the intrinsic desires of many institutions to remain affordable are too often overcome by the drivers of growth: for example, the arms race in spending and the pervasive desire to do more. This subsection describes how astutely organized processes can give cost containment advocates, including trustees in many cases, a more prominent seat at the table where price increases are negotiated).

This can be accomplished by organizing the FP&B process into the five stages laid out in figure 5.5 and discussed in the following list. The resulting discipline is helpful for envisioning information about the university's complex and decentralized operations as well as essential for cost containment and dealing with tight resource constraints.

1. *Multiyear Forecasts* of market and other externally determined factors. This may require months of work by people with knowledge, for example, of institutional data, economics, market research, and statistics. It's important to get expert advice wherever possible. At Stanford, we brought members of our economics and business school faculties together for late-afternoon seminars (ending with wine and

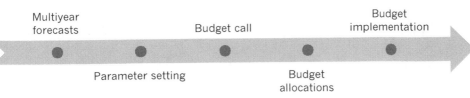

**Figure 5.5.** Stages of the FP&B process

cheese) to get their input on economic conditions and other conditions. In addition to the professional contribution, these consultations helped us gain faculty understanding and support. Exchanging ideas with other universities also pays dividends—so long as no antitrust violations are involved.

2. *Parameter Setting* for variables that are managed by the central administration. It is here that tuition rates are determined, along with the growth rate of salaries, the total amount of discretionary spending, and the target margin. The first-year parameters (for the year being budgeted) receive particular attention because they drive impending decisions; the outyears should not be neglected, however, because they place the budget in context and give operating units a heads-up about what to expect.

3. *Budget Call*, which describes the university's economic outlook and where it stands relative to prior-year expectations. The call ends by asking the operating unit heads for their input on priorities: in particular, on any changes in resourcing that they feel their units require. The first-year budget parameters represent a key input to this process because they indicate what the units can expect or, in cases where budgets need to be reduced, the sums that will need to be given up. The budget call is a primary vehicle for communicating the central administration's resource allocation strategy, and well-managed universities put a great deal of thought into its preparation.

4. *Budget allocations* determine the operating units' "authority to spend." This is the traditional work product of a budget process. The allocations may be made on a line-item basis, with a one-line budget, or through a system of RCM as described in the next section.

5. *Budget implementation*, which consists of technical tasks conducted mainly by people within the financial and operating departments.

Included under this rubric are individual salaries, detailed allocations for specific programs, and setting up spending controls in the accounting system. These tasks require enough time for them to be listed as a separate step in the budget process, but they are outside the scope of this book. We'll see that, in the decentralized environments of most universities, it is hard to get a handle on the operating units' planned use of restricted funds until this final FP&B stage has been completed.

Separating parameter setting (step 2) as a distinct element of the process is the key to restraining tuition growth. This makes it easier to have dispassionate discussions about tuition policy in relation to the institution's value system, as opposed to a means to the end of accommodating a greater number of budget requests. At Stanford, parameter setting was the stage where the board of trustees weighed in most strongly—to remind us of the university's broader social responsibility and also, because they voted on the parameters themselves, to hold us accountable for making balanced choices. Like Congress's overarching budget resolutions, the task was to set policy-based limits on overall spending before the pressure of special interest constituencies could be brought to bear.

### Approaches to Allocation

Allocation of general funds to operating units lies at the core of the budgeting process. This may be done by line-item allocation, a so-called one-line budget, RCM, or some combination of the three. The approaches are based on very different philosophies, but we will see shortly that, in the end, each requires that someone in the university allocate funds to individual activities.

Figure 5.6 illustrates the differences among the approaches: the degree to which decisions about revenues and/or expenditures are devolved to schools. RCM, represented by the dot at the top of the figure, uses formulas for devolving revenues to schools after deducting "taxes" (to fund central overhead expense) and "subventions" (to steer the institution when market forces don't reflect the school's priorities). Once revenue is decentralized, it is only the schools that can decide how the funds should be used. Jon Strauss, Edward Whalen, and Robert Zem-

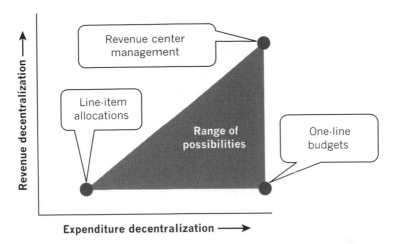

**Figure 5.6.** Approaches to resource allocation

sky introduced RCM at the University of Pennsylvania during the 1970s as a way of overcoming the complexity of a modern research university.[22] Zemsky and other RCM advocates belicve that it is a good, perhaps the best, way to stimulate revenue growth as called out in item three of the "seven budgeting goals" of table 5.2. Many others, including my colleagues at Stanford in the 1980s, have argued that RCM cedes too much of the central administration's ability to steer the institution.

Stanford adopted a variant of the one-line budget, which decentralizes decision-making responsibility for expenditures but not revenues. The central administration collects all general funds and distributes them to schools as judgmentally determined lump sums. In contrast, line-item allocation manages both revenues and expenditures centrally, as shown at the lower left of the figure. The three approaches can be combined as indicated by the "range of possibilities" shown in the triangle's interior. In a hybrid system, for example, some revenue streams are devolved by formulas and the remaining funds are distributed by a combination of one-line allocations (e.g., for major programs) and line-item budget entries.[23] I will assume a hybrid system in my illustrations from here on.

All three methods require the central administration to distribute at least some general funds to schools on the basis of judgment (i.e., through subventions, lump-sum allocations, or line-item budgets). They do differ in the *amount* of money that's allocated subjectively, however, and also in the degree to which expenditures are micromanaged by the central administration. One-line budgets give valuable spending discretion, but the central administration has few criteria for setting them other than last year's allocations adjusted for cost-rise. The same problem arises in RCM, but this doesn't matter so much because the (usually small) subventions are essentially "trim tabs" on a school's overall direction as determined by market forces. Line-item systems allocate everything judgmentally, but at the level of individual activities.

Line-item allocation is sometimes cited as an advantage in universities' efforts to improve productivity by stopping certain activities that are no longer a high priority: a process called "growth by substitution." Such systems provide at least two ways for allocators to impose such reductions as the "price" of funding for new activities. One way is to require each operating unit to offer up a list of items for possible elimination and then make selections from that list right along with the selections for funding increments. (This is a mild form of "zero-based budgeting" [ZBB] in that only a portion of the existing base is considered for defunding.) Another way is to apply a small across-the-board cut (1 percent, say) as a "haircut" to the existing base and then leave it up to the operating unit to decide on the needed savings. These tools are not directly available to the central administration in formula-based systems, but they can be applied by deans or others because all systems require line-item allocation somewhere in the organizational hierarchy. A central administration that cares about growth by substitution can require, as a matter of policy, that one tool or another be used in every line-item allocation exercise, regardless of level.

### Setting the Budget Limit

The allocation process itself starts with a budget limit, the maximum amount of money that can be used to fund the items that have been requested. The limit is based on the central university's target general funds operating margin (surplus or deficit, adjusted for any restricted funds that have been brought into the picture) after deducting all mandatory, formulaic, and discretionary expenses. Determining the proper target is a policy matter that depends on the assessment of future trends

| Table 5.4. The general funds allocation limit | | |
|---|---|---|
| | Base year | Proposed |
| Sources of funds | | |
|   Operating revenue | Data | Fcst |
|   Nonoperating income | Data | Fcst |
|   Total sources | Σ | Σ |
| Uses of funds | | |
|   Mandatory expenditures | Data | Fcst |
|   Contributions to the capital budget | Data | Input (policy) |
|   Entitlements | Data | Fcst |
|   Discretionary allocations | Data | Limit (residual) |
|   Margin | Data | Input (policy) |
| Total uses (= Total sources) | Σ | Σ |

and risks (discussed earlier) and any expected increase or decrease in restricted funds balances. The mechanics of making these margin calculations is not much different than the one used in for-profit businesses, but, of course, their purpose is to nourish the university's own operations rather than to distribute money to shareholders. These considerations generally require strong participation by the chief financial officer as well as the provost.

The tableau in table 5.4 is similar to one I use when helping universities redesign their budget processes. (Once again, some readers may wish to skim the details.) The two columns display the "base year" data (for the current year, included for comparison) and the values proposed for the following year. The first calculation, shown at the top of the table, totals up the anticipated sources of funds. (The Σ symbol in the tables means summation.) Then, the resulting uses of funds (which must equal the sources just calculated) are apportioned into the following five categories:

1. *Mandatory expenditures.* Items about which the university has little or no choice (e.g., debt service and the funding of pension plans and self-insurance reserves).
2. *Contributions to the capital budget.* Sums transferred to plant accounts to provide general funds support for capital projects (may represent "funded depreciation" but most institutions use other criteria).[24]
3. *Entitlements.* Sums due to lower-level operating units as the result of previous policy decisions. The most important entitlements for present

purposes are the distributions of revenue to schools under RCM formulas.

4. *Discretionary allocations.* Sums distributed to lower-level units on the basis of judgment (e.g., as line-item approvals, one-line allocations, and RCM subventions).

5. *Margin.* The surplus or deficit that adds to or subtracts from the university's general funds operating reserve.

Importantly, the proposed margin is entered as an input. The discretionary allocation is calculated as a residual once the other variables have been projected.

It's impossible to overemphasize that both the target margin and the tuition rate should be determined, on the basis of comprehensive financial plans, *before* the budget allocation process begins. Failure to do so invites a loss of financial discipline as manifested, for example, by excessive tuition increases or risk-taking. This discipline is critical for universities because the market forces that constrain price are weak and, unlike for publicly owned companies, there is no market-driven criterion for how much margin is enough. Failure to separate financial planning from resource allocation has helped drive universities to charge higher tuition rates than are socially optimal or prudent, and while borrowing covenants may put a floor under margins, for most universities these limits are well below the values that are truly prudent.

The most difficult part of budget management is apportioning the approved allocation limit among the various claimants for discretionary funds. A tableau to assist in this task is presented in table 5.5, and a worksheet to help make the trade-offs needed to populate the tableau is presented in table 5.6. The table has been designed with four principles in mind.

First, the sums needed for special purposes such as items 4 and 5 in table 5.2 need to be included. These funds are retained by the central administration and disbursed during the year as needed to achieve the programs' goals.

Second comes the need to focus on the share of general funds spending for academic units versus administrative and support units.[25] This breakdown has significant strategic consequences. It's important to track it explicitly because there is a tendency for administrative

**Table 5.5. The general fund allocation tableau**

|  | Allocations | | | | Contribution margins | |
|---|---|---|---|---|---|---|
| Allocation targets | GF Alloc. | Other | Restr'd | Total | Direct | Burdened |
| For special purposes | $\Sigma$ | $\Sigma$ | $\Sigma$ | $\Sigma$ | NA | NA |
|    Project funding | Input | Est. | Est. | $\Sigma$ | NA | NA |
|    Incentive pools | Input | Est. | Est. | $\Sigma$ | NA | NA |
| To academic units | $\Sigma$ | $\Sigma$ | $\Sigma$ | $\Sigma$ | $\Sigma$ | $\Sigma$ |
|    School A | Input | Est. | Est. | $\Sigma$ | Calc. | Calc. |
|    School B . . . etc. | Input | Est. | Est. | $\Sigma$ | Calc. | Calc. |
|    Other academic unit A . . . etc. | Input | Est. | Est. | $\Sigma$ | Calc. | Calc. |
| To admin. and support units | $\Sigma$ | $\Sigma$ | $\Sigma$ | $\Sigma$ | $\Sigma$ | $\Sigma$ |
|    Unit 1 | Input | Est. | Est. | $\Sigma$ | Calc. | NA |
|    Unit 2 . . . etc. | Input | Est. | Est. | $\Sigma$ | Calc. | NA |
| Campus consolidated | Calc. (control*) | $\Sigma$ | $\Sigma$ | $\Sigma$ | | $\Sigma$ |

*Must equal the allocation limit from table 5.4.

and support requirements to appear to budget-makers as more urgent than academic ones, thus producing an upward creep in their share of expenditures.

Third, as noted under all funds budgeting, it's important to manage general funds allocations in context of estimated usage of other sources. ("Other" includes the entitlements of table 5.4 as an important element.) The fact that the latter figures must be estimated rather than determined with certainty at this stage of the analysis does not detract from this principle.

The final principle is that the operating units' projected general fund contribution margins need to be considered when making the allocations. Positive margins indicate receipt of cross subsidies and negative ones indicate units that are net donors. The right-hand panel of table 5.5 contains the margin information. The "direct" column displays the general fund revenues attributable to the unit (whether supplied to it as an entitlement or not) minus the sum of entitlements and allocations. The "burdened" column allocates administrative and support costs to the academic units in accordance with standard accounting principles. (Burdens for the administrative and support unit source are calculated using the so-called "step-down procedure" that is familiar to users of OMB circular A-21.) Chapter 4 described the main calculations and, also, the

| Table 5.6. Allocation worksheet for one-line and line-item budgeting | | | | |
|---|---|---|---|---|
| Units and items | Amount requested | Gen. fund allocation | Other funding | Not funded |
| Organizational unit A | Σ | Σ | Σ | Σ |
|    Program 1 | Data | Input | Input | Calc. |
|    Program 2 . . . etc. | Data | Input | Input | Calc. |
|    Line item 1 | Data | Input | Input | Calc. |
|    Line item 2 . . . etc. | Data | Input | Input | Calc. |
| Organizational unit B . . . etc. | Σ | Σ | Σ | Σ |
|    Program 1 | Data | Input | Input | Calc. |
|    Program 2 . . . etc. | Data | Input | Input | Calc. |
|    Line item 1 | Data | Input | Input | Calc. |
|    Line item 2 . . . etc. | Data | Input | Input | Calc. |

situations in which direct and burdened margins should be used. How margin and mission come together to determine the amount of cross-subsidy to be provided to each academic unit was described chapter 1.

The subtotals in table 5.5 for allocations to special purposes, academic units, and administrative and support units play an important role in some institutions' planning. For example, a school may wish to limit expenditures for administrative and support units to a preset percentage of the total budget. This approach speaks to the concerns voiced by many faculty members that "administrative and support costs are out of control," which AGB's Barbara Taylor and I addressed in *Strategic Indicators for Higher Education*.[26]

The worksheet represented by table 5.6 aggregates the allocations to individual funding requests in one-line and line-item budgeting. (Such requests usually are not part of RCM systems, so the subventions are entered as lump sums.) The requests may be for program support, individual line items of expenditure, or a combination of the two. By "program," I mean a bundle of line items that relate to one another in service of some articulated mission objective. University strategic planning processes often identify major program initiatives, which then are carried forward into the annual budget processes. Program descriptions often include a revenue component, and it's important that the margins be net of expected revenues. In contrast, line items typically stand on their own; they are viewed as furthering the unit's general education, research, or support objectives and do not have specifically associated revenues. I think the trend in universities is moving in the direction of program-related planning and budgeting, but line-item budgeting remains appropriate for many purposes.

The worksheet has a separate line for each request, with the first column being the amount of general funds being requested by the unit head ("data"). The remaining three columns show whether the requests will be funded centrally, through an agreed usage of restricted and other funding, or not funded. (The first two are inputs, and the last is a calculated residual.) The general funds figures should be posted to the "input" cells of table 5.5 (e.g., through the use of linked spreadsheets or as part of an integrated decision-support system). Immediate posting ensures that the allocation limit is not exceeded. The worksheet can be used for administrative and support as well as academic units, because even the former may be able to tap restricted funds or reserves in some cases.

Many of the concepts presented here have been applied by one institution or another, but to my knowledge they have not been put together into a seamless software application.[27] Growing experience levels, data availability, computing power, and software development capacity will change that sooner or later.

## A Model for Balancing Mission and Margin

We now come to the crux of the traditional university's resource allocation problem: apportioning scarce general funds among the plethora of requests in a way that balances contribution to the institution's mission with contribution to margin. These decisions pit the advocates of mission enhancement against the guardians of financial prudence. They require the comparison of basically incommensurate variables—because mission assessments are inherently subjective, and margin is inherently quantitative. The resulting tension between mission and margin spawns confusion and conflict in university budgeting—thus the need for new tools and concepts. The problem exists in all universities, regardless of their budgeting styles. It exists even in RCM, the most formula-based type of budgeting, because somewhere in the organization people must allocate pots of money to particular activities.

I'll begin by addressing the mission-money problem in practical terms. The "basic trade-off model," to be presented first, is easily applied in any college or university. I then embed the basic method in a full-scale decision support model that, though not for the faint of heart analytically, adds substantial power to the analysis. I call this the "mission-margin trade-off model."

### The Basic Trade-Off Model

Remember what it was like as a child to walk into a penny candy store with a dollar bill in your pocket and an insatiable longing for all you saw? All the items looked good, but some looked better than others. Each had a different price, and your dollar would only go so far. It's all very complicated, but that's what it's like to set the budget in a traditional university. Worse, in a university there are always people (e.g., deans) who urge you to accept their proposals and proclaim dire consequences if you fail to do so.

Let's take a moment to formalize the situation. There is a list of potential items ("alternatives"), each of which has a priority (your preference) and a financial consequence (the acquisition price). You have a budget limit (that dollar bill). Your problem is to choose a set of items that will satisfy your preferences to the greatest extent possible given the budget limit. You might attempt this by grabbing whatever seems best at the moment until the proprietor says you're out of money, but surely there are better ways.

What's needed is to balance the benefits of the various alternatives against their costs in what's called a "trade-off analysis." The sidebar (opposite) describes the basic method for making the trade-offs. The procedure may exceed the grasp of that child in the candy store but surely not the capacity of a skilled university budgeter. (I apply the method to a real-world budgeting problem shortly.) The approach does more than improve one's ability to make selections; it has a good claim to be the best that can be devised without stretching the bounds of practicality.

The essential strategy is to "divide and conquer": that is, to break the problem into bite-sized pieces and make judgments about the pieces instead of the whole. The heavily academic judgments about priorities occur in step 2, unencumbered by money issues. Trading the priorities off against money takes place in step 5, where judgment is applied to only the shortlisted items. The other steps are clerical or require only objective reasoning.

> ## The Basic Trade-Off Model in a Nutshell
>
> 1. List the alternatives if you haven't done so already.
> 2. Rank order the alternatives in terms of their priorities without regard to their monetary consequences.
> 3. Enter the money data (prices or margins) into the list.
> 4. Identify the short list of affordable alternatives that are both more preferred and less costly than any others.
> 5. Choose the one item on the short list that you like the most—now considering money as well as preference.
> 6. Deduct the cost from your running total of available funds.
> 7. Repeat steps 4–6 until you have exhausted your budget.

Ignoring money when making the initial priority judgments and then focusing on only a small number of items when the time comes to consider priorities and money together are what make the method practical. The key fact is that *all the relevant alternatives, and only the relevant alternatives*, are considered at each stage of the trade-off process. ("Relevance" is deduced using the so-called "principle of dominance"—to be described shortly.) The many items that are irrelevant at this stage can be ignored for the moment, which represents a huge savings of cognitive effort. Other approaches to simplification, such as choosing items in order of preference, ignore the possibility that a high ranking but expensive item will preempt multiple lower-ranked but cheaper ones that, in the aggregate, would produce a better outcome.

### Budget Alternatives and Their Attributes

The mission-margin trade-off model is fundamentally similar to the penny-candy example, but there are three important differences: (i) the varied character of the alternatives being considered, (ii) use of margin (not simply cost) as the metric for monetary consequence, and (iii) the possibility that some alternatives are attractive not because of their intrinsic value, but because they promise to make lots of money for the institution. Each requires amending a particular step of the basic method. The amendments are minor in principle but of significant importance in practice. I believe that they cover all the special cases that are likely to arise in traditional-university budgeting.

An alternative may represent the addition of a single line item or it may be a collection of items bundled together to form a program. Examples of line items and programs include a new faculty or staff position, or the creation of a new degree program or research center. My proposed method places no limit on the number of alternatives, and programs can be intermixed freely with line items in the list of budget proposals.

Proposals that involve a continuum of values (e.g., the number of new dollars to be spent on financial aid) should be divided into discrete sub-proposals before being entered into the list of alternatives (step 1). The first tranche of financial aid might be $500,000, for example, and this could be followed by additional tranches of varying size. Each tranche has its own margin and each is ranked separately in comparison with the other budget requests, but otherwise the basic method is not affected. Some proposals must enter the budget in a particular order: for example, as when the first tranche of a given activity must be funded before subsequent tranches can be considered. Such requirements are handled by amending step 4 to read: "Identify the short list of affordable alternatives that are both preferred to and less costly than any others, and meet all applicable precedence constraints."

Finally, certain alternatives may involve budget reductions as opposed to additions. The need for such reductions and the means of generating downsizing proposals have been discussed elsewhere. Step 6 can handle such "growth by substitution" by augmenting the running total of available funds with savings achieved by the reduction.

Preferences represent more than the decision-maker's personal feelings. They are tied to the institutional value proposition that was introduced in chapter 2: what in this chapter I am calling "mission." (Henceforth, I'll refer to these values as "contributions to mission.") The ranking process (step 2) can be anchored to criteria that were, or at least should have been, discussed extensively before the onset of budgeting. Furthermore, a well-managed university will have developed metrics for gauging performance in relation to various mission elements. Such metrics can stimulate focused thought even when they are less than comprehensive or precise.

The set of ranks is tangible despite being based on highly subjective judgments. Arguments will proliferate, of course, but the discipline of ranking can help prevent the discussion from becoming chaotic. One can declare the rankings of certain proposals to be tied, but doing this too many times limits the power of the analysis. (Ties are accommodated by amending step 4 to say "not less preferred.") The ranking process may appear daunting at first, but this is what decision-makers must do anyway at an intuitive level. What the new method does is make the priority-setting process explicit and thus subject to more thoughtful analysis and review.

Ranking can be done in many ways, but perhaps the easiest approach is to: (i) array the proposals on a spreadsheet or as cards on a tabletop; (ii) organize them into coarse subgroups based on priority in relation to mission; (iii) sort within the subgroups; and (iv) reslot the packages among the subgroups until the ranker is comfortable with the overall list. Members of the budgeting team might be requested to do the ranking separately and then come together in a group session to reconcile differences. This is a variation on the so-called Delphi method of judgmental evaluation, which was developed to pool subjective data in forecasting and decision-making.[28]

Some programs may be disliked in absolute terms yet deemed worthy of consideration because they make money that can be used for other purposes. For example, a routine training or testing program performed for a certain company might not reach the normal threshold of academic desirability, but, being lucrative, the university might view it as preferable to downsizing. Such considerations necessitate a slight amendment in step 7 of the basic trade-off procedure, the so-called "stopping rule," as will be described later.

There is a profound difference between the ranking of preferences and the kind of thinking that takes place in for-profit resource allocation. The most difficult for-profit judgments pertain to the marketplace: how customers will react to the company's product or service. They are rooted in the user value function of chapter 2. Universities also make market-oriented judgments, but they relate to resource generation rather than the university's objectives per se. It's very important that preference rankings be based on the institutional value proposition and not the user one. In my experience, it's usually the program's proposers who evaluate market demand—after which higher-level decision-makers judge its contribution to the university's objectives. This division of labor cannot be hard and fast, but the distinction is useful as a hedge against confounding institutional and market-based value.

University budgeters should use margin as their measure of monetary consequence to cater to proposals that are expected to make money (i.e., to produce a positive margin). Proposals without revenue, or where cost exceeds revenue, show up as having negative margins. The existence of positive as well as negative margins poses no problem for the selection procedure. One simply amends step 6 to augment the running total of available funds by the amount of any positive margin. The initial available funds figure equals the budget limit (i.e., the total amount of money to be allocated). Negative margins count against the budget limit and positive ones offset it. How to set the limit was addressed earlier in this chapter.

Margin calculations generally should not include overhead allocations unless care is taken to use only the portion of overhead that varies with changes in activity (in which case the support service budgets should be adjusted accordingly). Where overheads are not differentiated as fixed versus variable, it is best to exclude their allocation entirely—except, perhaps, in "self-financing" activities that are supposed to be run like independent businesses. This is because the budget limit is expressed in terms of incremental net costs and not fully loaded ones.

Financial consequences may vary over time. I've been treating "margin" as a static concept, which works fine for activities and programs that are in a more or less steady state (i.e., where costs and revenues are not expected to change except for normal inflationary factors). These represent the vast majority of budget alternatives but by no means all of them. For example, newly launched programs typically are characterized by large losses at the beginning and smaller losses or even surpluses later. Comparing only the first-year margins (often quite negative) with the expected mission contributions would bias decisions against innovation.

The standard method of evaluating time-varying margins is to discount them back to present values, but that won't work here because the budget limit is based on current cash flow rather than the present value of future cash flows. Hence the use of discounted margin is limited to situations, such as those in certain support service areas, where projects stand on their own financially and mission contribution is not a factor. Appendix F describes what I consider to be a more appropriate approach for handling margins that are expected to vary over time.

Table 5.7 provides a hypothetical yet realistic dataset for illustrating the trade-off procedure. The items are listed in order of their rank (one is best), which is shown in the left-hand column. Shorthand descriptions of the activities appear next, followed by any precedence requirements (e.g., the item ranked twenty-fifth cannot enter the budget before the one ranked fifteenth has been funded). The estimated margins, expressed in thousands of dollars, are shown in the right-hand column. As mentioned previously, negative margins indicate losses and positive ones indicate profits. The budget limit of $6,500,000, shown as "($6,500) thousand," appears at the bottom of the "margin" column.

### Dominance, Affordability, and Sufficiency

A glance at table 5.7 confirms the need to narrow the range of judgment required at each stage of the decision-making process. Psychologist George Miller claimed that "humans can hold seven items in short-term memory, plus or minus two,"[29] and even this, the simplest of datasets, has many more line items than that. It's impossible to juggle more than a few elements at the same time, so some systematic rules are needed. The rules appear at steps 4 and 5 of the basic trade-off procedure. They require one to identify the dominant and affordable alternatives to be short-listed for selection, and eventually to decide when to end the process.

One alternative dominates another if it is both preferred and less costly. Plotting the points in a scatter diagram with rank on the vertical axis and margin on the horizontal axis makes the dominance relation easy to see. Figure 5.7 shows the five highest-ranked alternatives from table 5.7. Item 2, with its margin of +$150, dominates items 3 and 4, which have losses of −$4,000 and −$2,500, but not items 1 and 5. The general rule is that an alternative is dominant if the quadrant to the northeast of it is empty. If two items are tied in terms of ranking, the one with the better margin dominates. If two items are tied in terms of ranking, the one with the better margin dominates.

Affordability is determined by comparing the alternatives' margins with the running budget limit. For example, item 1's margin (−$6,984) exceeds the original budget limit (−$6,500); thus, though dominant, it

| Rank | Budget proposal | Precedence | Margin ($000) |
|---|---|---|---|
| 1 | Reduce both teaching loads and adjunct usage | | (6,984) |
| 2 | Eliminate a faculty position in geology | | 150 |
| 3 | * | | (4,000) |
| 4 | Increase financial aid: increment 1 | | (2,500) |
| 5 | * | | 1,000 |
| 6 | Reduce faculty teaching loads | | (6,182) |
| 7 | * | | 0 |
| 8 | Reduce the use of adjuncts | | (2,061) |
| 9 | * | | 15 |
| 10 | * | | (1,050) |
| 11 | Increase financial aid: increment 2 | | (2,500) |
| 12 | * | | (750) |
| 13 | Create a social science research center | | (501) |
| 14 | * | | (3,000) |
| 15 | Software certification training: increment 1 | | 150 |
| 16 | Downsize the Ancient Languages program | | 1,450 |
| 17 | * | | (50) |
| 18 | Add a master's degree in financial management | | 3,065 |
| 19 | Add a faculty position in economics | | (280) |
| 20 | * | | (5,000) |
| 21 | Reduce undergraduate student body | | (3,120) |
| 22 | * | | 61 |
| 23 | Build a fitness facility | | (1,500) |
| 24 | * | | 0 |
| 25 | Software certification training: increment 2 | Item 15 | 500 |
| 26 | Lease unused portions of university buildings | | 1,000 |
| | Budget limit | | (6,500) |

Table 5.7. Hypothetical budget data

*The names of these proposals are not relevant to the illustration.

is not initially affordable. The result is a shortlist consisting of items 2 and 5. Points 3 and 4 are dominated, and item 1 is not affordable. Notice that shortlist determination requires only clerical operations and that the affordability calculation need only be performed for dominant alternatives.

The result of shortlisting is that the user need only chose between items 2 and 5. The decision is purely judgmental, but, as noted earlier, one need only think about the shortlisted items. Once a choice has been made, the dominance and affordability rules are reapplied with the chosen item excluded from consideration and the budget limit updated. This process repeats until one of two sufficiency conditions is satisfied:

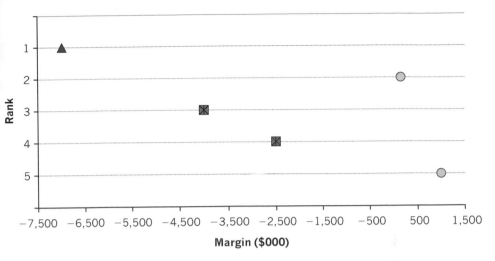

**Figure 5.7.** Dominance and affordability for alternatives 1–5

1. The running total of available funds is drawn down to zero or
2. The remaining alternatives are so unpalatable that they're judged to be not worth doing.

As is explained later on, the second possibility arises only for alternatives that have positive margins. These could have been chosen before stopping, but they weren't. Now, at the end of the analysis, it has become apparent that the profit to be made from the alternatives is not sufficient to overcome their intrinsic undesirability. How do we know these items are intrinsically undesirable? The answer may sound circular, but it isn't. The user has "revealed" a preference not to fund the item despite its positive margin, which can only happen if its contribution to mission is judged to be negative. Reaching this point, or simply exhausting the budget limit, signals "sufficiency" (i.e., that the choice process has been completed).

*An Interactive Trade-Off App*

University budgeting usually involves a group of senior leaders—headed by, say, the provost or dean—sitting together to review the proposed alternatives that already have been vetted by staff for basic acceptability, technical accuracy, and market viability. The group proceeds down the list of items, comparing them and looping back as needed. Some items may be accepted quickly and others rejected, but a large "swim" group will remain. This process requires many iterations and may extend over multiple meetings, which makes it hard to maintain consistency. Too often closure is reached because it must be (i.e., a budget must be produced) rather than from a sense of mastery.

The mission-margin trade-off model was designed for use in such situations. But how? The fact that the model is systematic, some might say tedious, is both a help and a hindrance: a help because it focuses thought and a hindrance because its mechanics may in some cases impede the conversation. Imagine, however, that the process's clerical elements have been programmed into a simple app that can be used during the budget meetings.[30] How would this work?

The first step would be to display the budget data graphically in the form of an "options chart" that can be projected and discussed at the budget meeting. Figure 5.8 extends the scatter diagram presented earlier to include all the alternatives in table 5.7. The dominant-and-shortlisted alternatives are represented by squares, the dominant-but-unaffordable one by a triangle, and all the others by boxed stars. Looking at the mission-margin trade-offs this way elicits more fruitful discussion than simply scanning up and down the list of alternatives. It may be impossible to project the whole diagram at once when there are many alternatives, but the app can be designed to allow navigation and enlargement—just like a Google map. Having such a display allows the budget group to focus on the dominant and affordable alternatives, knowing that the other alternatives will come up for consideration in due course.

But wait, there's more. Imagine that the group decides to select a certain alternative (e.g., the item ranked second) and now wants to move forward. The person operating the app double-clicks on the selected item, which posts that item to the tentative list of funded alternatives, recalculates the dominance relations, and updates the running total of available funds. The group now focuses on the new short list of items, and the process proceeds until one of the two aforementioned stopping conditions is met: (i) none of the remaining alternatives is affordable given the budget limit or (ii) none of the remaining affordable alternatives is judged to be desirable. The first condition is signaled when all

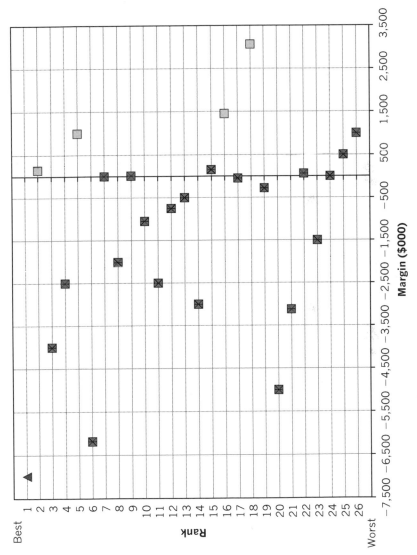

**Figure 5.8.** Options chart at the start of the trade-off analysis

the undominated items show up as triangles (which means none can be selected) and the second was discussed earlier. The app has pushed the mechanics of the trade-off process into the background, which allows judgments about costs in relation to benefits to be made without distraction. This saves a great deal of time; most importantly, it's likely to produce a budget that is more closely aligned with the university's institutional value proposition as seen by the participants.

Figure 5.9 shows one possible result of the iterative process. The fifteen filled circles depict alternatives that have been selected for inclusion in the budget, and the three alternatives depicted as triangles are unaffordable. The alternatives that are depicted as boxed squares are dominated by others and thus are not eligible for selection. The three depicted as squares have been judged to be "undesirable" in the sense of the second condition discussed earlier. This means that their contribution to the user value proposition has to be negative, because otherwise there would have been no reason not to select them.

Why, then, were the items with negative value contributions put on the original list of potential alternatives? The answer comes in two parts: (i) the alternative is not so bad as to defy consideration, and (ii) it can make money that might be used to fund other alternatives. (Indeed, the fact that the values are negative does not show up in the ranking process and thus is not really known until the end of the selection process.) This result harks back to the so-called "love-money" relationship of chapter 1, where I described how every decision in a market-based not-for-profit represents a combination of intrinsic and pecuniary value— where the latter can be either a net cost or a net profit. What we see in figure 5.9 are three alternatives for which net profit is not sufficient to offset their negative contribution to the mission.

### Mathematical Extensions

Using the trade-off app requires nothing more than common sense, but this does not exhaust the mission-margin model's potential. Applying mathematical analysis to quantify the trade-off relations that were reported in figure 5.9, and using the results in an optimization model, can achieve greater power. I'll summarize the extensions briefly, with details being presented in appendix G. What follows may be challenging

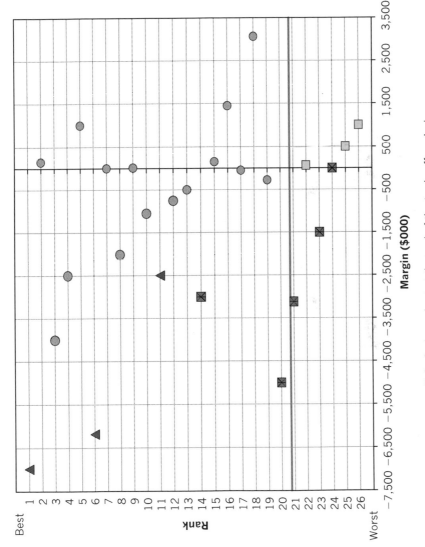

**Figure 5.9.** Options chart at the end of the trade-off analysis

analytically, but even scanning the material may provide some useful insight about what's involved.

An additional motivation for the extended model is to solve a problem with the trade-off app that some readers already may have identified: that changing the budget limit or any part of the options chart requires the process to be redone from the stage where the change first takes effect. This is because revising any selection will change the dominance and affordability calculations from that point forward. It's true that making selections will get easier with practice, but busy budgeters will become impatient with repeating the same task multiple times. The extended model allows one to change almost anything and then redo the analysis with the push of a button.

The model calculates the so-called "frontier curve" shown in figure 5.10. Appendix G describes how the curve is determined from the set of data points depicted by the large icons in the figure. (These are the points that were on the cusp of being selected in the original trade-off analysis.) Once determined, the curve can be used to calculate mission contribution as a mathematical function of rank. I have scaled the function so that calculated contribution (on the upper horizontal axis of the figure) equals the negative of margin ("−Margin"), which is consistent with the "decision rule" equations in chapter 1 and appendix G, and also have set the "zero value" point at the breakeven margin—both operations being permitted by the model's mathematics. All points lying to the right of the frontier curve have been included in the budget, and those to the left of the curve have not. This is consistent with the notion that an alternative for which mission contribution exceeds cost should be selected and vice versa.

The frontier curve is not changed by modifications to the list of alternatives or their margins, provided that the budget remains unchanged and the original analysis continues to reflect a valid interpretation of the institutional value proposition, given the information available when the analysis was performed. What this means is that the frontier curve can be used to inform judgments about a revised list of alternatives, ranks, and margins—which greatly simplifies the reanalysis. This eases the decision-maker's task when alternatives are added to or subtracted from the options chart, or when their margins are changed. To subtract an alternative, one simply removes it from the

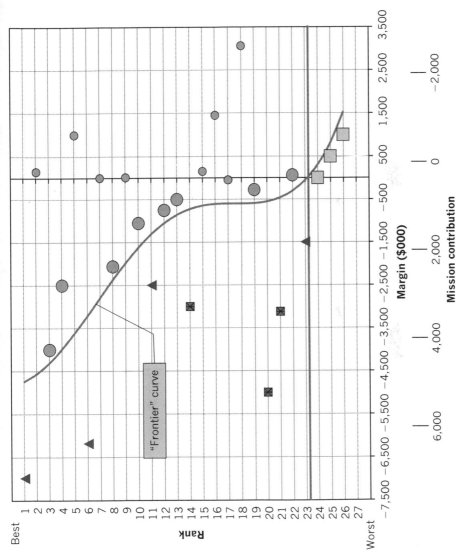

**Figure 5.10.** The frontier curve

dataset. To add an alternative, one simply judges its rank relative to the alternatives already present (e.g., "it's between alternatives 3 and 4 but considerably closer to 4," in which case 3.75 might be used). Changing an alternative's margin involves nothing more than entering the new figure into the dataset. The new margin data can be used to determine whether an alternative lies to the left or to the right of the frontier curve.

While useful, the aforementioned result does not completely determine which alternatives in the revised dataset should be chosen. This is because, by itself, position relative to the frontier curve does not take account of the budget limit. It's entirely possible that selecting all of the points in the revised dataset that lie to the right of the frontier curve would overspend the budget. One solution is simply to go back to the trade-off app, this time armed with the knowledge that points far to the northwest of the frontier curve are very likely to be in the final budget and thus can be selected without a great deal of thought. (*This solution is valid only for the original budget limit.* The case of a revised budget is addressed in the next paragraph.) One can concentrate on the points near the curve, which produces big savings in time and effort.

The frontier curve also enables the construction of an "optimization app" for finding the set of alternatives that produces the largest possible mission contribution given any specified budget limit. The procedure maximizes the sum of the chosen alternatives' mission contributions subject to the available funds. Optimization is faster and more powerful than the dominance-based trade-off analysis (it also is more demanding analytically), and it is impervious to the "constant budget limit" requirement that applied to the previous paragraph. Readers are referred to appendix G for a description of the procedure and how to use it.

The optimization app can be used to demonstrate chapter 1's assertion that a traditional university's ability to support money-losing programs—to exert its values over those of the marketplace—is directly proportional to its degree of budget flexibility. (Again, see appendix G.) What happens is that increasing budget flexibility rotates the frontier curve counterclockwise until it coincides with the horizontal axis in figure 5.10. This means that only alternatives with positive mission contributions get selected, which is equivalent to having no budget limit. Conversely, tighter and tighter budgets rotate the curve clockwise until it coincides with the vertical axis: the line depicting zero margin. This means that only items with positive margins can be selected, which is equivalent to profit maximization.

# Conclusion

The goal of this book has been to share my ideas about how traditional universities work, why their strengths are so important, what needs to be changed, and how the changes can be accomplished. I've tried to combine "soft" insights based on informed observation and experience with "hard" analytics based on microeconomics and management science. Hopefully, the result has been a roadmap for the way forward and guidelines for how to proceed at each stage. My approach recognizes institutions' need to chart their own courses, thus honoring the dictum of respected higher education insider Ellen Chaffee: "We don't need a bunch of solutions from outsiders; we need a bunch of tools for people to find their own solutions."[1] If this book stimulates deep conversations and serious tryouts, I will end my career on a happy note.

Let's reflect briefly on the key messages of the book's five chapters. I'll summarize the key material in each chapter and then list what I consider to be the overarching takeaways—the "metaconclusions," so to speak. I view these as "elevator speeches," short snippets that can be recounted during the time it takes to get from the ground floor lobby to one's office.

Chapter 1, "Understanding the Traditional University," started with a brief review of the problems and opportunities faced by traditional universities. The problems include massive market failures, loss of political confidence, clear and present threats by disruptive innovators such as for-profits and MOOC providers, and insufficient responses to these problems by senior administrators, board members, and faculty. Yet there are grounds for optimism. Most faculty do care sincerely about their responsibilities as teachers to help students learn, for example, and faculty principal investigators have demonstrated their ability to manage costs. The advantages offered by traditional universities, which make reform efforts immensely worthwhile, include on-campus learning, faculty resources, research and scholarship, and the not-for-profit organizational form—all of which could be undermined if the traditional university loses its relevance and is replaced with, say, mostly industrial-style institutions that operate mainly online.

> *Given the right concepts and tools, faculty and administrators can make great progress on reengineering in a relatively short period of time. It is vitally important that they do so.*

The chapter goes on to describe why universities do what they do: the principles by which not-for-profit universities should, and often do, set their priorities. This was followed by a discussion of the principles' implications for tuition policy and cost containment. The chapter ended by considering the two kinds of "value propositions" that most universities live by: the intrinsic values that underpin their missions and the instrumental values that drive their appeals to the marketplace.

> *There are good reasons why not-for-profit entities behave differently than for-profit ones. While some of the implications are problematic, reformers should take care not to compromise the pursuit of mission-related values in a rush to make institutions responsive to the marketplace and bottom line.*

Chapter 2, "The Reengineering Challenge," took up the "what" and "how" of reengineering. It began by examining some important flaws in the academic business model that need to be corrected. Overdecentralization of teaching activity perpetuates fragmentation and less-than-effective pedagogy, and unmonitored joint production can slowly shift the emphasis to research and scholarship—which makes it harder to improve teaching. The faculty's tendency to dissociate quality from cost means that cost containment is "someone else's problem," which further inhibits innovation. Additionally, the lack of good learning metrics means faculty get insufficient feedback on the effects of new teaching approaches. This leads to an overreliance on market forces (themselves uninformed by good data on learning), which in turn has triggered an arms race in prestige and student amenities.

*The academic business model is not perfect. It harbors flaws that make it increasingly difficult for traditional universities to fulfill their missions and fend off political and public criticism. The goal of reengineering is to investigate and correct these flaws.*

Doing the job will require multiple initiatives in each of three classes: teaching and learning improvement, activity and cost analysis, and comprehensive budget modeling. I described how to combine the initiatives into an affordable "reengineering portfolio" that allows an institution to manage its evolution in an orderly way and exploit the synergies among them. This led to consideration of how innovations get adopted, the importance of pilot projects, and the concepts of an improvement cycle and capability maturity metrics.

*Reengineering can be approached strategically by developing a portfolio of initiatives that span the three classes listed previously, following demonstrable good practice in getting them implemented, and monitoring the degree to which they have become embedded in university operations.*

The chapter ended by emphasizing the responsibilities of senior university leaders, starting with the president and provost. These leaders must both "talk the talk" and "walk the walk"—not allowing their many other challenges and responsibilities to drive reengineering from the institution's agenda. Governing boards should play a proactive role in seeing to it that this responsibility is discharged. In addition, oversight bodies such as accreditors and state agencies should monitor and, where necessary, stimulate progress.

*Senior university leaders bear ultimate responsibility for the reengineering strategy. Governing and oversight boards should take the steps needed to ensure that reengineering receives its needed high priority.*

Chapter 3, "The New Scholarship of Teaching," addressed the all-important matter of teaching effectiveness. Once again, we started with conceptual underpinnings: Kaizen (continuous improvement), systems thinking, service science, and learning science. These and similar concepts broaden and modernize Ernest Boyer's scholarship of teaching. It's becoming clear that boosting the quality of teaching means using the

# JOHNS HOPKINS

**Johns Hopkins University Press**
2715 N. Charles Street
Baltimore MD 21218
**www.press.jhu.edu**

*Now in paperback*

REENGINEERING THE UNIVERSITY
How to Be Mission Centered, Market Smart, and Margin
Conscious

William F. Massy

978-1-4214-2274-9     $29.95 paperback

broadened scholarship, and, therefore, that doctoral programs in every field concerned with undergraduate education should bring it into their curricula. This discussion was followed by three illustrative applications: course redesign as practiced by the National Center for Academic Transformation and a good many individual institutions, the Science Education Initiative at the Universities of Colorado and British Columbia, and the Open Learning Initiative at Carnegie Mellon University. Next came new proposals for the creation of departmental teaching improvement portfolios and the development of generally accepted learning assessment principles, which are intended to accelerate progress on teaching improvement.

*Effective programs for teaching improvement require a significantly broadened scholarship of teaching. Universities that don't embrace the scholarship and propagate it across their campuses will not be able to transform teaching to the extent needed to fulfill their missions and maintain competitiveness.*

The chapter ended by describing how universities can organize for teaching improvement by developing a program of "academic quality work" (AQW), a suite of activities that has proven to be effective in the United States and overseas. AQW systematizes the institution's approach to quality instead of leaving it mainly to self-initiated and self-monitored individual initiative. It extends beyond curriculum to include learning objectives, teaching methods, learning assessment, and quality assurance—all of which are necessary to sustain effective teaching and learning. Organizing to accomplish these tasks systematically is the best way to counteract the tendency for other activities (especially research and scholarship) to crowd out educational quality improvement.

*Universities need to organize systematically to apply the new scholarship of teaching at a scale that is sufficient to get the results they need. There is a practical method for doing this that has proven to be effective.*

Chapter 4, "The Cost of Teaching," addressed the problem of cost escalation and what can be done to contain it—without sacrificing quality, if at all possible. I started by showing why a number of widely used cost metrics are not helpful for tracking and comparing costs as well as why they may, in fact, do more harm than good. There is one approach to cost measurement that does work, however: activity-based costing (ABC). It looks at the structure of teaching activities with an eye for understanding both cost and quality rather than simply aggregate cost statistics. I described how ABC works at the course level (where it is an integral part of course redesign) and contrasted it with traditional top-down costing methods. (Full details of course-based ABC are provided in appendix B.) Next came consideration of four "design levels" that are important for thinking about the cost and quality of teaching. The "nano" and "micro" levels, which focus on individual learning activities and single courses, respectively, were discussed extensively in chapter 3. The "mezzanine" level focuses on groups of courses, and the "macro" level focuses on portfolios of courses for various degree programs. Applying ABC at these higher levels offers significant new opportunities for quality-conscious cost containment.

*Activity-based costing (ABC), the methodology used in course redesign, offers the best approach for campus-wide, quality-conscious cost measurement and cost containment. It avoids the serious problems associated with ratios, such as cost per credit hour, and opens the way to better design of course portfolios for departments and degree programs.*

The largest section of the chapter described my research on how to use university transactions data in a "course-based activity and cost model"—a faculty-friendly model with demonstrated usefulness for academic decision-making as well as financial analysis. The model combines timetabling and student registration data with general ledger, HR, and facilities data to model teaching activities and cost on a "bottom-up" basis. All the data obtainable from ratios such as cost per credit hour, and much more, can be calculated as by-products for any level in the organization. The discussion ended with consideration of how the course-based model can be deployed campus-wide, quickly and at relatively low cost, and how it can be used in departmental planning, degree program and student segmentation analysis, and university budgeting.

*It is now practical to deploy campus-wide course-based ABC models that provide enough detail about teaching activities, resource utiliza-*

*tion, and cost to make the trade-offs needed for quality-conscious cost containment. These models also provide a needed platform for bench-marking and course redesign.*

Chapter 5, "Financial Planning and Budgeting," extended our discussion from teaching activity and cost modeling at the departmental and degree-program level to include revenues, costs, and margins for the campus as a whole. It began by describing ways to envision university information at the central and operating-unit levels through the use of multiple data views, dashboards, and navigation. Next came discussions of "coherent financial planning" (including new strategies for program investment, financial sustainability, and risk) and "coherent resource allocation" (all funds budgeting, separating tuition decisions from spending allocations, and setting the budget limit). Most of the ideas have been applied piecemeal in one university or another, and the time has come to use the power of IT to bring everything together.

*Resource allocation in traditional universities will be greatly improved by deploying integrated financial planning and budgeting models that use state-of-the-art concepts and methods. Such improvements are badly needed given today's stringent financial environment and the prospects of increasing competition in the marketplace and for public funding.*

The chapter's final section presents a logically grounded model I have developed for "trading off" the subjective priorities of mission against numerically defined margins. The model implements the principles of resource allocation in not-for-profit entities that I introduced in chapter 1. This question has been the subject of much misunderstanding. Many people within the academy seem to believe that mission should trump margins ("We simply must do this thing, regardless of the cost"), while many others worry about financial viability and sustainability. Among other things, the new model provides insight about the cases in which mission should rule and, in any case, what the impact of "doing this thing" on other outcomes will be. It provides clear descriptions of how to make the trade-offs. A simple graphical version (possibly supplemented by a simple app) can be used to inform judgments at any budget level in any college or university, or else universities with management science capability can construct a more powerful mathematical version.

> *How to combine the incommensurates of mission and margin is a core problem of traditional university budgeting. A new model offers practical guidance for how to make these trade-offs. Universities that use the principles represented by the model, or implement the model itself, will save time and effort and make better resource allocation decisions than those that don't—which has important implications for being "mission centered, market smart, and margin conscious."*

The book's overarching argument is that traditional universities need to reform themselves to meet the economic, competitive, technological, and political challenges of the twenty-first century, and that this needs to be done in a way that preserves their most precious assets and sustains their essential values. That is what I mean by "reengineering the university."

I am pleased to report that some significant progress is being made as this book goes to press. The University of California's Riverside campus has embarked on a trial of the activity and cost model presented in chapter 4—and there is an expectation that the model will be extended to other UC campuses if the trial is successful. In addition to the direct benefits expected from this action, adoption of the model shows promise of defusing what has been an uncomfortable standoff between the university and the governor over cost-driven increments to tuition. The ramifications have yet to play out, but the experience appears to confirm the proposition that focusing on relevant facts can sometimes resolve thorny political issues.

The Lumina Foundation's proposed "Traditional Higher Education Model Redesign Challenge" represents another development. The Foundation has engaged the Education Design Lab of Washington, DC, to help guide its future grant-making by "articulating opportunities for traditional model reinvention" through the use of "design thinking" and "design-build strategies."[2] The Studio Design Team meeting held in Washington on June 24 and 25, 2015, brought together a group of innovators and consultants with track records of success in implementing the kinds of ideas presented in this book. I participated in the meeting and found the discussion to be intensely interesting and reinforcing.

It seems fitting to close this conclusion by recounting my good friend Dean Hubbard's philosophy about how to change a university. He began his twenty-five-year presidency of Northwest Missouri State University at a time when it urgently needed to do the kinds of things described in this book. Dean proposed numerous reforms, but an entrenched faculty rejected most of them. Indeed, the faculty senate enacted a vote of no confidence early in his tenure. All this had passed and change was in full swing by the time I conducted interviews at the university. The senate chair described what had happened: "Dean is very persistent," he said. "We learned eventually that, while he certainly listened to us, he wouldn't take 'no' for an answer unless he agreed that 'no' was truly justified. He would just keep coming back—with a smile and new facts or arguments—until he finally wore us down. What happened then was especially revealing. He kept right on listening, and if the idea didn't work he would be quick to admit it and make corrections. We finally decided that there's much benefit and little risk in working with him, and that it's easier to engage with his ideas than force drawn-out negotiations that mostly end up in the same place." Dean succeeded in transforming a university on the verge of bankruptcy to a robust campus that reflects what everyone who is familiar with it agrees combines exemplary academic values with market prowess and fiscal responsibility.

# Teaching and Learning Principles

## Learning Principles

The following list presents the basic principles that underlie effective learning. These principles are distilled from research from a variety of disciplines.

*1. Students' prior knowledge can help or hinder learning.*

Students come into our courses with knowledge, beliefs, and attitudes gained in other courses and through daily life. As students bring this knowledge to bear in our classrooms, it influences how they filter and interpret what they are learning. If students' prior knowledge is robust and accurate *and activated at the appropriate time*, it provides a strong foundation for building new knowledge. However, when knowledge is inert, insufficient for the task, activated inappropriately, or inaccurate, it can interfere with or impede new learning.

*2. How students organize knowledge influences how they learn and apply what they know.*

Students naturally make connections between pieces of knowledge. When those connections form knowledge structures that are accurately and meaningfully organized, students are better able to retrieve and apply their knowledge effectively and efficiently. In contrast, when knowledge is connected in inaccurate or random ways, it is possible that students will fail to retrieve or apply it appropriately.

*3. Students' motivation determines, directs, and sustains what they do to learn.*

As students enter college and gain greater autonomy over what, when, and how they study and learn, motivation plays a critical role in guiding the direction, intensity, persistence, and quality of the learning behaviors in which they engage. When students find positive value in a learning goal or activity, expect to successfully achieve a desired learning outcome, and perceive support from their environment, they are likely to be strongly motivated to learn.

Source: Eberly Center for Teaching Excellence & Educational Innovation, Carnegie Mellon University, 2014.

*4. To develop mastery, students must acquire component skills, practice integrating them, and know when to apply what they have learned.*

Students must develop not only the component skills and knowledge necessary to perform complex tasks; they must also practice combining and integrating them to develop greater fluency and automaticity. Finally, students must learn when and how to apply the skills and knowledge they learn. As instructors, it is important that we develop conscious awareness of these elements of mastery so as to help our students learn more effectively.

*5. Goal-directed practice coupled with targeted feedback enhances the quality of students' learning.*

Learning and performance are best fostered when students engage in practice that focuses on a specific goal or criterion, targets an appropriate level of challenge, and is of sufficient quantity and frequency to meet the performance criteria. Practice must be coupled with feedback that explicitly communicates about some aspect(s) of students' performance relative to specific target criteria, provides information to help students progress in meeting those criteria, and is given at a time and frequency that allows it to be useful.

*6. Students' current level of development interacts with the social, emotional, and intellectual climate of the course to impact learning.*

Students are not only intellectual but also social and emotional beings, and they are still developing the full range of intellectual, social, and emotional skills. While we cannot control the developmental process, we can shape the intellectual, social, emotional, and physical aspects of classroom climate in developmentally appropriate ways. In fact, many studies have shown that the climate we create has implications for our students. A negative climate may impede learning and performance, but a positive climate can energize students' learning.

*7. To become self-directed learners, students must learn to monitor and adjust their approaches to learning.*

Learners may engage in a variety of metacognitive processes to monitor and control their learning—assessing the task at hand, evaluating their own strengths and weaknesses, planning their approach, applying and monitoring various strategies, and reflecting on the degree to which their current approach is working. Unfortunately, students tend not to engage in these processes naturally. When students develop the skills to engage these processes, they gain intellectual habits that not only improve their performance but also their effectiveness as learners.

## Teaching Principles

Teaching is a complex, multifaceted activity, often requiring us as instructors to juggle multiple tasks and goals simultaneously and flexibly. The following small but powerful set of principles can make teaching both more effective and more efficient, by helping us create the conditions that support student learning and minimize the need for revising materials, content, and policies. While implementing these principles requires a commitment in time and effort, it often saves time and energy later on.

*1. Effective teaching involves acquiring relevant knowledge about students and using that knowledge to inform our course design and classroom teaching.*

When we teach, we do not just teach the content; we teach students the content. A variety of student characteristics can affect learning. For example, students' cultural and generational backgrounds influence how they see the world; disciplinary backgrounds lead students to approach problems in different ways; and students' prior knowledge (both accurate and inaccurate aspects) shapes new learning. Although we cannot adequately measure all of these characteristics, gathering the most relevant information as early as possible in course planning and continuing to do so during the semester can (i) inform course design (e.g., decisions about objectives, pacing, examples, format), (ii) help explain student difficulties (e.g., identification of common misconceptions), and (iii) guide instructional adaptations (e.g., recognition of the need for additional practice).

*2. Effective teaching involves aligning the three major components of instruction: learning objectives, assessments, and instructional activities.*

Taking the time to do this up front saves time in the end and leads to a better course. Teaching is more effective and student learning is enhanced when (i) we, as instructors, articulate a clear set of learning objectives (i.e., the knowledge and skills that we expect students to demonstrate by the end of a course); (ii) the instructional activities (e.g., case studies, labs, discussions, readings) support these learning objectives by providing goal-oriented practice; and (iii) the assessments (e.g., tests, papers, problem sets, performances) provide opportunities for students to demonstrate and practice the knowledge and skills articulated in the objectives, and for instructors to offer targeted feedback that can guide further learning.

*3. Effective teaching involves articulating explicit expectations regarding learning objectives and policies.*

There is amazing variation in what is expected of students across American classrooms and even within a given discipline. For example, what constitutes evidence may differ greatly across courses; what is permissible collaboration in one course could be considered cheating in another. As a result, students' expectations may not match ours. Thus, being clear about our expectations and communicating them explicitly helps students learn more and perform better. Articulating our learning objectives (i.e., the knowledge and skills that we expect students to demonstrate by the end of a course) gives students a clear target to aim for and enables them to monitor their progress along the way. Similarly, being explicit about course policies (e.g., on class participation, laptop use, and late assignments) in the syllabus and in class allows us to resolve differences early and tends to reduce conflicts and tensions that may arise. Altogether, being explicit leads to a more productive learning environment for all students.

### 4. Effective teaching involves prioritizing the knowledge and skills we choose to focus on.

Coverage is the enemy: Don't try to do too much in a single course. Too many topics work against student learning, so it is necessary for us to make decisions—sometimes difficult ones—about what we will and will not include in a course. This involves (i) recognizing the parameters of the course (e.g., class size, students' backgrounds and experiences, course position in the curriculum sequence, number of course units), (ii) setting our priorities for student learning, and (iii) determining a set of objectives that can be reasonably accomplished.

### 5. Effective teaching involves recognizing and overcoming our expert blind spots.

We are not our students! As experts, we tend to access and apply knowledge automatically and unconsciously (e.g., make connections, draw on relevant bodies of knowledge, and choose appropriate strategies) and so we often skip or combine critical steps when we teach. Conversely, students don't yet have sufficient background and experience to make these leaps and can become confused, draw incorrect conclusions, or fail to develop important skills. They need instructors to break tasks into component steps, explain connections explicitly, and model processes in detail. Though it is difficult for experts to do this, we need to identify and explicitly communicate to students the knowledge and skills we take for granted, so that students can see expert thinking in action and practice applying it themselves.

### 6. Effective teaching involves adopting appropriate teaching roles to support our learning goals.

Even though students are ultimately responsible for their own learning, the roles we assume as instructors are critical in guiding students' thinking and behavior. We can take on a variety of roles in our teaching (e.g., synthesizer, moderator, challenger, commentator). These roles should be chosen in service of the learning objectives and in support of the instructional activities. For example, if the objective is for students to be able to analyze arguments from a case or written text, the most productive instructor role might be to frame, guide, and moderate a discussion. If the objective is to help students learn to defend their positions or creative choices as they present their work, our role might be to challenge them to explain their decisions and consider alternative perspectives. Such roles may be constant or variable across the semester depending on the learning objectives.

### 7. Effective teaching involves progressively refining our courses based on reflection and feedback.

Teaching requires adapting. We need to continually reflect on our teaching and be ready to make changes when appropriate (e.g., something is not working, we want to try something new, the student population has changed, or there are emerging issues in our fields). Knowing what and how to change requires us to examine relevant information on our own teaching effectiveness. Much of this information already exists (e.g., student work, previous semesters' course evaluations, dynamics of class participation), or we may need to seek additional feedback with help from the university teaching center (e.g., interpreting early course evaluations, conducting focus groups, designing pre- and posttests). Based on such data, we might modify the learning objectives, content, structure, or format of a course, or otherwise adjust our teaching. Small, purposeful changes driven by feedback and our priorities are most likely to be manageable and effective.

# Course-Based ABC

Imagine that a small group of faculty, or even a single professor, has decided to dig deeply into the question of teaching cost—perhaps, but not necessarily, as part of a course redesign project. Working with an analyst from the dean's office, the group begins by focusing its attention on a single course. How should the analysis proceed? The steps are straightforward, albeit unfamiliar to anyone who has not previously been involved in course redesign. This appendix describes how to build a basic course-based ABC model. A fully comprehensive Excel implementation can be found on the Johns Hopkins University Press website. Tables B.1 through B.3 of this appendix present a somewhat simplified version, and further simplifications can be effected, if desired.

## Characterization of Activities

To set ideas, let's assume that the goal is to describe a large science course—although the approach can be tailored to courses of any size in any subject. Deciding what activities to consider is the first step in building a course-based ABC model. This is a sensitive issue because defining activities at too high a level limits the model's usefulness, while defining them in too much detail makes the model difficult to construct and understand. There are three basic types of categories:

1. *Group activities (traditional classes, online classes conducted synchronously, and organized teamwork).* Class sections appearing in the registrar's timetable provide the classic example of contact activity. They are characterized by frequency and duration of meetings, class size, the number of replications ("sections") offered, and whether the contact is F2F or online. This basic structure also applies to certain kinds of asynchronous group work: for example, where teams are organized in advance (and thus are controlled for size) and advised by a teacher who may attend some but not all the group meetings.
2. *"Individual" activities where the effort varies on a per-student basis (out-of-class work by students and grading by instructors).* They are characterized by the time students spend doing assignments (not included in the simplified template) and the time faculty and TA's use to grade and provide feedback on student work.

3. *Fixed activities (ones that don't depend on enrollment)*. These are primarily administrative in nature: for example, organizational work before the semester begins, management during the semester, and wrap-up after the semester. Preparation for in-class teaching is included in the group category because it depends on the frequency and durations of classes.

The three represent a refinement of the *synchronous activities, asynchronous activities: students*, and *asynchronous activities: teachers* categories in text figure 3.1 of chapter 3. Notice that categories 1 and 2 depend on enrollment: the first through the relation between class size and section counts and the second through the "minutes per student" construct.

Suppose that the analysis team has decided to model the activities listed on the rows of table B.1. Italicized figures represent calculations. All the other figures are inputs. The activities are primary class sections (lectures), two kinds of secondary sections (discussion sessions and labs), organized teamwork, grading and related work, course administration, and provision of financial support (operating cost). Student work is ignored in this basic model, but it is included in the extensive one provided online. Part A of the table allows users to characterize the activities that are performed on a group basis.

- *Meetings per week*: average over the semester
- *Duration*: average minutes per meeting
- *Group size*: based on educational considerations and room size
- *Replications needed*: the calculated number of sections that must be offered in order to handle the expected enrollment at the desired class size

   Part B of the table allows users to input the resources required for group activities.

- *Contact*: the time spent directly with the group, calculated from the frequency and duration data
- *Office*: teacher office hours, per assigned replication, per week
- *Preparation*: time spent by teachers preparing for the activity, per group meeting
- *% dual preparation*: percentages of cases in which the teacher handles more than one section, which offers an economy in preparation
- *Other staff*: time of technicians, and others, who support the teacher, per section, per week
- *Support—Operating $*: expenditures on supplies, and so forth, per section per week
- *Support—Facilities SF*: room size in square feet in which the group is expected to meet (usually supplied from the university's facilities records)

   Part C of the table allows users to input data on effort that varies in direct proportion to enrollment or is fixed regardless of enrollment and the number of sections. Per-student data are entered on a weekly basis (ten minutes per week per student for grading and $5.00 for variable operating costs like laboratory supplies). Fixed-cost data are entered as hours or dollars for the semester as a whole.

## Table B.1. Activities and resource requirements

### A. Description of Group Activities

| Activity name | Meetings per week | Duration (minutes) | Group size (students) | Replications needed | Comments |
|---|---|---|---|---|---|
| Lecture | 1 | 60 | 120 | 4 | Standard room—limited lecture format |
| Discussion | 1 | 60 | 25 | 20 | Standard breakout session |
| Laboratory | 1 | 120 | 18 | 28 | Wet lab session |
| Organized items | 0.333 | 30 | 7 | 71 | Teacher attends for 30 minutes every 3 weeks |

### B. Resources Required for Group Activities

| Requirements per wk per replication | Contact | Office | Preparation | Dual prep. (%) | Other staff | Operating Expense ($) | Facilities size (SF) |
|---|---|---|---|---|---|---|---|
| Lecture | 60 | 60 | 90 | 30 | 0.5 | 2,000 | 2,600 |
| Discussion | 60 | 120 | 60 | 75 | 0.0 | 0 | 500 |
| Laboratory | 120 | 30 | 60 | 50 | 0.0 | 500 | 800 |
| Organized items | 30 | 0 | 0 | 0 | 0.0 | 0 | 0 |

### C. Other Resource Requirements

| Requirements not related to groups | Type | Metric | Pre-semester | During semester | | Post-semester | Grand total (Hours) |
|---|---|---|---|---|---|---|---|
| | | | | Per wk | Total | | |
| Grading, etc. | Per student | Minutes | 0 | 10 | 100 | 30 | 1,083 |
| Administration | Fixed | Hours | 16 | 4 | 40 | 8 | 64 |
| Other oper. cost | Per student | Dollars | $0 | $5 | $50 | $0 | $25,000 |
| Other oper. cost | Fixed | Dollars | $0 | $250 | $2,500 | $0 | $2,500 |

### D. Other Data

Expected enrollment 500  Hourly cost of other staff $50

Weeks in semester: 10

Facilities cost per square foot (SF)  Lecture: $8  Discussion: $7  Laboratory: $12

Part D of the table allows users to enter data not elsewhere classified: specifically, for semester length, expected enrollment, and hourly facilities costs (operating cost plus depreciation as estimated by the finance office). Finally, I must emphasize that the figures in table B.1 are illustrative only and do not represent any particular course or institution.

The estimates of teacher office hours, effort on preparation and grading, and fixed effort are obtained by talking with faculty who currently teach the course or have done so in the recent past. While these variables are less easily quantified than the ones that characterize group activities, experience shows that people who are familiar with a given course can estimate them in reasonable ways. But while these data are relatively easy to collect, it's not all that common to do so—which is precisely the reason for using a template in the first place. Once the data have been input, spreadsheet formulas calculate the relationships among enrollment, group characteristics, and teacher effort that are needed to do the costing.

The data for group size and number of replications can be observed directly when working with historical data, but switching to a predictive model is a little more complicated. First, users must choose whether to control for class size or section counts when making their projections. Controlling for class size lets the number of sections, and hence resourcing requirements, vary with enrollment. The user sets a target class size, and the model calculates the number of sections needed to accommodate the enrolled students without exceeding the target. However, the model can be modified to control the number of sections so that class size varies with enrollment. (Class size equals the chosen section count divided by enrollment.) Which approach is better depends on the circumstances, as discussed in chapter 4.

People usually build more detail into models used for designing courses (a special kind of predictive modeling) than is typical for analyzing existing courses. The extra detail may use a finer set of activity definitions or characterize activities on a week-by-week basis rather than as averages over the semester. This helps one visualize the design when the incidences or durations of activities are allowed to vary over the semester. It's best to design courses "brick by brick," one week at a time, rather than by assuming that all activities proceed in lockstep. This is particularly important when novel technology applications are being considered. The template that is available online provides for week-by-week variation.

## Resources and Unit Costs

Modeling resources and unit costs is easier than characterizing activities. Again, the first step is to decide on the amount of detail to be considered. The main columns of table B.2 list the human resource types that have been important in a number of my modeling projects. There are two levels of regular faculty, (paid) adjunct faculty, TAs, and an "other teaching" polyglot category that includes administrators and unpaid adjuncts.

The percent of effort figures allow users to specify how each resource type contributes to the teaching tasks for each activity: for example, to the percent of sections taught by the indicated type. Let's say the table indicates that 10 percent of lectures are

## Table B.2. Resource utilization and unit costs

| % personnel assignments by type | Total hours needed | Senior faculty | Junior faculty | Adjunct faculty | Other teaching | Teaching assistant | Total assigned |
|---|---|---|---|---|---|---|---|
| Lecture | 122 | 10% | 50% | 30% | 10% | 100% | 200% |
| Discussion | 650 | 0% | 10% | 20% | 0% | 70% | 100% |
| Laboratory | 840 | 0% | 10% | 0% | 0% | 90% | 100% |
| Organized teams | 355 | 10% | 25% | 25% | 10% | 30% | 100% |
| Grading, etc. | 1,083 | 0% | 10% | 0% | 0% | 100% | 110% |
| Administration | 64 | 100% | 0% | 0% | 0% | 0% | 100% |
| Unit cost (per hour) | | $150 | $100 | $75 | $110 | $35 | NA |

## Table B.3. Total and average costs

| Activity | Total cost ($) | | | | | Average cost ($) | |
|---|---|---|---|---|---|---|---|
| | Teacher | Other staff | Operating | Facilities | Overall | Per student | Per section |
| Lecture | 12,871 | 1,000 | 8,000 | 10,408 | 32,279 | 65 | 8,070 |
| Discussion | 32,175 | 0 | 0 | 10,007 | 42,182 | 84 | 2,109 |
| Laboratory | 34,860 | 0 | 14,000 | 22,412 | 71,272 | 143 | 2,545 |
| Organized teams | 28,489 | 0 | 0 | 0 | 28,489 | 57 | 401 |
| Grading, etc. | 77,729 | 0 | 0 | 0 | 77,729 | 155 | NA |
| Admin. & other | 9,600 | 1,000 | 22,000 | 42,827 | 251,951 | 504 | NA |
| All activities | 195,724 | 2,000 | 44,000 | 85,654 | 503,902 | 1,008 | NA |

taught by senior faculty, 50 percent by junior faculty, 30 percent by adjuncts, and 10 percent by other teaching staff. For noncontact activities, they are percentages of the estimated total minutes required to perform the task. The percentages sum to more than one when team teaching or other needs put multiple staff members on a task at the same time. The table assumes that a TA will be present along with faculty at all primary class sessions, and that junior faculty guide and spot-check the grading performed by TAs.

The teacher effort figures can accommodate more innovation than meets the eye. It's usual to think of an instructor as taking a given discussion section for the whole semester, for example, but this is by no means necessary. Suppose that some group sessions are conducted virtually (e.g., by means of videos) and that the freed-up professorial time is applied to team-teach discussion sections on a rotating basis along with the regular TA. This would give both students and TAs more intimate contact with the professor, to the benefit of both. I recently had occasion to talk with my wife's granddaughter (an undergraduate at a state flagship university) who had just experienced a discussion-section "drop-in" by her literature professor. She said it made a huge difference.

The bottom row of table B.2 gives the unit costs ($ per hour) of the various resources. Preparation of these data is more technical than we've seen up to this point. It falls in the province of university cost accountants, but departmental and school model builders would do well to provide the accountants with the following instructions: (i) personnel costs should include salaries, benefits, and perhaps an allocated share of departmental support, such as administration, secretaries, supplies, and travel; (ii) overheads above the level of the department should not be allocated to personnel or other operating costs; and (iii) both organized and departmental research should be excluded from the faculty salary data for reasons that were discussed in chapters 4 and 5.* (The treatment of overhead stems from the need to estimate the direct cost of teaching—overheads can be allocated later if desired. Departmental research is handled by defining the faculty hourly rate in terms of a "normal teaching load"—so to add it in separately would be double counting.) With the unit costs in hand, it is a simple matter to calculate a blended cost per section or cost per minute or hour for each activity—which then can be applied to the activity requirements that were calculated in table B.1.

The activity and resourcing data are all that's necessary to build a rich bottom-up ABC model for a particular course. Table B.3 illustrates the kinds of results that can be calculated from the earlier tables. The *total Cost—teacher* figures reflect the sum of hours for each staff type multiplied by its hourly rate, plus the *other expenditures* figures in table B.1, and similarly for the other cost types. The *average cost* figures are calculated by dividing overall cost by the enrollment and section counts, respectively. Average costs based on other volume measures, such as student credit hours (SCH), can be obtained if desired.

---

*Organized research is identified in the general ledger and thus can easily be excluded. Departmental research can be excluded by means of a notional or survey-based allocation scheme. See Anguiano, "Cost Structure of Post-Secondary Education," and the top-down allocation section of chapter 4.

# Computer-Aided Course Design

It doesn't take much experience with spreadsheet templates like the one shown back in tables B.1 and B.2 to know that these tools become unwieldy as course designs get more complex. This manifests itself in two ways: (i) the activities on the rows of the table proliferate, and (ii) the assignments of activities to time periods (on the columns of the table) become much more variegated. (An example of the latter is that an activity may occur in some weeks but not in others or have different durations from week to week.) All this could be handled on a spreadsheet (as in the online template mentioned in appendix B), but the sheet eventually may become unwieldy and the formulas difficult to maintain.

About fifteen years ago, I envisioned a computer-aided course design tool ("course CAD") that could facilitate and automate the work currently being done on spreadsheet templates. The idea was for users to configure a custom list of activities, drag and drop them on an appropriate time line, assign resources, and then push a button to perform the ABC calculations. That design concept is presented here. Lack of time and development tools, coupled with doubts about whether the tool would be adopted in the then-prevailing environment, led me to set the idea aside—but now its pursuit seems eminently worthwhile.

The scale of the programming task makes such an application amenable to distributed open-source development under a Creative Commons license.* Indeed, today's development tools might make the work feasible as a student computer science project. It seems to me that this kind of grassroots development would maximize the possibilities for getting a good product and, very importantly, getting it adopted by faculty.

My design concept for course CAD is illustrated in figure C.1. The illustration is based loosely on a five-week multimethod module of the kind outlined in figure C.1, but the ideas are easily generalized. I'll explain the elements in the order most users would encounter them.

---

*http://creativecommons.org. The automation tools of Microsoft Visio might be used to advantage.

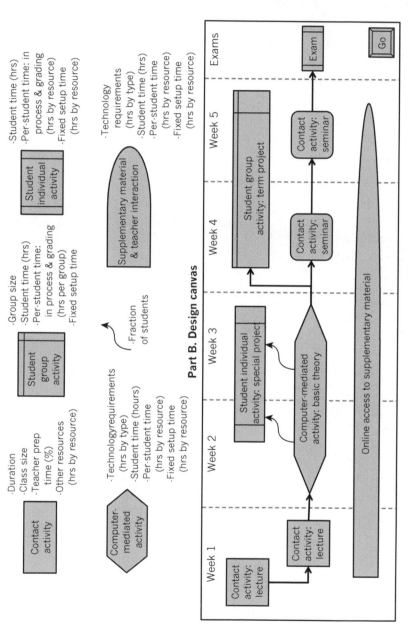

**Part A. Teaching and learning activities**

Contact activity
- Duration
- Class size
- Teacher prep time (%)
- Other resources (hrs by resource)

Student group activity
- Group size
- Student time (hrs)
- Per-student time: in process & grading (hrs per group)
- Fixed setup time

Student individual activity
- Student time (hrs)
- Per-student time: in process & grading (hrs by resource)
- Fixed setup time

Computer-mediated activity
- Technology requirements (hrs by type)
- Student time (hours)
- Per-student time (hrs by resource)
- Fixed setup time (hrs by resource)

Supplementary material & teacher interaction
- Technology requirements (hrs by type)
- Student time (hrs)
- Per-student time (hrs by resource)
- Fixed setup time (hrs by resource)

→ Fraction of students

**Part B. Design canvas**

Week 1 | Week 2 | Week 3 | Week 4 | Week 5 | Exams

Contact activity: lecture
Contact activity: lecture
Student individual activity: special project
Computer-mediated activity: basic theory
Student group activity: term project
Contact activity: seminar
Contact activity: seminar
Exam
Online access to supplementary material
Go

**Figure C.1.** Design concept for course CAD

1. *Teaching and learning activities* (part A). The module is assumed to involve six basic learning activities, each represented by a different "smart" shape (i.e., one containing customizable attributes that can be read from external code). Users customize the basic activities into specific ones like *contact activity: lecture* and *contact activity: seminar*, which appear in part B of the figure. Double-clicking a customized shape opens a dialog box where one can enter the activity's name and general attributes. The basic activities have slightly different attribute sets, as follows:

   a. *Contact activity*: can represent primary or secondary lecture-discussion classes, seminars, labs, and other class types. The attributes are duration, target and maximum class size, teacher preparation time as a percentage of contact time, and supplementary resources such as technicians and TAs who help the main teacher conduct the class. The distribution of teachers by type (e.g., adjunct vs. regular faculty) may be specified at this point or deferred for later designation.

   b. *Student group ("team") activity*: noncontact work that's done in organized groups. The attributes are target and maximum group size, total hours required for students over the course of the assignment (not per week), and total fixed and variable hours required for teachers and other resources. Variable time includes teachers' periodic visits to group meetings as well as emails and office hours specifically related to the assignment.

   c. *Student individual activity*: noncontact work done by students on an individual basis and/or in informal groups. The attributes are the same as those for group activity except there is no group size.

   d. *Computer-mediated activity*: work by students with software learning objects and similar resources as described in chapter 3. Attributes are the same as listed previously, plus any special resource requirements such as lab time and software licenses.

   e. *Early exit arrows*: curved arrows that show the fraction of students who leave an assignment early. *Straight arrows* represent precedence relations that apply to all students who exit in the normal way. Dropout and failure percentages also can be represented, if desired.

   f. *Supplementary material and teacher interaction*: access to syllabus materials (e.g., via a course management system) and to teachers through email and general office hours. Attributes are the same as for computer-mediated activities.

2. *Design canvas* (part B). The user drags activity shapes to the appropriate time slot(s) and connects the needed precedent arrows. The following features also can be activated:

   a. *Further customization*: double-clicking a shape situated on the design canvas allows the general attributes to be overridden or new ones to be added: for example, to amend an activity's duration or the fraction of students exiting in a particular week.

   b. *Set durations for noncontact activities*: done by stretching a shape to span a desired time interval. Resource requirements are prorated over whatever interval is chosen.

    c. *Teacher specification*: invokes a procedure (not shown) that specifies teacher type for activities where this decision has been deferred. The idea is to allow users to make global changes in estimated teacher-type distributions for specified activities and/or time periods.

3. *"Go" Button* (on the design canvas). Pushing this button activates an engine for totaling up resource requirements and costs, based on an assumed student through-put. This is analogous to preparing a bill of materials and costs in a conventional computer-aided design application.

Among other things, the engine will determine the number of sections and teams required to meet group size objectives as well as the number of students that leave each applicable assignment early. (Recall from the chapter 3 that students can move from computer-mediated work to special individual projects as soon as they demonstrate competence.)

A course-CAD developer will need to test the aforementioned elements against local requirements, and also add detail is needed to reduce the design concept to practice. I believe, however, that the material in this appendix and in appendix B should provide sufficient guidance and motivation to get development off the ground.

# Incremental Cost of Enrollment

Table 4 of chapter 5 presented sample results for the incremental cost of enrollment, but the method of calculation was described only in general terms. This appendix presents the method of calculation.

Accommodating a few students in a section with unused capacity incurs per-student costs such as grading, but adding more students will at some point require extra sections—with the extra cost that this entails. This formulation leads to two questions: (i) how should the number of extra students be characterized; and (ii) how should one determine the number of new sections that will be required? Adding the "new section cost" to the per-student cost (if any) will produce the overall incremental cost. (My prototype activity and cost model did not include per-student cost, so text table 4.4 reported only the "new section cost.")

It's possible to assume a series of specific values for the extra students and calculate the incremental cost associated with each, but this would be very tedious. A better approach is to assume a probability distribution for the number of extra students and calculate the resulting expected value for incremental cost. An "exponential distribution" offers simplicity, and it also appears to reflect the kinds of situations that will most likely be encountered: for example, that small enrollment changes are considerably more probable than larger ones. The distribution is characterized by a single parameter: E[x], where x is the expected number of extra students.

When the first extra section must be added depends either on (i) the total number of unused seats in the current sections or (ii) the department's policy for maximum class size (which may be less than the number of seats in the classroom). We'll call the unused capacity slack. An additional section will need to be added when the extra enrollment exceeds the available slack.

Figure D.1 depicts the scheme as it appears for positive enrollment changes. The solid curve shows an exponential probability density with mean $E[x] = 1/\lambda$ (shown on the x-axis to denote the scale). The formulas for the density function and distribution (cumulative density) function are:

$$f[x] = \lambda e^{-\lambda x}; \ F[x] = 1 - e^{-\lambda x}$$

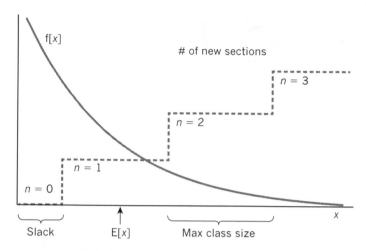

**Figure D.1.** Elements of the incremental cost algorithm

The dotted steps in the figure denote the extra sections that must be added to accommodate the new enrollments: none until the slack has been used up, and then one additional section when each max class size increment is reached.

We want to calculate the expected cost (*C*) per incremental student (*x*), which is obtained as follows:

$$E[C/x] = \Sigma_{n=0,1,2\ldots} n \cdot CpS \times E\left[\frac{1}{x} \middle| n\right] \cdot \Pr[n],$$

where $E[1/x \,|\, n]$ is the expectation of $1/x$ for the range of *x* included in *n*, $\Pr[n] = F[x_n] - F[x_{n-1}]$, and *CpS* is the cost of one section. (Notice that the expression for $n=0$ is zero.) $E[1/x]$ for an exponential distribution has no closed-form solution, and the series solution converges very slowly due to the alternating signs of its successive terms. Therefore, we get the solution by calculating $E[1/x]$ for many small intervals of *x*. It has proven to be practical to use a step size of one student, which, given that the solution must be integer, produces an exact result. A visual basic function is presented in the text box for readers who want to do the calculation in Excel.

The cost saved by reducing enrollments is obtained by applying a negative sign to the aforementioned calculation. In this case, *slack* means the amount by which classes can be made smaller without triggering the policy response of closing a section. While not discussed in the text, it's very likely that the incremental costs for adding and subtracting students will differ because of these differing interpretations of slack. For example, a class that's almost full will have little upside slack but potentially a lot of downside slack. This requires the calculation to take account of current class size as well as the upper and lower policy limits.

```
Public Function IncrementalCost(slack As Integer, sCapacity As Integer, CostPerSect,_
    expectedEnrChange, initialSlice As Integer)
Dim x As Integer, dx As Integer, nSects As Integer, lambda, sResult, lowFn, hiFn, midPt,_
    xLow, nResult

    Const threshold = 1e-10
    xPrint = False

    sResult = 1000000#
    lambda = 1 / expectedEnrChange

    'Iterate over incremental sections (ignore slack, since cost is zero)
    While sResult > threshold                   'go until change is negligible
        xLow = slack + nSects * sCapacity       'beginning enr for section
        nSects = nSects + 1                      'now increment the section count
        dx = initialSlice '* nSects              'slice size for this section
        x = xLow
        hiFn = Exp(-lambda * x)
        sResult = 0

    'Loop for enrollment slices
    While x < xLow + sCapacity
        If x + dx > xLow + sCapacity Then x = xLow + sCapacity Else x = x + dx      'ending x
        lowFn = hiFn                             'beginning prob Fn
        hiFn = Exp(-lambda * x)                  'ending prob Fn
        midPt = x + (initialSlice - 1) / 2       'point for evaluating 1/x
        sResult = sResult + (lowFn - hiFn) / midPt      'expected 1/x
    Wend

    nResult = nResult + sResult * nSects         'expected cost/student for the section
    Wend

incrementalCost = CostPerSect * nResult
End Function
```

# Smart What-Ifs in the Course-Based ABC Model

This appendix describes the "smart what-if" model in general terms but hopefully in enough detail for a management science professional to be able to re-create the procedure. I prototyped the model as part of my research but for technical reasons did not include it in the software used for the pilot test described in chapter 4.

Step one is to decide which variables should be used as criteria and controls for the optimization. There are many possibilities, but the model as prototyped works well with only these:

Criterion Variables
1. *Percentage of sections* in each course category
2. *Average class size* for each category
3. Percentage of adjunct sections for each category
4. Faculty teaching load for the department

Control Variables
1. *Number of sections* offered in each activity category
2. Number of adjunct sections in each category

The enrollment forecast for each instructional category and the total number of sections that can be taught by the department's regular faculty are taken as given ("exogenous").

The procedure adjusts the control variables to meet the criteria as closely as possible, based on the target and exception-reporting thresholds presented in text figure 4.7. A variable's *target* is the figure that the department wants to achieve, but it would be a miracle if the exogenous factors allowed the targets for all criterion variables and course categories to be hit exactly. Hence we model the degree of discomfort ("regret") associated with deviations from the targets—a quantity it's assumed the department wants to minimize. Reasonable assumptions are that: (i) regret rises at an increasing rate as a variable gets further from its target, and (ii) the effect is inversely proportional to the length of the variable's normal range.

This leads to what's called a "quadratic ideal point model":

minimize $regret = \Sigma_i w_i \left( x_i - x_i^T \right)^2$,

where the control index $i$ runs over the control variables, $x_i$ are the criterion variables, $x_i^T$ are the targets, and $w_i$ are the weights described under point (ii) in the previous paragraph.

Minimization will be facilitated if the variables are transformed so that the criteria are linear functions of the control variables. The linearity requirement is violated for some of the criteria described in the text, but this is remedied by approximations such as the following for the first criterion: $\%Sects_i = Sects_i/Sects$.

$$\left( \frac{Sects_i}{Sects} - \%Sects_i^T \right) \rightarrow \left( \frac{Sects_i - \%Sects_i^T \times Sects}{Sects} \right) \rightarrow \left( \frac{Sects_i - \%Sects_i^T \times \Sigma Sects_1}{\Sigma Sects_i^T} \right)$$

The transformation introduces only small errors while producing a strictly quadratic objective function.

It's possible to limit the amount a department can pay to hire adjuncts. First, determine the average cost per adjunct section, which may vary by course category. The minimization algorithm then constrains *average compensation $\times$ number of adjunct sections* to stay within the available funds. Such adjunct budgets are common in today's universities.

So far, the unacceptability thresholds have not entered the picture, but that can be taken care of by adding additional constraints that require each variable to come in above its minimum acceptability threshold and below its maximum threshold. The resulting model, a quadratic objective function with linear constraints, is easy to minimize using a standard quadratic programing algorithm.

To summarize, the smart forecasting procedure minimizes regret with respect to the control variables for each year in the planning period, subject to the budget and policy constraints. The optimizer can be run in either of two modes: (i) where the control variables must be integer, which, of course, is a condition of the real world; or (ii) as a noninteger approximation. The second mode runs much more quickly and may be acceptable for routine forecasting, though it might be risky to rely on it in some situations.

# Margin Equivalents for Start-Up Programs

This appendix presents my proposed method for summarizing a stream of time-varying margins in terms of a single budget-base allocation. This is applicable to the mission-margin trade-off model discussed in chapter 5, and more generally. I assume that revenues and costs vary erratically during a "start-up" period and then settle down to a steady state. The method funds the initial deficits from a revolving fund, which is paid back by an annual allocation that is determined at the project's outset and runs to the end of the its estimated lifetime. The calculations are done in constant dollars, but a university inflation rate can be applied to costs, revenues, and the budget allocation.

The procedure consists of five steps, as follows.
1. Forecast the revenues and costs separately for each start-up year and for the steady state. Include the unknown operating budget allocation as a revenue item.
2. Fund the initial deficits (offset by any surpluses) from a revolving fund, with interest charged (or earned) added to the outstanding balance each year.
3. Amortize the outstanding balance at the beginning of the steady state over the remaining life of the project. This can be done using Excel's FV (future value) function.
4. Use Excel's Solver Add-in to find the (constant) annual budget allocation that brings the future value of cash flows to zero at the end of the project's life. In Solver, set the cell for this future value (step 4) to a Value Of 0, set the Changing Variable Cells to the operating budget allocation cell (step 1), and uncheck the Make Unconstrained Variables Non-Negative box.
5. Use the budget allocation as the item's margin in the mission-money model, and add it into the operating budget base if the project is chosen.

An annotated illustration can be found in the mission-market trade-off file cited in footnote 30 of chapter 5.

The use of year-to-year forecasts followed by a steady state is consistent with normal financial practice. The calculations are similar to those used for the well-known internal rate of return measure, except that the result is an ongoing cash flow rather than a discount rate. (Businesses don't typically think in base budget terms.) The method appears to be highly robust as well as appropriate to the not-for-profit world. There are no constraints on the pattern of revenues and expenditures; for example, the University could choose to supply startup capital from a separate fund that does not require repayment. Finally, the operating budget allocation can turn out to be positive or negative, which is consistent with the margin specification of the mission-market model.

# Extensions to the Mission-Margin Model

I introduced the mission-margin model in chapter 1 under the rubric of nonprofit enterprise theory ("why universities do what they do") and used it in chapter 5 when constructing a trade-off model for balancing budget proposals' promised value contributions against their financial consequences. This appendix justifies the ideas presented in those chapters and extends them into some previously unexplored terrain. Specifically, it performs four tasks:

1. provides the mathematical and conceptual underpinnings for the economic theory of not-for-profit enterprises discussed in chapter 2,
2. shows how to quantify the frontier curve ("mission contribution function" described at the end of chapter 5,
3. describes the budget optimization tool also described at the end of chapter 5, and
4. justifies the assertions of chapter 2 about the relation between financial affluence and the ability to further mission-related values. I won't repeat those descriptions here, so readers should read the material in conjunction with the respective chapters.

The discussion is intended for economists and management scientists who wish to learn more about the principles and/or implement the methods.

## Nonprofit Enterprise Theory

The for-profit decision rule is derived by maximizing the entity's profit function, *Profit* $(x)$, where $x$ is the vector of activities that might be undertaken. Let $R(x)$ represent the revenue produced by the activities ("demand function") and $C(x)$ the costs incurred by them ("cost function"). Then:

maximize: $profit\ (x) = R(x) - C(x)$ with respect to $x$.

The maximum occurs where the partial derivatives of the profit function vanish (i.e., where $marginal\ profit\ (x_i) = 0$ for every activity $x_i$). This requires the derivatives of the revenue and cost functions to equal one another, or in more familiar terminology:

$MR(x_i) = MC(x_i)$, for all $i$,

which is *marginal revenue = marginal cost*, as used in the text.

Not-for-profit entities, such as traditional universities, maximize an *institutional value function* rather than profits while requiring revenues equal to costs ("budget balance"). Let V(x) be the value function. Then, the maximization is:

maximize: V(x) with respect to x.
subject to
R(x) − C(x) = 0.

We proceed by adding the product of the constraint (which equals zero at the maximum but is nonzero elsewhere) and a "Lagrangian undetermined multiplier" ($\lambda$) to the objective function that is to be maximized:

maximize: *value* (x) + $\lambda$ {R(x) − C(x)} with respect to x.

Setting the derivatives with respect to both x and $\lambda$ to zero yields the following system of equations:

$$MV(x) + \lambda \{MR(x_i) - MC(x_i)\} = 0 \text{ for each } i$$

$$R(x) - C(x) = 0$$

The Lagrangian, $\lambda$, can be interpreted as the *marginal value of money* because it is the extra value created by an extra dollar of margin. The last step is to divide the first part of the formula by $\lambda$ to obtain:

$$MV(x_i)/\lambda + MR(x_i) = MC(x_i)\} \text{ for each } i.$$

This is the equation given in the text for the nonprofit decision rule:

*value added + incremental revenue = incremental cost.*

An alternative's contribution to mission now is revealed as the ratio of the *slope of the value function* for each activity to the *marginal value of money*.

## Quantifying a Budget Alternative's Mission Contribution

Text figure 5.10 introduced two elements that were not a part of the previous results:

- Feasible alternatives that were "on the cusp" of being selected (i.e., were just in the money) are indicated by larger icons than the others. They are called *frontier points*.
- A curve that lies slightly *below and to the left* of the points that were selected, and slightly *above and to the right* of the ones that were feasible but not selected at the end of the exercise. This is called the "frontier curve." Points that lie above and to the right of the curve are included in the budget and vice versa.

The frontier curve can be viewed as estimating an alternative's "mission contribution" (heretofore referred to as "value") as a function of its rank. Hence, it may be referred to as the "mission contribution function."

The frontier curve is estimated from the frontier points using a special least squares procedure. The procedure forces the curve into a path between the selected and unselected frontier points and prevents it from "bending backward." (Bending backward means travel in a northeasterly rather than southwesterly direction, which would violate the principle of dominance.) The estimation can be performed using Excel's Visual Basic capability, but, as with the trade-off analysis, it would be better to create a specialized app.

The procedure's first step is to postulate a mathematical form for the frontier curve. Let this function be denoted by $V[R]$, where $R$ stands for rank. The simplest possible function is a linear one, where each change in ranking contributes the same amount to the institution's mission. If one starts the metric at 100 and sets the increment to, say, $-4$, then $V[R] = 100 - 4\,(R-1)$ so that $V[1] = 100$, $V[2] = 96$, and so on down to $V[26] = 0$. (Larger numerical ranks produce lower contributions.) A bigger increment allows for negative mission contributions as discussed earlier. For example, $V[R] = 100$ $-5.5\,(R-1)$ makes $V[R]$ negative for all ranks greater than 22.

While good for illustration, the linear function is too restrictive to be used in practice. For example, there may be very little difference among the top-ranked packages and/or very large differences among the low-ranked ones. Such variations can be accommodated by a polynomial of sufficiently high order.

$$V[R] = b_0 + b_1\,R + b_2\,R^2 + b_3\,R^3 + b_4\,R^4 + b_5\,R^5 + \ldots$$

The next step is to substitute the fitted polynomial, for $V[R]$, in place of the *mission contribution* term of the "nonprofit decision rule" given earlier. The result is:

$$margin = b_0 + b_1\,R + b_2\,R^2 + b_3\,R^3 + b_4\,R^4 + b_5\,R^5 + \ldots,$$

where *margin* has been placed on the left-hand-side and given a positive sign to reflect its role as the model's dependent variable. This formulation defines the *contribution* metric in the same units as $-margin$, but the units can be changed through multiplication by any positive constant. Notice that all the variables are readily available in text table 5.7.

The unknown parameters ($b$-values) are estimated from the frontier points by minimizing the sum of squared deviations between the equation's left- and right-hand sides. Two constraints are added to the minimization in order to handle the following requirements.

1. The contribution function should be monotonic with respect to $R$: that is, it should not bend backward. Violation of this condition would mean that an alternative further down on the ranking scale would have a larger contribution metric than one higher up, which is not acceptable. The estimator prevents this condition by minimizing the sum of squared deviations subject to the condition that the slope of the contribution function be nonnegative for every decision package. That is:

$$dV[R]/dR = b_1 + 2\,b_2\,R + 3\,b_3\,R^2 + 4\,b_4\,R^3 + 5\,b_5\,R^4 + \ldots \geq 0.$$

The constraint does not bind in the case of zero derivatives, which indicate tied rankings and thus pose no problem.

2. The contribution function must lie to the left of the funded points and to the right of the unfunded ones. That is:

$V[R] \leq margin - k$ for the funded (green) frontier points

$V[R] \geq margin + k$ for the unfunded (yellow) frontier points,

where $k$ is a small nonnegative "buffer constant" to be discussed later.* (The results presented in the text are based on $k = -300$.)

The constrained minimization problem can be solved by using a quadratic programming procedure of the kind included in Excel's Solver tool.

The coefficients for the preference function illustrated in the text are shown in table G.1. (Term 0 in the polynomial's constant term, Term 1 the linear term, etc.) The *Rank* value used with these coefficients has been transformed to the interval between 1.0 (best) and 2.0 (worst) in order to reduce rounding errors. Contribution is expressed in "margin-equivalent" terms, with negative contributions being better than positive ones. The coefficients' alternating signs would be worrisome in many studies, but that's not a problem here because the objective is simply to interpolate between the frontier points without trying to infer anything about structure. As noted in the text, the equation can be used to calculate $V[R]$ for a new decision package once it has been slotted it into the list of ranks.

The usual desiderata for defining a "preference function" (e.g., that it be convex) don't apply in this case, because the curve does nothing more than establish a metric for preferences already determined by the ranking process. The best fit to the dataset may involve tight curvature and one or more inflection points, which in the present case required the thirteen terms shown in the table. The fact that there are thirteen data points leaves us with zero degrees of freedom, but that's not a problem given that our task is essentially one of interpolation. The thirteen points represent only decision alternatives that are close to the frontier. Alternatives further from the frontier are not relevant for this part of the analysis—although they do figure in the optimization to be described in the next section.

The resulting mission contribution equation allows us to plug in an alternative's rank and estimate its contribution. I have already explained why this works for the frontier points, but how about the other points? Consider two frontier points with rank $X$ and $X+2$ and one nonfrontier point with rank $X+1$. The equation gives estimated values for $X$ and $X+2$, and we know that *value* for $X+1$ must lie between $X$ and $X+2$.

---

*Some nonlinear programming algorithms have trouble finding a feasible solution. If that happens, try eliminating this constraint *except* for the dominant points that have not been selected (i.e., the ones for which mission contribution must be negative); this produces a considerably simpler problem.

| Table G.1. Coefficients for the mission contribution function | | | |
|---|---|---|---|
| Term | Value | Term | Value |
| 0 | +6.001 | 7 | +9.507 |
| 1 | −6.276 | 8 | −25.663 |
| 2 | −12.108 | 9 | +12.958 |
| 3 | −3.202 | 10 | −3.047 |
| 4 | −2.176 | 11 | +3.065 |
| 5 | +17.184 | 12 | −1.875 |
| 6 | +0.556 | 13 | +0.338 |

Hence it is sensible to interpolate between these two numbers.* The equation converts the rank-order information about direction of preference into quantitative information about degree of preference or dislike. For example, it shows that the higher-ranked points produce considerably greater mission contribution than the lower-ranked ones. This is not a necessary outcome, however. An economist would say that the original trade-off analysis, used to estimate the *mission contribution* curve, has "revealed" the university's underlying preferences.[†]

## A Budget Optimization Tool

The estimated contribution function enables the construction of a budget optimization tool for finding the budget alternatives that produce the largest possible contribution given the university's available funds. The procedure maximizes the sum of the estimated mission contributions of the chosen alternatives subject to the budget limit. Management scientists call this a "knapsack problem": one wants the total contribution of chosen items to be as large as possible without exceeding the knapsack's capacity. Our problem differs from the classic knapsack one because some contribution and/or margins can be negative, but that poses no difficulty. Implementation proceeds by defining each decision alternative as a binary variable that equals 1 if it is chosen and 0 if it's not, and then maximizing the sum of the included mission contributions subject to the prespecified budget limit and any precedence relations. The optimization can be performed using Excel, but, as with the previous analyses, a user-friendly app that decision-makers could use hands-on would pay dividends.

The optimization can be formulated as the following integer programming problem. Define:

*I*:  the *index* of the decision package

$X_i$:  the package's *decision variable*: $X_i = 1$ if the it is included in the optimized budget and $X_i = 0$ if not

---

*The nonprofit decision rule for discreet alternatives is an inequality rather than an equality, so the nonfrontier points conform to the rule just as the frontier ones do.
[†]Nobelist Paul Samuelson introduced this notion of "revealed preference" in his *Foundations of Economic Analysis* (Cambridge, MA: Harvard University Press, 1947).

$v_i$: the package's *mission contribution* as determined by V[R]

$m_i$: the package's *margin*

$p_i$: the package's *precedence variable*, if any: $P_i = X_j$, where $X_j$ refers to the package pointed to by $i$'s precedence relation and $P_i = 0$ if $i$ has no precedence relation

B:  the budget limit

Now the problem can be stated as:

Maximize $\Sigma_i \{v_i \times X_i\}$ with respect to the $X_i$, subject to the constraints

| | |
|---|---|
| $X_i$ is Integer | *To prevent fractional choices* |
| $0 \leq X_i \leq 1$ *(all i)* | *Upper and lower limits for the integer definitions* |
| $X_i \leq p_i$ *(all i)* | *Precedence requirements* |
| $\Sigma_I \{-m_i \times X_i\} \leq B$ | *Budget limit* |

This maximizes the sum-product of the decision variables ($X_i$) multiplied by their contributions ($V_i$), subject to the four constraints. The first two constraints enforce the variable definitions. The third keeps $X_i$ at 0 unless (i) the package preceding it already has been selected or (ii) it has no precedence relation. ($P_i = 1$ in either of these cases, whereas $P_i = 0$ if there is a precedence relation and that package is not in the budget.) The fourth constraint ensures that the sum of the margins for the chosen alternatives does not exceed the available budget. This is a variation on the classic knapsack problem in that some $v$ and $m$ may be negative and there is an extra constraint, but integer programming can still obtain a solution.

Optimization is faster and more powerful than the dominance-based trade-off app discussed in the text, although it also is more demanding analytically. The algorithm always gets the right answer for the data fed into it, but one must remember that the estimated mission contribution function is simply an approximation. Hence the tool may not quite replicate the list of selected alternatives obtained in the underlying dominance-based analysis. (The difference in total mission contribution achieved will be minor, however.) But while users lose the "hands-on control" that characterizes the trade-off app, the optimization tool offers the huge advantage of performing sensitivity analysis at the push of a button—which gives users a much better opportunity to envision the consequences of changes in the dataset. Importantly, the tool allows one to change the budget limit as well as other elements of the dataset.

Users can overcome the loss of hands-on control by considering the optimization app's calculated budget as being only a recommendation: the penultimate rather than the ultimate step in the process. The results should be entered on a new options chart and changes made as desired. (The frontier curve isn't needed for this purpose, so changes in the budget limit are perfectly admissible.) Combining the optimizing and dominance methods provides users with a great deal of power without the loss of hands-on control.

As mentioned previously, the optimization result may not quite replicate the selected alternatives from the underlying dominance-based analysis. However, it may be possible to improve the situation by adding terms to the function's polynomial (if sufficient degrees of freedom are available) and/or adjusting the "buffer constant" (*b*) in subparagraph 2 of the estimator description. (It's also possible that the subjective analysis itself lacked perfect consistency.) But while the two lists of selected alternatives may vary to some extent, the differences in contributions attained are likely to be quite small. This suggests that the fine structure of choices may not make a lot of difference. Large errors caused by making choices piecemeal are the real value killers, and these are avoided in both the integer programming and subjective procedures.

## Effects of Financial Affluence and Stringency

I asserted in chapter 1 that the traditional university's ability to support money-losing programs—to exert its values over those of the marketplace—is directly proportional to its degree of budget flexibility. How this works is illustrated by the five scenarios called out in figure G.1, which shows the frontier curve associated with each.

- *Base case* (the result shown in text figure 5.10). The budget limit is $6,500, which is sufficient to fund a goodly fraction of the proposed items but by no means all of them.
- *Very loose budget.* Money is so easy that all alternatives with positive *mission contribution* can be funded, and there is no need to fund any with negative contributions. The frontier curve is a horizontal line, at the point where the curve crosses the zero-margin line. It is obtained by dividing the base-case curve by a number very close to zero: so that any upward shift on the *rank* scale translates to a very large *mission contribution*.
- *Relaxed budget* (compared to the base case). Money is easy but it's not unlimited. In this case, $15,000 is available for distribution (as opposed to the $6,500 in the base case), which produces a divisor of 0.27. The curve, which has been rotated downward so that small changes in rank produce big changes in mission contribution, permits more alternatives to be funded than in the base case.
- *Stringent budget.* The limit assumed for this case is to require a profit of $1,500. The divisor is 1.85, which rotates the curve upward so fewer alternatives can be funded.
- *Very tight budget.* The university wants to harvest all possible positive margins and incur no liabilities—perhaps because it is threatened with bankruptcy. This requires a vertical frontier that coincides with the zero-margin axis (in effect dividing by a number close to infinity). All alternatives to the right of the line are accepted and none of those to the left, which amounts to profit maximization.

The frontier curves in figure G.1 were generated by dividing the base case curve by a constant called the "incremental value of money," which represents the amount of extra mission contribution attainable by adding to the budget limit.* The incremental

*I say "in principle" because the concept relates to a continuous model rather than the discreet one used here. The difference is not important for present purposes, however.

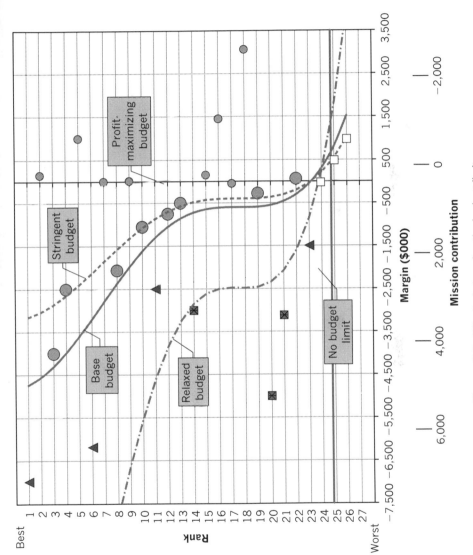

**Figure G.1.** Effect of changing the budget limit

value of money approaches zero when funds are very loose (the university already is doing all it knows how to do) and infinity when funds are very tight (the university teeters on the brink of bankruptcy). For purposes of drawing the figure, the incremental value of money was determined as follows: (i) run the optimization tool for the indicated budget limits and note the final objective function values, (ii) fit a smooth curve to these values (the curve is convex from above), and (iii) calculate the slopes of the curve at the indicated points.

## Preface

1. Jeremy N. Smith, "When 'Money Ball' Meets Medicine," *New York Times*, April 5, 2015, Review Section, 2. See also Stephen Matchett, "Cover All Bases for Productivity," *The Australian*, January 13, 2010, in which Matchett compared me to Billy Beane.

2. Terry Eagleton, "The Slow Death of the University," *Chronicle of Higher Education*, April 10, 2015, B-6.

## Chapter 1. Understanding the Traditional University

1. Kelly Field, *Chronicle of Higher Education* blog, August 28, 2013. Scott Jaschik, *Inside Higher Education*, August 22, 2013.

2. "FACT SHEET on the President's Plan to Make College More Affordable: A Better Bargain for the Middle Class," White House Office of the Press Secretary, Washington, DC, August 22, 2013.

3. Henceforth, the term "university," as opposed to the unwieldy "colleges and universities," will refer to all kinds of traditional higher education institutions.

4. See Robert Zemsky, Gregory R. Wegner, and William F. Massy, *Remaking the American University: Market-Smart and Mission-Centered* (New Brunswick, NJ: Rutgers University Press, 2005).

5. I want to note Derek Bok's comprehensive and insightful *Higher Education in America* (Princeton, NJ: Princeton University Press, 2013), however, because I will make liberal use of his arguments as context for my proposals. Another touchstone is Robert Zemsky's characterization of higher education's problems in terms of four pithy chapter titles: "A Faculty Encamped at Just North of Armageddon," "A Federalized Market with Little Incentive to Change," "A Regulatory Quagmire," and "A Troublesome Fractiousness." See *A Checklist for Change* (New Brunswick, NJ: Rutgers University Press, 2013). I agree with his conclusion that the traditional sector's problems cannot be solved until these issues are dealt with.

6. A second market failure stems from externalities vis-à-vis university market incentives and the benefits of an educated citizenry to a democracy. The details are fraught with political controversy, however, and, because the arguments of this book don't depend on it, I have chosen not to press the matter.

7. See John V. Lombardi, *How Universities Work* (Baltimore: Johns Hopkins University Press, 2013), ch. 10.

8. Zemsky, *A Checklist for Change*, 15.

9. *The New English Bible*, standard edition (New York: Cambridge University Press, 1970), 788.

10. Zemsky, *A Checklist for Change*, 159, with slight editing.

11. Bok, *Higher Education in America*, 202. Perhaps this is due to the emphasis placed on professional responsibility by proponents of academic freedom. See William G. Bowen and Eugene M. Tobin, *Locus of Authority: The Evolution of Faculty Roles in the Governance of Higher Education* (Princeton, NJ: Princeton University Press, 2015), 50; and Donald Kennedy, *Academic Duty* (Cambridge, MA: Harvard University Press, 1997), ch. 1.

12. Bok, *Higher Education in America*, 203.

13. William F. Massy, *Initiatives for Containing the Cost of Higher Education*, Special Report 1, Stretching the Higher Education Dollar (Washington, DC: American Enterprise Institute, 2013).

14. Ibid., 1.

15. Ibid., 3.

16. Frank H. T. Rhodes, *The Creation of the Future: The Role of the American University* (Ithaca, NY: Cornell University Press, 2001), xi.

17. Zemsky, *A Checklist for Change*, 168–69, elaborates extensively on my description.

18. Clayton M. Christensen and Henry Eyring, *The Innovative University: Changing the DNA of Higher Education from the Inside Out* (San Francisco: Jossey-Bass, 2011), 332–36.

19. Maya Jasanoff, "Globalization, Then and Now," presented at the Aspen Forum for Higher Education Futures, Aspen, CO, June 17, 2015.

20. "Stranded capital" refers to resources that have been made obsolete or irrelevant but which cannot easily be repurposed.

21. This is an example of what Nobel Prize–winning economist Paul Samuelson calls the "Generalized le Chatelier Principle": that removing a constraint from an optimization problem can't make things worse and may make them better.

22. See, for example, William F. Massy, *Honoring the Trust: Quality and Cost Containment in Higher Education* (Bolton, MA: Anker, 2003).

23. See Bowen and Tobin, *Locus of Authority*, for an extensive discussion of faculty governance and its benefits.

24. National Research Council, *Improving Measurement of Productivity in Higher Education. Panel on Measuring Higher Education Productivity: Conceptual Framework and Data Needs*, ed. Teresa A. Sullivan, Christopher Mackie, William F. Massy, and Esha Sinha. Committee on National Statistics and Board on Testing and Assessment, Division of Behavioral and Social Sciences and Education. Washington, DC: National Academies Press.

25. Bok, *Higher Education in America*, 31.

26. The benefits of research for universities and the broader society are well summarized by Michael M. Crow and William B. Dabars, *Designing the New American University* (Baltimore: Johns Hopkins University Press, 2015); and Jonathan Cole, *The Great American University: Its Rise to Preeminence, Its Indispensable National Role, and Why It Must Be Protected* (New York: Public Affairs, 2009).

27. See Michael S. Roth, *Beyond the University: Why Liberal Education Matters* (New Haven, CT: Yale University Press, 2014), as cited in ch. 1, for example.

28. Ernest L. Boyer, *Scholarship Reconsidered: Priorities of the Professoriat* (Princeton, NJ: Carnegie Foundation for the Advancement of Teaching, 1991).

29. Quoted in Roth, *Beyond the University*, 108.

30. Harry Hansmann, "The Role of Nonprofit Enterprise," in *The Economics of Nonprofit Institutions*, ed. S. Rose-Ackerman (New York: Oxford University Press, 1986), 57–84. See also Harry Hansmann, "The Rationale for Exempting Nonprofit Organizations from Corporate Income Taxation," *Yale Law Journal* 91 (November 1981): 54–100, for more on the benefits of the nonprofit organizational form.

31. Clark Kerr, "A General Perspective on Higher Education and Service to the Labor Market," unpublished paper excerpted in "Distillations," *Policy Perspectives* (Philadelphia: Institute for Research on Higher Education, University of Pennsylvania, September 1988), 1.

32. Gordon Winston, *Why Can't a College Be More Like a Firm?* Discussion Paper DP-42 (Williamstown, MA: Williams College, Williams College Project on the Economics of Higher Education, 1997).

33. Estelle James and Egon Neuberger, "The University Department as a Non-profit Labor Cooperative," *Public Choice* 36 (1981): 585–612; David S. P. Hopkins and William F. Massy, *Planning Models for Colleges and Universities* (Stanford, CA: Stanford University Press, 1981), ch. 3.

34. Adapted from William F. Massy, "*Collegium economicum*: Why Institutions Do What They Do," *Change* 36, no. 4 (July–August 2004): 26.

35. For example, see Bowen and Tobin, *Locus of Authority*.

36. The for-profit model applies most directly to public corporations, where the owners are relatively distant from the entity and its mission and the managers are subject to the full force of return-on-investment criteria. The possibility of hybrid companies, privately owned by individuals with a strong societal as well as monetary objective, is ignored.

37. This usually is stated as "marginal cost = marginal revenue." The terminology used in the text is consistent with other usage in this book, which is motivated by the need to avoid confusion with "margin" as used in the book's title.

38. Bok, *Higher Education in America*, 35, makes this point, among others.

39. James and Neuberger, "The University Department as a Non-profit Labor Cooperative," characterize the academic department as a nonprofit labor cooperative. This is consistent with nonprofit theory as outlined here. It simply reflects a particular—and self-serving—choice of value function, but this characterization is not consistent with government's and society's view of universities, nor with the substantial subsidies and

tax advantages granted to them. Events since 1981 have discredited the labor coop-erative idea as a normative principle, though, of course, it still arises occasionally in practice. Similar governance issues are described by Bowen and Tobin, *Locus of Authority*.

40. I once served as an associate dean under Arjay Miller of the Stanford Business School. Years later, when I was vice president for Business and Finance, I found myself renegotiating the School's revenue-sharing formula. Arjay was a tough negotiator, but in the end, he graciously stated: "A great business school needs to be part of a great university." That said, one must be careful that the sharing formulas for schools that are well positioned in the marketplace maintain their incentives to achieve maxi-mum performance.

41. The exception, of course, is where a company subsidizes now in anticipation of future gain. My analysis is of the "comparative statics" kind, however, in which such considerations don't arise.

42. See William F. Massy, "Cost and Pricing in Higher Education," in *Handbook of Research in Educational Finance and Policy*, ed. Edward Fiske and Helen Ladd (New York: Routledge, 2007).

43. Howard Bowen, *Costs of Higher Education: How Much Do Universities and Col-leges Spend per Student and How Much Should They Spend?* (San Francisco: Jossey-Bass, 1980).

44. Cf. Robert Zemsky and William F. Massy, "Cost-Containment: Committing to a New Economic Reality," *Change* 22, no. 6 (November–December 1990): 16–22.

45. Private communication with Henry R. Levin, Columbia Teachers College and formerly Stanford University. See also William F. Massy, "Markets in Higher Educa-tion: Do They Promote Internal Efficiency?," in *Markets in Higher Education: Rhetoric or Reality?* ed. P. Teixeira, B. Jongbloed, D. Dill, and A. Amaral (Dordrecht, The Neth-erlands: Kluwer Academic Publishers, 2004), 13–35.

46. Bowen and Tobin, *Locus of Authority*, 181.

47. Robert S. Kaplan and David P. Norton, *Strategy Maps: Converting Intangible As-sets into Tangible Outcomes* (Cambridge, MA: Harvard Business Press, 2004), 10; em-phasis added.

48. Quoted in Roth, *Beyond the University*, 153.

49. Howard R. Bowen and Paul Servelle, *Who Benefits from Higher Education—and Who Should Pay?* (Washington, DC: American Association for Higher Education, 1972), provided some classic examples.

50. The historical and current heterogeneity in curricular objectives, and the contro-versies that swirl around them, are summed up by Roth, *Beyond the University*, esp. ch. 3.

51. Quoted in ibid., 84. I might have added Jane Addams's concerns, also quoted by Roth at p. 85, about the "tragic failure of people from different groups to understand one another" and her admonition that "illiberal education should continually confront us with the perspicacious divergences that strengthen our ability to understand differ-ences from various perspectives even as we learn to understand commonalities."

52. Roth, *Beyond the University*, 189 (the quotation sums up the very important insights expressed on pages 180–89).

53. Robert D. Putnam, *Our Kids: The American Dream in Crisis* (New York: Simon & Schuster, 2015), 190. The statistic is from the National Education Longitudinal Study of 1988, Fourth Follow-Up.

54. While I believe my list of value propositions captures the essence of the subject, changes in particulars would not change the force of my overall argument.

## Chapter 2. The Reengineering Challenge

1. For a discussion of "reinvention" in the business context, see Mark W. Johnson, Clayton M. Christensen, and Henning Hagerman, "Reinventing Your Business Model," *Harvard Business Review*, August 31, 2013, 1–11. They cite the reasons for reinvention as "(i) addressing needs of large groups who find existing solutions too expensive or complicated, (ii) capitalizing on new technology to leverage existing technologies in new markets, and (iii) bringing a job-to-be-done focus where it doesn't exist" (1). The reasons in academe are more complex, but they definitely include capitalizing on new technology and bringing a job-to-be-done focus where it doesn't exist.

2. The fact that curriculum is a collective responsibility doesn't necessarily hold the forces of fragmentation at bay. See Robert Zemsky, *Structure and Coherence: Measuring the Undergraduate Curriculum* (Washington, DC: Association of American Colleges, 1989).

3. See Bowen and Tobin, *Locus of Authority*, esp. 49–65.

4. Massy, *Honoring the Trust*, 103.

5. William F. Massy and Robert Zemsky, "Faculty Discretionary Time: Departments and the Academic Ratchet," *Journal of Higher Education* 65, no. 1 (1994): 1–22; William F. Massy and Andrea K. Wilger, "Improving Productivity," *Change: The Magazine of Higher Learning* (July–August 1995): 10–20; Massy, *Honoring the Trust*.

6. Adapted from Marc L. Nerlov, "On Tuition and the Cost of Higher Education: Prolegomena to a Conceptual Framework," *Journal of Political Economy*, Part II, 3 (1972): S178–S218.

7. Professors do have strong views about productivity, but these views revolve around the idea of improving quality rather than cost-effectiveness. See Massy, *Honoring the Trust*, ch. 4.

8. Richard M. Cyert and James G. March introduced the term in their 1963 book, *A Behavioral Theory of the Firm* (Englewood Cliffs, NJ: Prentice Hall). They emphasized that a certain amount of slack helps in problem solving and creativity, though of course undermines productivity.

9. National Research Council, *Improving Measurement of Productivity in Higher Education*, 52.

10. See ch. 8 of Massy, *Honoring the Trust*, for an early evaluation of the assessment movement.

11. National Governors Association, *Complete to Compete—from Information to Action: Revamping Higher Education Accountability Systems*, ed. Travis Reindl and Ryan Reyna (Washington, DC: NGA Center for Best Practices, 2011).

12. See, for example, Robert Zemsky, "The Dog That Doesn't Bark: Why Markets Neither Limit Prices nor Promote Educational Quality," in *Achieving Accountability in Higher Education: Balancing Public, Academic, and Market Demands*, ed. Joseph C. Burke et al. (San Francisco: Jossey-Bass, 2005), 275–95.

13. Zemsky, Wegener, and Massy, *Remaking the American University*, 34.

14. See Massy, "Cost and Pricing in Higher Education," for further discussion.

15. Akshay R. Rao, "The Quality of Price as a Quality Cue," *Journal of Marketing Research* 42, no. 5 (November 2005): 401–405.

16. Peter Ewell, "Assessment, Accountability, and Improvement: Revisiting the Tension," Occasional Paper No. 1, National Institute for Learning Outcomes Assessment, College of Education, University of Illinois at Urbana-Champaign, 2009, 16.

17. Clay Christensen classifies change as either evolutionary or disruptive. However, the intermediate "discontinuous" category is important for purposes of this book. See Clayton M. Christensen, *The Innovator's Dilemma: When New Technologies Cause Great Firms to Fail* (Boston, MA: Harvard Business School Press, 1997).

18. Dan Berrett, "How Big Money Can Encourage Calculated Risks in the Classroom," *Chronicle of Higher Education* 61, no. 18, December 11, 2014, A4.

19. The center was under the direction of Professor and Vice Provost for Education Randy Bass.

20. See, for example, Everett M. Rogers, *Diffusion of Innovations*, 5th ed. (New York: Free Press, 2003).

21. See ibid.; William F. Massy, "Innovation and Market Penetration," unpublished PhD thesis, Department of Economics, Massachusetts Institute of Technology, 1960; and Massy, *Honoring the Trust*, 125.

22. Christensen, *The Innovator's Dilemma*; Christensen and Eyring, *The Innovative University*.

23. Adapted from William F. Massy, "Life on the Wired Campus: How Information Technology Will Shape Institutional Futures," in *The Learning Revolution: The Challenge of Information Technology in the Academy*, ed. D. G. Oblinger and S. C. Rush (Bolton, MA: Anker, 1997), 197.

24. The term "demonstration project" is used in some contexts, but I will not make that distinction here.

25. William F. Massy, Steven W. Graham, and Paula Myrick Short, *Academic Quality Work: A Handbook for Improvement* (Bolton, MA: Anker Publishing Company, Inc., 2007), ch. 1.

26. Presentation at the Lumina-sponsored meeting on the redesign of public university educational delivery systems held in Washington, DC, on June 24 and 25, 2015.

27. See William F. Massy and Nigel J. French, "Teaching and Learning Quality Process Review: What the Program Has Achieved in Hong Kong," *Quality in Higher Education* 7, no. 1 (April 2001): 33–45; and William F. Massy, "Applying Business Quality

Principles to Academic Audit: Hong Kong's Second-Round TLQPR." Presented at the conference of the International Network for Quality Assurance Agencies in Higher Education, Bangalore, India.

## Chapter 3. The New Scholarship of Teaching

1. Boyer, *Scholarship Reconsidered*; Charles E. Glassick, Mary Taylor Huber, and Gene I. Maeroff, *Scholarship Assessed: Evaluation of the Professoriate* (San Francisco: Jossey-Bass, 1997). See Massy, *Honoring the Trust*, ch. 4, for additional discussion.

2. Robert Zemsky, *Making Reform Work: The Case for Transforming American Higher Education* (New Brunswick, NJ: Rutgers University Press, 2009), ch. 10.

3. Ibid., 169; from James Zull, *The Art of Changing the Brain: Enriching the Practice of Teaching by Exploring the Biology of Learning* (Sterling, VA: Stylus Publishing, 2002).

4. Carl Wieman and colleagues, Colorado Physics and Chemistry Research Group (PowerPoint, circa 2005).

5. From Carl Wieman, "Science Education for the 21st Century" (Undated Power-Point presentation, circa 2007, provided by personal communication.)

6. Ibid.

7. Eric Mazur, "Farewell, Lecture," *Science* 323, no. 5910 (January 2009): 50–51. In this mini-lecture, Mazur told us, in effect, that heating causes the metal's atoms to vibrate more vigorously, which causes the plate to expand. The question was when heating a similar plate with a large hole in the middle, would the diameter of the hole (i) get larger, (ii) stay the same, or (ii) get smaller. (The answer could have been given by a show of hands if the clickers had not been available.) I answered (iii) in the erroneous belief that the hole would be pressed in from all sides, but the correct answer is (i) because the atoms around the circumference of the hole require more space—a fact that came to me as I tried to explain my first answer.

8. *The Innovative University* by Christensen and Eyring provides a good example of how the new techniques can span the two kinds of outcome.

9. Kaizen Institute, "What Is Kaizen?" (http://www.kaizen.com/about-us/definition-of-kaizen.html).

10. Ibid.

11. NCPI was a federally funded educational research and development center that operated at Stanford University, the University of Pennsylvania, and the University of Michigan during the 1990s.

12. Detained descriptions can be found in Massy, Graham, and Short, *Academic Quality Work*.

13. Peter N. Miller, "Is 'Design Thinking' the New Liberal Arts?," *Chronicle Review*, March 26, 2015.

14. Example adapted from Massy, *Honoring the Trust*, 130–34.

15. Barbara Walvoord and Kirsten Pool, "Enhancing Pedagogical Productivity," in *Enhancing Productivity: Administrative, Instructional, and Technological Strategies*, New Directions for Higher Education, ed. James C. Groccia and Judith E. Miller (San Francisco, CA: Jossey-Bass, 1998), 35–48, and personal communications.

16. See Paul T. Magilo, Cheryl A. Kieliszewski, and James C. Spohrer, eds., *Handbook of Service Science* (New York: Springer, 2010).

17. Louis Soares and A. L. Ostrom, "College Is a Service," paper presented at the Lumina Foundation convening on service science, Indianapolis, April 4–5, 2013.

18. Robert F. Lusch and C. Y. Wu, "A Service Science Perspective on Higher Education: Linking Service Productivity Theory and Higher Education Reform," paper presented at the Lumina Foundation convening on service science, Indianapolis, April 4–5, 2013.

19. Paul A. Kieliszewski, John A. Bailey, and Jeanette Blomberg, "A Service Practice Approach: People, Activities and Information in a Highly Collaborative Knowledge-based Service Systems," in *Handbook of Service Science*, 284.

20. The need for "location and context awareness" is another principle of service science. See Robert J. Glushko, "Seven Contexts for Service System Design," in *Handbook of Service Science*, 219–50.

21. James C. Spohrer and Paul P. Maglio, "Toward a Science of Service Systems: Value and Symbols," in *Handbook of Service Science*, 167.

22. Rogelio Oliva and John D. Sterman, "Death Spirals and Virtuous Cycles: Human Resource Dynamics in Knowledge-Based Services," in *Handbook of Service Science*, 323.

23. See Massy and Wilger, "Improving Productivity," for a discussion of the research effect.

24. Olivia and Sterman, "Death Spirals and Virtuous Cycles: Human Resource Dynamics in Knowledge-Based Services," 354.

25. Mary Jo Bitner, A. L. Ostrum, and R. Burkhard, "Service Blueprinting: Transforming the Student Experience," presentation at the Lumina Foundation Convening on Service Science, April 4–5, 2013, 1.

26. Zull, *The Art of Changing the Brain*.

27. Ibid., quoted in Zemsky, *Making Reform Work*, 170.

28. George Siemans, Shane Dawson, and Grace Lynch, "Improving the Quality and Productivity of the Higher Education Sector: Policy and Strategy for Systems-Level Deployment of Learning Analytics," Australian Government, Office for Learning and Teaching, December, 2013, 8.

29. National Research Council, *Discipline-Based Education Research: Understanding and Improving Learning in Undergraduate Science and Engineering*, ed. S. R. Singer, N. R. Nielsen, and H. A. Schweingruber, Committee on the Status, Contributions, and Future Directions of Discipline-Based Education Research, Board on Science Education, Division of Behavioral and Social Sciences and Education (Washington, DC: National Academies Press).

30. Ibid., 2.

31. Carl Wieman and Sarah Gilbert, "The Teaching Practices Survey: A New Tool for the Evaluation and Improvement of College and University Teaching in Mathematics and Science," unpublished Science Education Initiative at the University of British

Columbia, undated, 2. See also Carl Wieman, "A Better Way to Evaluate Undergraduate Teaching," *Change* (January–February 2015): 1.

32. Dan Berrett, "A New Kind of Study Seeks to Quantify Educational Quality," *Chronicle of Higher Education* 60, no. 21 (February 7, 2014). Professor Corbin Thompson of Columbia Teachers College serves as principle investigator for the project.

33. AAU Undergraduate STEM Initiative website (January 2014). Launched in 2011, the initiative is funded by a grant from the Leona M. and Harry B. Helmsley Charitable Trust.

34. Announcement of the Simon Initiative Learning Engineering Ecosystem, Carnegie-Mellon University, June 15, 2015, distributed at the Aspen Forum for the Future of Higher Education.

35. Ibid.

36. Ibid.

37. Cf. Jack M. Wilson, "Reengineering the Undergraduate Curriculum," in *The Learning Revolution: The Challenge of Information Technology in the Academy*, ed. Diana G. Oblinger and Sean C. Rush (Bolton, MA: Anker, 1966), 107–28.

38. National Research Council, *Improving Measurement of Productivity in Higher Education*, appendix B.

39. Ibid.

40. Carol Twigg, communication to the NRC Panel.

41. National Research Council, *Improving Measurement of Productivity in Higher Education*, appendix B.

42. Carol Twigg, communication to the NRC Panel.

43. All quotations are from Carl Wieman, Katherine Perkins, and Sarah Gilbert, "Transforming Science Education at Large Research Universities: A Case Study in Progress," *Change: The Magazine of Higher Learning* (March–April 2010): 9.

44. Ibid.

45. Ibid., 11.

46. Carl Wieman, Louis Deslauiers, and Brett Gilley, "Use of Research-Based Instructional Strategies: How to Avoid Faculty Quitting," table 1. *Physical Review ST Physics Education Research* 9 (September 19, 2013): 023102.

47. Wieman, Perkins, and Gilbert, "Transforming Science Education at Large Research Universities," 14.

48. OLI website: http://oli.cmu.edu/get-to-know-oli/learn-more-about-oli/. See also Candace Thille, "Surfing the Tsunami: A Study of Faculty Engagement with the Open Learning Initiative," unpublished doctoral dissertation in higher education management, University of Pennsylvania Graduate School of Education, 2013; and Steve Arnold, Kevin Guthrie, and Candace Thille, "Effective Use of New Learning Media and Technology," in *Forum Futures* (Cambridge: Forum for the Future of Higher Education, 2012).

49. Thille, "Surfing the Tsunami."

50. Ibid., 112.

51. This and the following quote are from Thille, "Surfing the Tsunami," 119.

52. Ibid., 13.

53. Ibid., 150–51.

54. Adapted from Peter Ewell, "Evidence Guide: A Guide to Using Evidence in the Accreditation Process," prepared for the Accrediting Commission for Senior Colleges and Universities, Western Association of Schools and Colleges, 2002, 8–12.

55. Massy, Graham, and Short, *Academic Quality Work*.

56. David D. Dill, "Quality by Design: Toward a Framework for Academic Quality Management," in *Higher Education: Handbook of Theory and Research*, ed. John C. Smart (New York: Agathon Press, 1992), 37–83; and Frans van Vught, "The New Context for Academic Quality," in *Emerging Social Demands and University Reform: Through a Glass Darkly*, ed. David D. Dill and Barbara Sporn (New York: Pergamon Press, 1995), 194–211.

57. Adapted from Massy, *Honoring the Trust*, 159, and Massy, Graham, and Short, *Academic Quality Work*, 27. The materials on AQW were first developed as part of my work in Hong Kong and then modified in Missouri and Tennessee. (The version presented here is based on the Tennessee experience.) See Massy, Graham, and Short, *Academic Quality Work*, for more detail.

58. Massy, Graham, and Short, *Academic Quality Work*, ch. 2.

59. A detailed description of the self- and peer-review processes, including templates, training instructions, and sample self-studies, can be found in Massy, Graham and Short, *Academic Quality Work*.

60. See ibid., ch. 4.

61. Described in William F. Massy, "Academic Audit for Accountability and Improvement," in *Achieving Accountability in Higher Education: Balancing Public, Academic, and Market Demands*, ed. Joseph C. Burke (San Francisco: Jossey-Bass, 2005), 173–97; and William F. Massy, "Education Quality Audit as Applied in Hong Kong," in *Public Policy for Academic Quality: Analysis of Innovative Policy Instruments*, ed. David D. Dill and Maarja Beerkens (New York: Springer, 2010), 203–26. Arguments about whether audits of teaching methods and improvement processes, as opposed to learning outcomes themselves, represent effective quality assurance have raged for decades. Hence, it was satisfying to see Carl Wieman weigh in on the side of teaching method reviews (Carl Wieman, "A Better Way to Evaluate Undergraduate Teaching").

## Chapter 4. The Cost of Teaching

1. Adapted from William Massy, "Creative Paths to Boosting Productivity," in *Reinventing the American University: The Promise of Innovation*, ed. Ben Wildavsky, Andrew P. Kelly, and Kevin Cary (Cambridge, MA: Harvard Education Press, 2011), 84.

2. Michael F. Middaugh, *Understanding Faculty Productivity: Standards and Benchmarks for Colleges and Universities* (San Francisco: Jossey-Bass, 2001). His table 3.3 presents a list of metrics for measuring "productivity": for example, "credit hours per faculty FTE" and "direct expense per FTE students taught."

3. Cf. National Research Council, *Improving Measurement of Productivity in Higher Education*, 30.

4. Ibid., 80.

5. Ibid., ch. 4.

6. Ibid.

7. Ibid., 80.

8. William F. Massy, Teresa A. Sullivan, and Christopher Mackie, "Improving Measurement of Productivity in Higher Education," *Change: The Magazine of Higher Learning* 45, no. 1 (2013): 15–23; and William F. Massy, Teresa A. Sullivan, and Christopher Mackie, "Data Needed for Improving Productivity Measurement in Higher Education," *Research and Practice in Assessment* 7 (Winter): 5–15.

9. Sandra R. Sabo, *Coming to Terms*. Washington, DC: National Association of College and University Business Officers, March 2014. Pattison is executive director of NACUBO.

10. The methodology is described in NACUBO, *Explaining College Costs: NACUBO's Methodology for Identifying the Cost of Delivering Undergraduate Education* (Washington, DC: National Association of College and University Business Officers, 2002).

11. Quoted in Gary Cokins, "What Is Activity-Based Costing . . . Really?," keynote address, Institute of Management Accountants 75th Anniversary Conference, June 1994. See also Gary Cokins, *Activity-Based Cost Management: Making It Work* (Chicago: Irwin Professional Publishing, 1996).

12. Maria Anguiano, "Cost Structure of Post-Secondary Education: Guide to Making Activity-Based Costing Meaningful and Practical," policy paper from the Bill and Melinda Gates Foundation: Post–Secondary Education Success, December 2013.

13. Dennis Weisman and T. Mitchell, "Texas Instruments Recalculates Their Costing System," *Journal of Cost Management* 9, no. 2 (Spring 1986): 63–68; M. Hearth, R. Kaplan, and J. Waldon, "New Costing Systems?," *Journal of Accounting Historians* 4, no. 1 (1991): 6–22. Also described in Massy, *Honoring the Trust*, 255–59.

14. William F. Massy and Robert Zemsky, *Using Information Technology to Enhance Academic Productivity*, occasional paper (Washington, DC: Educom, 1995).

15. Zemsky, *Structure and Coherence*.

16. Cf. David F. Swenson, *Pioneering Portfolio Management* (New York: Free Press, 2000); for an early account, see William F. Massy, *Endowment: Perspectives, Policies, and Management* (Washington, DC: Association of Governing Boards of Universities and Colleges, 1990).

17. Richard Light et al., "Reducing Class Size: What Do We Know?" undated working paper and personal communication. "Case method" teaching as practiced in many law and business schools represent an exception, but these courses are carefully designed to promote interaction and taught by faculty skilled in the Socratic management of large groups.

18. The module approach also is being used in a number of overseas venues.

19. Anguiano, "Cost Structure of Post-Secondary Education," 5.

20. Bill Gates, "The Future of College," remarks delivered at the annual meeting of the National Association of College and University Business Officers (NACUBO). Nashville, TN, July 21, 2014.

21. Quantrix, an IDBS company (Portland, ME): http://www.quantrix.com.

22. William F. Massy, "Modeling Instructional Productivity in Traditional Universities," unpublished discussion paper prepared for the Lumina Foundation, March 2012. The implemented prototype included the model's kernel and most, but not all, of the other functionality described in the paper.

23. The variables definitions are straightforward except for the unit cost of faculty, $C_{FAC,T}$. This is the cost of a full-time, tenure-line faculty member teaching a normal load, after deducting research and departmental administration as described in table B.2. The formula produces the "direct cost of teacher time" for the people responsible for teaching the various sections. TA costs are included if they handle, for example, labs or breakout sections, but they fall into "other teaching costs" (which are allocated later) if the work is grading or other general assistance. The unit costs should include salaries and benefits as a minimum, but they also may include support costs that vary directly with faculty numbers.

24. Economists call these "reduced form models." Books on econometrics describe the many dangers of using reduced form models for policy purposes.

25. "Nonstructural models" are called "reduced-form models" in econometrics, but that expression is insufficiently descriptive for the present context.

26. Targets were set equal to the variables' time series average values over years and academic-year semesters (i.e., excluding summer), separately for primary and secondary sections. Thresholds were based on the variables' standard deviations: pooled (to improve stability) over instruction modes, class-size categories, course levels, and instructor types. A graphic slider allowed users to adjust the sensitivity of the exception reporting.

27. "Slack" also can be defined in terms of room capacity, or any other way of describing an acceptable maximum class size.

28. The incremental cost figures presented at the departmental meetings described in the next section were based on an earlier algorithm, but the impression conveyed was qualitatively similar.

29. John Immerwahr, "Report to the Lumina Foundation," April 2013, Public Agenda, unpublished. John is a former philosophy department chair at Villanova University.

30. Ibid.

31. Ibid.

32. David S. P. Hopkins and William Massy, *Planning Models for Colleges and Universities* (Stanford, CA: Stanford University Press, 1981), ch. 2.

33. Cf. NACUBO, "Explaining College Costs."

34. National Research Council, *Improving Measurement of Productivity in Higher Education*, Section 5.2.

35. The allocation rule for departmental research might be based on policy (e.g., faculty should spend $x$ percent of their time on research) or periodic time surveys. See also National Research Council, *Improving Measurement of Productivity in Higher Education*, Section 5.2.2, for an adjustment to take account of unfunded sponsored obligations.

36. See www.Pilbaragroup.com for detailed descriptive materials.

37. Matt Easdown, "Data-Driven Decision Making," Annual Meeting of the National Association of College and University Business Officers (NACBBO), Chicago, 2013.

38. Whether building one's own model is a good idea is not necessarily clear. Much of the cost lies in developing algorithms, data extraction routines, and interfaces that won't contribute greatly to the institution's stock of intellectual capital. The cost of such development will be substantial, and continual maintenance and upgrading efforts will be needed. Finally, my work at Stanford taught me how hard it is to sell the software or build a consortium to amortize the cost over multiple users.

39. Cf. Cyert and March, *A Behavioral Theory of the Firm*.

40. See also National Research Council, *Improving Measurement of Productivity in Higher Education*, Section 4.5.

41. See ibid., 78–79, for further discussion.

42. Paul Tough, "Who Gets to Graduate?," *New York Times Magazine*, May 18, 2014, 28–33. The first long quotation is on p. 29 and the second is on p. 30.

43. Results from the Pilbara model could be used to develop a successor to "Virtual U," a university simulation game I helped develop with Sloan Foundation support during the 1990s. They would replace the game's complex core production function with a much simpler algorithm based on the activities and costs described in this chapter, which would open the way for additional innovations aimed at enhancing the game's utility as a tool for teaching and training. Virtual U was an example of what now are called "serious games"; simulations of real-world events are processes that address policy and management issues—in this case, particularly in the area of resource allocation. The best-known examples of the serious games in general are "Games for Health" and "Games for Change," which focus on medical care and social change, respectively.

## Chapter 5. Financial Planning and Budgeting

1. Edward R. Tufte, *Envisioning Information* (Cheshire, CT: Graphics Press, 1990), introduction.

2. Edward R. Tufte, *Beautiful Evidence* (Cheshire, CT: Graphics Press, 2006), 162–63.

3. The 2014/15 book can be obtained at http://web.stanford.edu/dept/pres-provost /budget/plans/BudgetBookFY15.pdf.

4. Most new information system applications use some variant of the CMM (e.g., IBM's common data model or one of Microsoft's implementations of extensible markup language [XML]).

5. Nathan Dickmeyer, David Hopkins, and I introduced the PPV idea in "TRADES: A Model for Interactive Financial Planning," in *Financial Planning Models: Concepts and Case Studies in Colleges and Universities*, ed. Joe B. Wyatt, James C. Emery, and Carolyn P. Landis (Princeton, NJ: EDUCOM, InterUniversity Communications Council, 1979). A more advanced approach for making PPV trade-offs can be found in Donald A. Wehrung, David S. P. Hopkins, and William F. Massy. "Interactive Preference Optimization for University Administrators," *Management Science* 24 (1978): 599–611.

6. Oracle Hyperion and a few other currently available models include drill capability, but they would need to be enhanced to provide all my envisioned functionality.

7. Kellogg Commission on the Future of State and Land-Grant Universities, "Returning to Our Roots: Toward a Coherent Campus Culture," National Association of State Universities and Land-Grant Colleges, 2000, 10 and 13. Sponsorship was by the National Association of State Universities and Land Grant Colleges (NASULGC), now the Association of Public and Land-Grant Universities (APLU).

8. Joseph C. Burke, ed., *Fixing the Fragmented University: Decentralization with Direction* (Bolton, MA: Anchor Publishing, 2007).

9. James J. Duderstadt, "Fixing the Fragmented University: A View from the Bridge," in *Fixing the Fragmented University: Decentralization with Direction*, ed. Joseph C. Burke (Bolton, MA: Anker, 2007), 49.

10. Massy, *Improving Measurement of Productivity in Higher Education*, 122.

11. Hopkins and Massy, *Planning Models for Colleges and Universities*, ch. 6.

12. See Massy, *Endowment*, and the references cited there.

13. Hopkins and Massy, *Planning Models for Colleges and Universities*, ch. 6.

14. David Hopkins and I described the basic ideas in *Planning Models for Colleges and Universities*, 282.

15. Richard C. Grinold, David S. P. Hopkins, and William F. Massy, "A Model for Long-Range University Budget Planning under Uncertainty," *Bell Journal of Economics* 9 (1978): 396–420; and William F. Massy, Richard C. Grinold, David S. P. Hopkins, and Alejandro Gerson, "Optimal Smoothing Rules for University Financial Planning," *Operations Research* 29 (1981): 1121–36.

16. For a primer on endowment spending policies, see Massy, *Endowment*, ch. 2, and the references cited there.

17. Sam L. Savage, *The Flaw of Averages: Why We Underestimate Risk in the Face of Uncertainty* (New York: Wiley, 2009).

18. William F. Massy, "Capital Structure and Risk Management," in *Higher Education Finance Forum 2008* (Cambridge, MA: Forum for the Future of Higher Education, 2008), 13. See also, John Core, "Capital Structure and Risk Management Discussion," in *Higher Education Finance Forum 2008* (Cambridge, MA: Forum for the Future of Higher Education, 2008), 25.

19. John Augustine, "Capital Structure and Risk Management Preface," in *Higher Education Finance Forum 2008*, 4.

20. John Curry, "Capital Structure and Risk Management Introduction," in *Higher Education Finance Forum 2008*, 10. John Curry, currently director of strategic initia-

tives in higher education for Deloitte Consulting, remains a thought leader in financial planning and modeling.

21. I am grateful to Tim Warner, Stanford's vice provost for budget and auxiliaries management, and Andrew Harker, director of budget management, for bringing the scheme to my attention as part of our joint work for the National University of Singapore.

22. Cf. Jon Strauss, John Curry, and Edward Whalan, "Revenue Responsibility Budgeting," in *Resource Allocation and Higher Education*, ed. William F. Massy et al. (Ann Arbor: University of Michigan Press, 1996), 163–90; and Zemsky et al., *Remaking the American University*, ch. 4. RCM also is called "responsibility center management," but "revenue center management" is more descriptive and more in line with the materials in this book.

23. For more detail, see William F. Massy, "Value Responsibility Budgeting," in *Resource Allocation and Higher Education*, 293–324.

24. Formula-determined depreciation is a mandatory item in for-profit accounting principles but not for universities.

25. Cf. Barbara E. Taylor and William F. Massy, *Strategic Indicators for Higher Education, 1996: Vital Benchmarks and Information to Help You Evaluate and Improve Your Institution's Performance* (Princeton NJ: Peterson's, 1996), 22–29.

26. Ibid.

27. Advanced models such as Oracle's Hyperion go part of the way, but I believe that significantly more powerful and user-friendly approaches are possible.

28. Cf. Harold A. Linstone and Murray Turoff, *The Delphi Method: Techniques and Applications* (Reading, MA: Addison-Wesley, 1975).

29. George A. Miller, "The Magical Number Seven, Plus or Minus Two: Some Limits on Our Capacity for Processing Information," *Psychological Review* 63 (1956): 81–97.

30. A simple version of the model, based on Excel for Windows, is available on the Johns Hopkins University Press website: www.press.jhu.edu. Developing a more robust and user-friendly app might be a good exercise for a computer science student.

## Conclusion

1. *Chronicle of Higher Education*, March 14, 2014, A4.
2. Key words and phrases from the meeting materials.

Anguiano, Maria. (2013, December). "Cost Structure of Post-Secondary Education: Guide to Making Activity-Based Costing Meaningful and Practical." Policy paper from the Bill and Melinda Gates Foundation: Post–Secondary Education Success.

Arnold, Steve, Kevin Guthrie, and Candace Thille. (2012). "Effective Use of New Learning Media and Technology." In *Forum Futures*. Cambridge, MA: Forum for the Future of Higher Education.

Augustine, John. (2008). "Capital Structure and Risk Management Preface." In *Higher Education Finance Forum 2008*. Cambridge, MA: Forum for the Future of Higher Education (available on the web through EDUCAUSE), 3–8.

Berrett, Dan. (2014, February 7). "A New Kind of Study Seeks to Quantify Educational Quality." *Chronicle of Higher Education, 69*(21).

———. (2014, December 11). "How Big Money Can Encourage Calculated Risks in the Classroom." *Chronicle of Higher Education, 61*(18), A4.

Bitner, Mary Jo, A. L. Ostrom, and R. Burkhard. (2013, April 4–5). "Service Blueprinting: Transforming the Student Experience." Presentation at the Lumina Foundation convening on service science, Indianapolis.

Bok, Derek. (2013). *Higher Education in America*. Princeton, NJ: Princeton University Press.

Bowen, Howard. (1980). *Costs of Higher Education: How Much Do Universities and Colleges Spend per Student and How Much Should They Spend?* San Francisco: Jossey-Bass.

Bowen, Howard R., and Paul Servelle. (1972, August). *Who Benefits from Higher Education—and Who Should Pay?* Washington, DC: American Association for Higher Education.

Bowen, William G., and Eugene M. Tobin. (2015). *Locus of Authority: The Evolution of Faculty Roles in the Governance of Higher Education*. Princeton, NJ: Princeton University Press.

Boyer, Ernest L. (1991). *Scholarship Reconsidered: Priorities of the Professoriate*. Princeton, NJ: Carnegie Foundation for the Advancement of Teaching.

Burke, Joseph C. (Ed.). (2007). *Fixing the Fragmented University: Decentralization with Direction*. Bolton, MA: Anker.

Christensen, Clayton M. (1997). *The Innovator's Dilemma: When New Technologies Cause Great Firms to Fail*. Boston: Harvard Business School Press.

Christensen, Clayton M., and Henry Eyring. (2011). *The Innovative University: Changing the DNA of Higher Education from the Inside Out*. San Francisco: Jossey-Bass.

Cokins, Gary. (1994, June). "What Is Activity-Based Costing . . . Really?" Keynote Address, Institute of Management Accountants 75th Anniversary Conference.

———. (1996). *Activity-Based Cost Management: Making It Work*. Chicago: Irwin Professional Publishing.

Cole, Jonathan. (2009). *The Great American University: Its Rise to Preeminence, Its Indispensable National Role, and Why It Must Be Protected*. New York: Public Affairs.

Core, John. (2008). "Capital Structure and Risk Management Discussion." In *Higher Education Finance Forum 2008*. Cambridge, MA: Forum for the Future of Higher Education (available on the web through EDUCAUSE), 25.

Crow, Michael M., and William B. Dabars. (2015). *Designing the New American University*. Baltimore: Johns Hopkins University Press.

Curry, John. (2008). "Capital Structure and Risk Management Introduction." In *Higher Education Finance Forum 2008*. Cambridge, MA: Forum for the Future of Higher Education (available on the web through EDUCAUSE), 9–11.

Cyert, Richard M., and James G. March. (1963). *A Behavioral Theory of the Firm*. Englewood Cliffs, NJ: Prentice-Hall.

Dickmeyer, Nathan, David S. P. Hopkins, and William F. Massy. (1979). "TRADES: A Model for Interactive Financial Planning." In Joe B. Wyatt, James C. Emery, and Carolyn P. Landis (Eds.), *Financial Planning Models: Concepts and Case Studies in Colleges and Universities*. Princeton, NJ: EDUCOM, InterUniversity Communications Council.

Dill, David D. (1992). "Quality by Design: Toward a Framework for Academic Quality Management." In John C. Smart (Ed.), *Higher Education: Handbook of Theory and Research* (pp. 37–83). New York: Agathon Press.

Duderstadt, James J. (2007). "Fixing the Fragmented University: A View from the Bridge." In Joseph C. Burke (Ed.), *Fixing the Fragmented University: Decentralization with Direction* (pp. 49–69). Bolton, MA: Anker.

Eagleton, Terry. (2015, April 10). "The Slow Death of the University." *Chronicle of Higher Education*, B-6.

Easdown, Matt. (2013). "Data-Driven Decision Making." Annual Meeting of the National Association of College and University Business Officers (NACBBO), Chicago.

Ewell, Peter. (2002). "Evidence Guide: A Guide to Using Evidence in the Accreditation Process." Prepared for the Accrediting Commission for Senior Colleges and Universities, Western Association of Schools and Colleges.

———. (2009). Assessment, Accountability, and Improvement: Revisiting the Tension." Occasional Paper No. 1, National Institute for Learning Outcomes Assessment, College of Education, University of Illinois at Urbana-Champaign.

Gates, Bill. (2014, July 21). "The Future of College." Remarks delivered at the annual meeting of the National Association of College and University Business Officers (NACUBO). Nashville, TN.

Glassick, Charles E., Mary Taylor Huber, and Gene I. Maeroff. (1997). *Scholarship Assessed: Evaluation of the Professoriate.* San Francisco: Jossey-Bass.

Grinold, Richard C., David S. P. Hopkins, and William F. Massy. (1978). "A Model for Long-Range University Budget Planning under Uncertainty." *Bell Journal of Economics, 9,* 396–420.

Hansmann, Harry. (1981, November). "The Rationale for Exempting Nonprofit Organizations from Corporate Income Taxation." *Yale Law Journal, 91,* 54–100.

———. (1986). "The Role of Nonprofit Enterprise." In S. Rose-Ackerman (Ed.), *The Economics of Nonprofit Institutions* (pp. 57–84). New York: Oxford University Press.

Hearth, M., R. Kaplan, and J. Waldon. (1991). "New Costing Systems?" *Journal of Accounting Historians, 4*(1), 6–22.

Hopkins, David S. P., and William F. Massy. (1981). *Planning Models for Colleges and Universities.* Stanford, CA: Stanford University Press.

Immerwahr, John. (2013, April). "Report to the Lumina Foundation." Public Agenda, unpublished.

James, Estelle, and Egon Neuberger. (1981). "The University Department as a Nonprofit Labor Cooperative." *Public Choice, 36,* 585–612.

Jasanoff, Maya. "Globalization, Then and Now." Presented at the Aspen Forum for Higher Education Futures, Aspen, CO, June 17, 2015.

Johnson, Mark W., Clayton M. Christensen, and Henning Hagerman. (2013, August 31). "Reinventing Your Business Model." *Harvard Business Review,* 1–11.

Kaplan, Robert S., and David P. Norton. (2004). *Strategy Maps: Converting Intangible Assets into Tangible Outcomes.* Cambridge, MA: Harvard Business Press.

Kellogg Commission on the Future of State and Land-Grant Universities. (2000, January). "Returning to Our Roots: Toward a Coherent Campus Culture." National Association of State Universities and Land-Grant Colleges.

Kennedy, Donald. (1997). *Academic Duty.* Cambridge, MA: Harvard University Press.

Kerr, Clark. (1988, September). "A General Perspective on Higher Education and Service to the Labor Market." Unpublished paper excerpted in "Distillations," *Policy Perspectives.* Philadelphia: Institute for Research on Higher Education, University of Pennsylvania.

Light, Richard, et al. (n.d.). "Reducing Class Size: What Do We Know?" Working paper.

Linstone, Harold A., and Murray Turoff. (1975). *The Delphi Method: Techniques and Applications.* Reading, MA: Addison-Wesley.

Lombardi, John V. (2013). *How Universities Work.* Baltimore: Johns Hopkins University Press.

Lusch, Robert F., and C. Y. Wu. (2013, April 4–5). "A Service Science Perspective on Higher Education: Linking Service Productivity Theory and Higher Education Reform." Presented at the Lumina Foundation convening on service science, Indianapolis.

Maglio, Paul P., Cheryl A. Kieliszewski, and James C. Spohrer (Eds.). (2010). *Handbook of Service Science*. New York: Springer.

Massy, William F. (1960). "Innovation and Market Penetration." Unpublished PhD thesis, Department of Economics, Massachusetts Institute of Technology.

———. (1990). *Endowment: Perspectives, Policies, and Management*. Washington, DC: Association of Governing Boards of Universities and Colleges.

———. (1996). "Value Responsibility Budgeting." In William F. Massy (Ed.), with collaborators, *Resource Allocation and Higher Education* (pp. 293–324). Ann Arbor: University of Michigan Press.

———. (1997). "Life on the Wired Campus: How Information Technology Will Shape Institutional Futures." In D. G. Oblinger and S. C. Rush (Eds.), *The Learning Revolution: The Challenge of Information Technology in the Academy* (pp. 195–210). Bolton, MA: Anker.

———. (2001, March). "Applying Business Quality Principles to Academic Audit: Hong Kong's Second-Round TLQPR." Presented at the conference of the International Network for Quality Assurance Agencies in Higher Education, Bangalore, India.

———. (2003). *Honoring the Trust: Quality and Cost Containment in Higher Education*. Bolton, MA: Anker.

———. (2004, July–August). "*Collegium economicum*: Why Institutions Do What They Do." *Change, 36*(4), 26.

———. (2004). "Markets in Higher Education: Do They Promote Internal Efficiency?" In P. Teixeira, B. Jongbloed, D. Dill, and A. Amaral (Eds.), *Markets in Higher Education: Rhetoric or Reality?* (pp. 13–35). Dordrecht, The Netherlands: Kluwer Academic Publishers.

———. (2005). "Academic Audit for Accountability and Improvement." In Joseph C. Burke (Ed.), *Achieving Accountability in Higher Education: Balancing Public, Academic, and Market Demands* (pp. 173–97). San Francisco: Jossey-Bass.

———. (2007). "Cost and Pricing in Higher Education." In Edward Fiske and Helen Ladd (Eds.), *Handbook of Research in Educational Finance and Policy*. New York: Routledge.

———. (2007). "Using the Budget to Fight Fragmentation and Improve Quality." In Joseph C. Burke (Ed.), *Fixing the Fragmented University: Decentralization with Direction* (pp. 122–44). Bolton, MA: Anker.

———. (2008). "Capital Structure and Risk Management." In *Higher Education Finance Forum 2008*. Cambridge, MA: Forum for the Future of Higher Education (available on the web through EDUCAUSE), 13–24.

———. (2010). "Education Quality Audit as Applied in Hong Kong." In David D. Dill and Maarja Beerkens (Eds.), *Public Policy for Academic Quality: Analysis of Innovative Policy Instruments* (pp. 203–26). New York: Springer.

———. (2011). "Creative Paths to Boosting Academic Productivity." In Ben Wildavsky, Andrew P. Kelly, and Kevin Cary (Eds.), *Reinventing the American University: The Promise of Innovation* (pp. 73–100). Cambridge, MA: Harvard Education Press.

———. (2012, March). "Modeling Instructional Productivity in Traditional Universities." Unpublished discussion paper prepared for the Lumina Foundation.

———. (2013, April). *Initiatives for Containing the Cost of Higher Education*. Special Report 1. Stretching the Higher Education Dollar. Washington DC: American Enterprise Institute.

Massy, William F., and Nigel J. French. (2001, April). "Teaching and Learning Quality Process Review: What the Program Has Achieved in Hong Kong." *Quality in Higher Education, 7*(1), 33–45. Original version was presented at the 1999 conference of the International Network for Quality Assurance Agencies in Higher Education, Santiago de Chile.

Massy, William F., Steven W. Graham, and Paula Myrick Short. (2007). *Academic Quality Work: A Handbook for Improvement*. Bolton, MA: Anker Publishing.

Massy, William F., Richard C. Grinold, David S. P. Hopkins, and Alejandro Gerson. (1981). "Optimal Smoothing Rules for University Financial Planning." *Operations Research, 29*, 1121–36.

Massy, William F., Teresa A. Sullivan, and Christopher Mackie. (2013, January). "Improving Measurement of Productivity in Higher Education." *Change: The Magazine of Higher Learning, 45*(1), 15–23.

———. (2013, Winter). "Data Needed for Improving Productivity Measurement in Higher Education." *Research and Practice in Assessment, 7*, 5–15.

Massy, William F., and Andrea K. Wilger. (1995, July–August). "Improving Productivity." *Change: The Magazine of Higher Learning*, 10–20.

Massy, William F., and Robert Zemsky. (1994, January–February). "Faculty Discretionary Time: Departments and the Academic Ratchet." *Journal of Higher Education, 65*(1), 1–22.

———. (1995). *Using Information Technology to Enhance Academic Productivity*. Occasional Paper. Washington, DC: Educom.

Mazur, Eric. (2009, January 2). "Farewell, Lecture." *Science, 323*(5910), 50–51.

Middaugh, Michael F. (2001). *Understanding Faculty Productivity: Standards and Benchmarks for Colleges and Universities*. San Francisco: Jossey-Bass.

Miller, George A. (1956). "The Magical Number Seven, Plus or Minus Two: Some Limits on Our Capacity for Processing Information." *Psychological Review, 63*, 81–97.

Miller, Peter N. (2015, March 26). "Is 'Design Thinking' the New Liberal Arts?" *Chronicle Review*.

NACUBO. (2002). *Explaining College Costs: NACUBO's Methodology for Identifying the Cost of Delivering Undergraduate Education*. Washington DC: National Association of College and University Business Officers.

National Governors Association. (2011). *Complete to Compete—from Information to Action: Revamping Higher Education Accountability Systems*. Edited by Travis Reindl and Ryan Reyna. Washington, DC: NGA Center for Best Practices.

National Research Council. (2012). *Discipline-Based Education Research: Understanding and Improving Learning in Undergraduate Science and Engineering*. Edited by S. R. Singer, N. R. Nielsen, and H. A. Schweingruber. Committee on the Status,

Contributions, and Future Directions of Discipline-Based Education Research. Board on Science Education, Division of Behavioral and Social Sciences and Education. Washington, DC: National Academies Press.

National Research Council. (2012). *Improving Measurement of Productivity in Higher Education. Panel on Measuring Higher Education Productivity: Conceptual Framework and Data Needs.* Edited by Teresa A. Sullivan, Christopher Mackie, William F. Massy, and Esha Sinha. Committee on National Statistics and Board on Testing and Assessment, Division of Behavioral and Social Sciences and Education. Washington, DC: National Academies Press.

Nerlov, Marc L. (1972). "On Tuition and the Cost of Higher Education: Prolegomena to a Conceptual Framework." *Journal of Political Economy*, Part II, 3, S178–S218.

*The New English Bible.* (1970). Standard Edition. New York: Cambridge University Press.

Putnam, Robert D. (2015). *Our Kids: The American Dream in Crisis.* New York: Simon & Schuster.

Rao, Akshay R. (2005, November). "The Quality of Price as a Quality Cue." *Journal of Marketing Research, 42*(5), 401–405.

Rhodes, Frank H. T. (2001). *The Creation of the Future: The Role of the American University.* Ithaca, NY: Cornell University Press.

Rogers, Everett M. (2003). *Diffusion of Innovations* (5th Ed.). New York: Free Press.

Roth, Michael S. (2014). *Beyond the University: Why Liberal Education Matters.* New Haven, CT: Yale University Press.

Sabo, Sandra R. (2014, March). *Coming to Terms.* Washington, DC: National Association of College and University Business Officers.

Samuelson, Paul. (1947). *Foundations of Economic Analysis.* Cambridge, MA: Harvard University Press.

Savage, Sam L. (2009). *The Flaw of Averages: Why We Underestimate Risk in the Face of Uncertainty.* New York: Wiley.

Siemans, George, Shane Dawson, and Grace Lynch. (2013, December). "Improving the Quality and Productivity of the Higher Education Sector: Policy and Strategy for Systems-Level Deployment of Learning Analytics." Australian Government, Office for Learning and Teaching.

Smith, Jeremy N. (2015, April 5). "When 'Money Ball' Meets Medicine." *New York Times*, Review Section, 2.

Soares, Louis, and A. L. Ostrom. (2013, April 4–5). "College Is a Service." Paper presented at the Lumina Foundation convening on service science, Indianapolis.

Strauss, Jon, John Curry, and Edward Whalan. (1996). "Revenue Responsibility Budgeting." In William F. Massy (Ed.), with collaborators, *Resource Allocation and Higher Education* (pp. 163–90.) Ann Arbor: University of Michigan Press.

Swenson, David F. *Pioneering Portfolio Management.* New York: Free Press, 2000.

Taylor, Barbara E., and William F. Massy. (1996). *Strategic Indicators for Higher Education, 1996: Vital Benchmarks and Information to Help You Evaluate and Improve Your Institution's Performance.* Princeton NJ: Peterson's.

Thille, Candace. (2013). "Surfing the Tsunami: A Study of Faculty Engagement with the Open Learning Initiative." Unpublished doctoral dissertation in higher education management at the University of Pennsylvania Graduate School of Education.

Tough, Paul. (2014, May 18). "Who Gets to Graduate?" *New York Times Magazine*, 28–33.

Tufte, Edward R. (1990). *Envisioning Information.* Cheshire, CT: Graphics Press.

———. (2006). *Beautiful Evidence.* Cheshire, CT: Graphics Press.

van Vught, Frans. (1995). "The New Context for Academic Quality." In David D. Dill and Barbara Sporn (Eds.), *Emerging Social Demands and University Reform: Through a Glass Darkly* (pp. 194–211). New York: Pergamon Press.

Walvoord, Barbara E., and Kirsten J. Pool. (1998). "Enhancing Pedagogical Productivity." In James C. Groccia and Judith E. Miller (Eds.), *Enhancing Productivity: Administrative, Instructional, and Technological Strategies* (pp. 35–48). San Francisco: Jossey-Bass.

Wehrung, Donald A., David S. P. Hopkins, and William F. Massy. (1978). "Interactive Preference Optimization for University Administrators." *Management Science, 24,* 599–611.

Weisman, Dennis L., and T. Mitchell. (1986, Spring). "Texas Instruments Recalculates their Costing System." *Journal of Cost Management, 9*(2), 63–68.

White House. (2013, August 22). "FACT SHEET on the President's Plan to Make College More Affordable: A Better Bargain for the Middle Class." White House Office of the Press Secretary, Washington, DC.

Wieman, Carl. (2015, January–February). "A Better Way to Evaluate Undergraduate Teaching." *Change*, 1.

Wieman, Carl, Louis Deslauiers, and Brett Gilley. (2013, September 19). "Use of Research-Based Instructional Strategies: How to Avoid Faculty Quitting." *Physical Review ST Physics Education Research, 9,* 023102.

Wieman, Carl, and Sarah Gilbert. (n.d.). "The Teaching Practices Survey: A New Tool for the Evaluation and Improvement of College and University Teaching in Mathematics and Science." Unpublished Science Education Initiative at the University of British Columbia, 2.

Wieman, Carl, Katherine Perkins, and Sarah Gilbert. (2010, March–April). "Transforming Science Education at Large Research Universities: A Case Study in Progress." *Change: The Magazine of Higher Learning.*

Wilson, Jack M. (1966). "Reengineering the Undergraduate Curriculum." In Diana G. Oblinger and Sean C. Rush (Eds.), *The Learning Revolution: The Challenge of Information Technology in the Academy* (pp. 107–28). Bolton, MA: Anker.

Winston, Gordon C. (1997). *Why Can't a College Be More Like a Firm?* Discussion Paper DP-42. Williamstown, MA: Williams College, Williams College Project on the Economics of Higher Education.

Zemsky, Robert (1989). *Structure and Coherence: Measuring the Undergraduate Curriculum.* Washington, DC: Association of American Colleges.

————. (2005). "The Dog That Doesn't Bark: Why Markets Neither Limit Prices Nor Promote Educational Quality." In Joseph C. Burke et al. (Eds.), *Achieving Accountability in Higher Education: Balancing Public, Academic, and Market Demands* (pp. 275–95). San Francisco: Jossey-Bass.

————. (2009). *Making Reform Work: The Case for Transforming American Higher Education.* New Brunswick, NJ: Rutgers University Press.

————. (2013). *A Checklist for Change.* New Brunswick, NJ: Rutgers University Press.

Zemsky, Robert, and William F. Massy. (1990, November–December). "Cost-Containment: Committing to a New Economic Reality." *Change, 22*(6), 16–22.

Zemsky, Robert, Gregory R. Wegner, and William F. Massy. (2005). *Remaking the American University: Market-Smart and Mission-Centered.* New Brunswick, NJ: Rutgers University Press.

Zull, James. (2002). *The Art of Changing the Brain: Enriching the Practice of Teaching by Exploring the Biology of Learning.* Sterling, VA: Stylus Publishing.

# Index

Page numbers in *italics* indicate figures and tables.